T0234872

Lecture Notes of the Institute for Computer Sciences, Social Informatics and Telecommunications Engineering 171

More information about this series at http://www.springer.com/series/8197

Roch Glitho · Marco Zennaro
Fatna Belqasmi · Max Agueh (Eds.)

e-Infrastructure
and e-Services

7th International Conference, AFRICOMM 2015
Cotonou, Benin, December 15–16, 2015
Revised Selected Papers

 Springer

Editors
Roch Glitho
Systems Engineering
Concordia University, EV006-227
Montreal, QC
Canada

Marco Zennaro
International Centre for Theoretical Physics
  (ICTP)
Trieste, Trieste
Italy

Fatna Belqasmi
Zayed University
Abu Dhabi
UAE

Max Agueh
ECE, Paris
Paris
France

ISSN 1867-8211   ISSN 1867-822X (electronic)
Lecture Notes of the Institute for Computer Sciences, Social Informatics
and Telecommunications Engineering
ISBN 978-3-319-43695-1   ISBN 978-3-319-43696-8 (eBook)
DOI 10.1007/978-3-319-43696-8

Library of Congress Control Number: 2016952886

Printed on acid-free paper

This Springer imprint is published by Springer Nature
The registered company is Springer International Publishing AG
The registered company address is: Gewerbestrasse 11, 6330 Cham, Switzerland

Preface

The deployment of efficient and effective information and communication technology (ICT) infrastructure and services in developing countries faces several obstacles. Cost, awareness, availability, affordability, and accessibility are some examples. Nevertheless, this deployment remains a pre requisite for development. High-quality venues are therefore needed to discuss research and experimental results, and AFRICOMM is among these venues.

The first edition of AFRICOMM, which took place in Maputo, Mozambique in 2009, was the beginning of an exciting journey. Five editions followed before the latest edition that was held in Cotonou (Republic of Benin). The hosts of these five editions were: Cape Town (South Africa) in 2010, Zanzibar (Tanzania) in 2011, Yaounde (Cameroon) in 2012, Blantyre (Malawi) in 2013, and Kampala (Uganda) in 2014.

The topics generally discussed at AFRICOMM include (but are not limited to) energy-aware ICT infrastructure, existing/emerging wireless broadband access technologies, WiMAX, LTE, IT security issues in developing countries, as well as affordable and relevant mobile technologies and solutions. Discussions on the role that emerging ICT technologies—e.g., cloud computing, network function virtualization (NFV), software-defined networks (SDN)—could play in developing countries have also begun.

We now proudly present the proceedings of AFRICOMM 2015, which took place in Cotonou (Republic of Benin), during December 15–16, 2015. They include very high quality papers. The acceptance rate is 33 % (17 long papers out of 51 submissions, plus short papers and posters). The authors are from various countries including the Republic of Benin, Burkina Faso, Nigeria, Cameroon, Mozambique, Uganda, Malawi, South Africa, Tunisia, Italy, Portugal, Poland, France, Germany, Sweden, Norway, Canada, and the USA.

The papers were presented in four sessions: communication infrastructure; access to information; green IT applications and security; and health and communication infrastructure. The posters they were shown in two sessions. There were also two enlightening keynotes speeches: The first was by Dr. Patrick Valduriez on cloud and big data in developing countries and the second by Prof. Nii Quaynor on Africa Internet technical institutions.

December 2015   Roch Glitho

Organization

General Chair

Roch Glitho — Concordia University, Montreal, Canada and IMSP, University of Abomey Calavi, Benin

Technical Program Committee Chair/Co-chairs

Marco Zennaro — ICTP, Italy
Fatna Belqasmi — Zayed University, United Arab Emirates
Max Agueh — ECE, Paris

Web Chair

Abbas Soltanian — Concordia University, Montreal, Canada

Publicity and Social Media Chair/Co-chairs

Omo Oaiya — WACREN, Nigeria
Marco Zenaro — ICTP, Italy
Ouoba Jonathan — VTT, Finland

Workshops Chair

Antoine Bagula — The Western Cape University, South Africa

Publications Chairs

Karl Jonas — Bonn-Rhein-Sieg University of Applied Science, Germany
Tegawendé F. Bissywende — University of Luxembourg, Luxembourg University of Ouagadougou, Burkina Faso

Conference Manager

Barbara Fertalova — European Alliance for Innovation (EAI)

Local Chair

Jules Degila — IMSP/UAC, Republic of Benin

Posters Chair

Muthoni Masinde   Central University of Technology, Bloemfontein,
                                   South Africa

Contents

Green IT Applications and Security

Health and Communication Infrastructure

Short Papers

Communication Infrastructure

TV White Space Networks Deployment: A Case Study of Mankweng Township in South Africa

Millicent T. Ramoroka[1], Moshe T. Masonta[2], and Adrian Kliks[3(✉)]

[1] TV White Spaces Centre, University of Limpopo, Polokwane, South Africa
millicent.ramoroka@ul.ac.za
[2] Meraka Institute, Council for Scientific and Industrial Research (CSIR), Pretoria, South Africa
mmasonta@csir.co.za
[3] Poznan University of Technology, Poznan, Poland
akliks@et.put.poznan.pl

Abstract. The role of cheap and easy access to various telecommunication facilities is crucial for further community development. Such an observation is of particular importance for the developing countries all over the world since reliable and open access to communication systems can fasten the reduction of the development gap. In this work we analyze the benefits that can be obtained by application of TV White Space network, i.e. the network that operates in vacated TV band in a cognitive manner. The whole analysis is conducted based on specific use-case, i.e. the test network deployed in the Mankweng Township.

Keywords: e-Learning · e-Surveillance · Mankweng Township · TV white spaces

1 Introduction

Recently, both developed and developing countries are experiencing unprecedented high urbanization rates due to 'modern community development' and high standard services provided in building smart town and cities through knowledge economy [1, 2]. Urban areas, mostly aspired smart towns and cities, have become places suitable for making a living as they effectively provide people with the services they want and need as compared to townships and rural areas [1–4]. As a result, the majority of people in developing countries reside in urban areas in search of quality life. At the same time policy development to curb urbanization and the decentralization of development to rural areas and townships has also attracted attention in many countries [3]. The latter is more focused, among others, on: (a) economic restructuring, (b) rural industrialization, (c) improved environmental and energy planning, (d) easy accessibility of public services and infrastructure, and (e) innovative Information and Communication Technologies (ICT) in townships and rural areas. In South Africa, high rates of rural-urban migration are a result of limited or lack of services and infrastructures in most rural areas and townships [4]. Although urban areas are associated with modern knowledge economy, they also have adverse effects such as congestion, environmental pollution and degradation, and high rates of crime, among others [2].

© ICST Institute for Computer Sciences, Social Informatics and Telecommunications Engineering 2016
R. Glitho et al. (Eds.): AFRICOMM 2015, LNICST 171, pp. 3–13, 2016.
DOI: 10.1007/978-3-319-43696-8_1

The decentralization of development from urban areas to townships and rural areas has been the most effective strategy in dealing with inequalities that exist between these areas [3]. Thus, bringing services and infrastructure that are key to knowledge economy development especially associated with smart towns and cities close to people in townships and rural areas is of importance in this regard. For the purpose of this paper, attention will be given to the decentralization of ICT through low cost Internet connectivity in order to achieve modern development in South Africa's townships. The paper argues that if people in townships are well connected through low cost Internet such as the TV White Space Networks (TVWSN), they will reduce the high rates of urbanization and mostly contribute to modern community development [5, 6]. The goal and originality of this paper stake out on the discussion about the idea of community development due to the deployment of TVWSN. Intentionally, the main attention is paid on the Mankweng Township as an example of developing region. Although we focus on the specific case, the conclusions drawn from this work can be easily projected to townships in other regions. Thus, in order to prove the practicality of this concept we will discuss intentionally the real implementation of TVWSN in the abovementioned scenario, i.e. Mankweng Township in the Limpopo Province in South Africa. Three use-cases will be discussed: delivery of broadband Internet for e-Learning, application of TVWSN for smart metering and e-Surveillance.

The remainder of this paper is organized as follows: Sect. 2 provides the motivation for this study. Section 3 discusses the technical, legal and economical enablers for real implementation of TVWSN. Section 4 presents how TVWSN can fasten the development of specific economy branches and in consequence of the certain region. Finally Sect. 5 concludes this paper.

2 Modern Community Development and TVWSNs

Urban development is characterized by a number of components which include reliable energy supply, public services and infrastructure; and transport and communication development, among others [1, 3]. These components rely on each other and work as a system in building towns and cities that are sustainable and further fulfill people's economic and social needs [4]. Urban areas are also expected to function as economic engines for surrounding townships and rural areas. Although economic development leads to increases in Gross Domestic Product (GDP) [1], it also leads to adverse structural changes [4]. Easy accessibility to basic public services such as water, electricity, health, education, transport and Information and communications technology (ICT) is one of the reasons for high urban migration [5, 6]. Today there is a growing need for access to ICT and its related infrastructure which is underlying the move towards smart towns and knowledge economy [2, 3]. In order to build smart towns and cities, emphasis is on improving communication channels through the adoption of affordable ICT [6].

The application of TVWSNs for further community development is currently considered all over the world; however in this paper it is intentionally analyzed in the context of developing regions, treating the Mankweng Township in South Africa as an arbitrarily selected representative. As it will be discussed later, TVWSN can be a beneficial solution for reduction of ICT gap in developing regions since it offers affordable Internet. In particular, utilization of TV band guarantees high signal coverage with the usage of relatively low power compared to higher frequency bands (OPEX reduction). Moreover, as the amount of white spaces (licensed, but unused frequency gaps) in developing countries is rather high, wider spectrum bands can be assigned for opportunistic data transmission and it is generally easier to design such networks. Finally, wireless networks are cheaper comparing to traditional wired solutions since they do not require any excavation (CAPEX reduction).

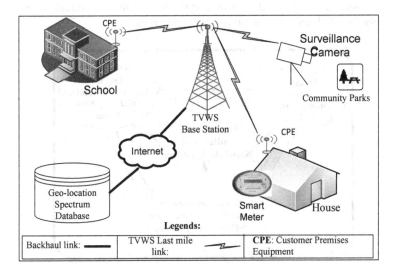

Fig. 1. A typical Modern Township with TVWSN coverage

Thus, let us present the concept of TVWSN which will be analyzed in the context of Mankweng Township, but can be straightforwardly adapted to any other developing region. For this region we have identified three essential services, which can be delivered by means of TVWNS. These are e-Learning facilities for schools, e-Surveillance to public centers, and smart metering from homes for municipal billing purposes. Proposed envisioned Modern Township in developing areas is depicted in Fig. 1, where a TVWS base station can be shared with existing cellular or municipality masts, or a completely new site can be erected. The customer premises equipment (CPE) communicates directly with the TVWS base station through the TVWS wireless link. At each CPE is then connected to a Wi-Fi access point for Internet distribution, and for e-Surveillance, a CPE is directly connected to the surveillance camera. Mankweng Township is only limited to providing Internet connectivity to schools, and other e-Services (shown in Fig. 1) are possible applications towards modern township. It is important to note that this concept can be easily modified in order to consider other services. As the key concept has been presented, in what follows we will discuss three enablers that are crucial from the perspective of practical deployment of TVWSN in developing areas.

3   Technical, Legal and Economical Enablers

The development of the ICT infrastructure and delivery of broadband Internet connectivity to a wide society is an effective way for reducing the development gap between countries and societies [7]. Let us however look at this concept from three perspectives – technological, legal and economical – which we consider as the pillars of reliable community development, as shown in Fig. 2. In all cases it is important to analyze the benefits from experiences from the developed nations. In what follows we will prove that existing technological, legal and economic solutions are mature enough to be applied successively for TVWSN deployment in developing regions.

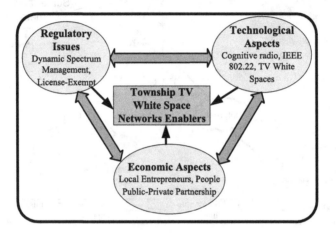

Fig. 2.   Three pillars of reliable community TVWSN deployment

3.1   Regulatory Issues – The First Pillar

Focusing first on the technological aspects, one can assume that modern countries suffer from the high scarcity of the available radio frequency (RF) spectrum although its effective utilization is very poor [8]. Thus, advanced and sophisticated technological solutions have been proposed both in North America and Europe to allow for opportunistic and flexible utilization of RF spectrum. These can be collected under the umbrella of cognitive radio (CR). Although pure CR concept is still on its research phase, it is worth mentioning the important steps towards its practical implementation.

Standard efforts towards the implementation of CR systems include the IEEE 802.22 which is a wireless regional area network (WRAN), whose amendment is on the final preparation stage. Other efforts are found in the documents with the requirements for the so-called white space devices [9], the family of standards for cognitive radio IEEE 1900.x [10], and the recent decision on assigning the bandwidth from 470 to 490 MHz for dynamic spectrum access solutions in the United Kingdom by the Office of Communications (Ofcom) [11]. These exemplary standards and regulatory documents can be treated as legal basis for the deployment of TVWSN in the nearest future even in developed countries (like South Africa).

As the legal solutions exist and can be applied easily, let us analyze the problem of opportunistic spectrum usage from different perspective. One can claim that many African regions do not suffer from the spectrum scarcity due to lack of telecommunication infrastructure. Thus, potentially there is no need for application of such mechanisms, and spectrum could be assigned in traditional, static way. While this is true, this problem has to be analyzed from the long term perspective, especially taking into account the rapidity of the countries' development. Thus, the authors of this work suggest gaining from the experience of other countries and working on such solutions that will allow for easy, cheap and fast deployment of telecommunication infrastructure, and at the same time will guarantee that the current problems of already developed countries will never come to life in Africa[1]. Application of such a solution could indeed reduce the widening gap in the ICT area in developing regions.

However, the presence of legal solutions is just one of many necessary conditions for enabling the ICT network deployment. Therefore, let us discuss the technological aspects from the perspective of developing countries in the next subsection.

3.2 Technological Aspects – The Second Pillar

Lack of fixed-line ICT infrastructure in rural and township areas coupled with recent advancements in wireless communications technology are among the reasons why wireless networks have become the most inexpensive and preferred solution to address broadband connectivity in underserved area [8]. Despite claims of 100 % cellular network coverage in South Africa, broadband access in rural and township areas remains a challenge. This is partly due to low average revenue per user (ARPU) in rural areas [7] and the high spectrum license fees which constitutes a barrier for new players to enter into the market [12]. While Wi-Fi is capable of providing low-cost broadband connectivity, it is limited to indoor or short range coverage due to its high operating frequency bands. Thus, the most preferred wireless communications solution for rural and township areas should operate in RF spectrum below the 1 GHz band (for greater coverage) and be license-exempted or at low spectrum license fee.

Recent digital migration of television broadcast has freed-up large blocks of RF spectrum in the 470–790 MHz band, and this spectrum promises to provide low cost broadband connectivity [13]. Thus, taking into account the above considerations, one of the promising technologies for application in South Africa for delivering broadband connectivity in rural and township areas is the deployment of TVWSNs. Such an alternative has been already considered by international companies, such as Microsoft and Google, which led some measurements campaigns for TVWSN communications [14]. Furthermore, various works have been carried out to adapt the existing guidelines for the devices operating in white spaces to the African situation, such as in [13].

---

[1] It is worth mentioning that analogous situation took place in Poland, the national country of the third author, where due to historical reasons decision on the adoption of MPEG2 or MPEG4 was made much later than in the west Europe. In consequence, Poland had newer standard earlier than many other west countries.

The TVWS pilot project has been deployed in Mankweng Township and the surrounding villages with special focus to selected secondary schools since 2014 [14]. As shown in Fig. 4 Limpopo TVWSN connects five secondary schools, of which four of these schools are in rural villages and one school is in the township. This proof-of-concept experiment shows the benefits of the TVWSN application for community development; it can be then treated as technical enabler, the second pillar needed for achieving this goal. It will be analyzed in more detailed way in the following sections.

3.3 Economical Aspects – The Third Pillar

Focusing only on the technical and legal aspects will not succeed in the long term perspective. Thus, the overall economic analysis of the proposed solutions shall be the third pillar of the way for country development through broadband Internet connectivity. As the concept of infrastructure deployment and network development relates various groups of the society we propose the People Public-Private Partnership (P4) model as the key economical solution. The P4 model will ensure community participation in the township projects and is contemporarily widely used as a promising solution for development of given region [15]. Involving the local community makes the community to have some sense of ownership to the network, thereby reducing the possibility of vandalism and mature project failures. Thus, the issues of ownership and management have to be split according to the P4 model.

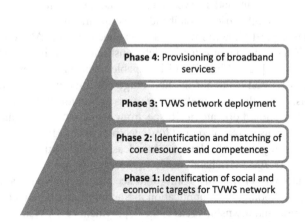

Fig. 3. P4 model for township TVWS network deployment

A typical P4 model (including consecutive phases of its implementation) is shown in Fig. 3. In such a model, local governments will co-invest for TVWSN to provide broadband access in the schools, health centers, and e-Government. Such co-investments will encourage the private sector, especially the small and medium enterprises and village entrepreneurs to enter into the ICT market by providing specialized Internet services within their townships. We believe that the P4 model is also suitable for building wireless community networks for townships and rural communities. Furthermore, community networks are mainly made for sharing the information among the community members and the network can be easily expanded as the community grows. We believe that the application of P4 model can be treated as the third pillar for practical TVWSN deployment.

4 TVWSN for E-Community

The previous section demonstrated that there exist technical, legal and economic instruments that can be applied for practical deployment of TVWSNs. Thus, let us now discuss the profits achieved by the whole community through deployment of the TVWSN. We will base on the specific use-cases, i.e. the TVWSN experiments conducted in Mankweng Township under the framework of TVWS pilot in the Limpopo Province. Application of the TVWSN for these exemplary situations should be treated as a way for building the knowledge economy, safety guarantee for society and as an incentive to implementation of innovative solutions for smart cities and towns.

4.1 E-Learning Facilities for Rural Regions

The goal of Limpopo TVWS pilot was to deliver access to broadband Internet to the students and teachers. The deployed TVWSN connected 5 schools, as shown in Fig. 4 with the offered average backhaul throughput of 7.21 Mbps per radio link [16]. The transmit power of each device was set to 20 dBm according to local agreements.

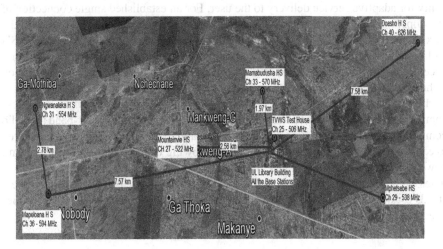

Fig. 4. Limpopo TVWSN topology showing all sites [16]

Among the student population, Grade 8 to 11 were selected using simple random sampling techniques. The student sampling frame of 2 979 was compiled from lists provided by the 3 sampled schools (Mamabudusha, Doasho and Mountain View High Schools), from which a decision was made to take a 20 % sample, representing 600 elements, for questionnaire survey. Similarly, a sampling frame of 124 educators was compiled from lists provided by the three schools; and, a total of 24 educators were selected through simple random sampling techniques for survey. Separate questionnaires were used for students and educators. The questionnaires covered a wide range of issues inclusive of the users' confidence in their technological abilities and skills, which is the focus of this article, to use TV White Space for learning and teaching. The questionnaires were loaded into android phones using the online data collection application, Open Data Kit (ODK). The UL Computer Science final year students were employed to administer the ODK-based questionnaires.

Based on the questionnaires collected of the experiences of the participants, most of the respondents (around 80 %) expressed that digital literacy is of highest importance [14]. Most of the respondents were also highly satisfied that they could easily access the word-wide resources. It means that delivering of facilities offered by the TVWSN is highly expected by the community. Students and teachers possessed the practical means for offline and online multimedia delivering and sharing, for circulation of important information and for accessing world-wide resources. As the conducted experiments focuses only on delivering Internet access to township areas, one important question that arose is to check if the e-Learning services could be delivered to the community by means of TVWSN.

Let us notice that by application of flexible spectrum usage the current needs for throughput (e.g. bidirectional video transmission) can be guaranteed by simply assigning more spectrum for this purpose at certain time and location. Such an observation together with the fact of Variable Bit Rates required for MPEG-4 transmission creates an opportunity for adaptive service delivery to the user. For an established single connection of 10 Mbps third level of baseline, extended and main profile can be achieved (with the maximum resolution of 720×576 with the frame rate of 25.0). Application of TVWSN will optimize the energy consumption and improve the effective usage of spectrum – once the higher throughput is needed more spectrum or more advanced transmission techniques will be applied.

It is important to note that the cost of deploying a wireless network is much less comparing to the cost of wired network. Moreover, by application of TV-band for radio communication, relatively high distances of signal delivery can be achieved compared to e.g. free Wi-Fi band. Let us consider the following example – for a given transmit power, distance and antenna gains, the path loss of such link will be approximately 3^ζ times higher for 2.4 GHz center frequency comparing to the 800 MHz one, where ζ stands for attenuation factor. It means that the transmit power can be reduced 3^ζ times to achieve the same range just by reducing the carrier frequency.

4.2 E-Surveillance Through TVWSN

A natural application of video-transmission through the TVWSN is the remote monitoring or e-Surveillance. As the crime problems are of highest importance in every country, and particularly in the regions where economical changes influences wide communities, safety guarantee to the citizens is crucial. As the presence of municipal services is necessary, the effectiveness of their work can be improved by delivering them the tools for remote monitoring of particularly dangerous areas. Omitting intentionally the privacy issues, which have to be also considered, the analysis of the applicability of the TVWSN for such a purpose will be similar as for e-Learning scenario. However, probably the scale problem could be the key issue here, since the number of video streams will be relatively much greater than for the e-Learning case. On the other hand the communication will be mainly one-directional in this case what eases the system design. Again, the flexibility of TVWSN allows for effective deployment of such a network for surveillance purposes. Based on the experiments conducted in Mankweng Township one can deduce that such an appropriately designed network can be applied also in this scenario.

4.3 Smart Metering for Water Resources

One of the key problems in African countries is the need for long-distance travelling by collectors in order to check the gauges (for example water consumption). Automation of this procedure will provide cost savings for the companies, and will guarantee timely and accurate delivering of the current meter readings. Application of TVWSN for these purposes seems to be fast and easy way for achieving this goal. Let us check the technical possibility of the deployed TVWSN in Mankweng Township for this scenario. In order to estimate the generated traffic, let us assume that each household is equipped with one gauge, and the meter readings are checked every hour. In order to send the measured values accurately each gauge needs to transmit its identity (arbitrarily set to 32 bits) and the value itself (again 32 bits). Having in mind the number of habitants in the considered Mankweng Township (33,738 of habitants in 2011 year, what results in the density of 2,800 people per km^2) the total average traffic that has to be served is approximately equal to $64 \cdot 2800 \frac{bph}{km^2} \approx 50 \frac{bps}{km^2}$. Please note that this value can be reduced by the average number of persons per one household and by the reduction of meter reading collection frequency (e.g., once per day). Finally, the application of TVWSN for smart metering seems to be a very promising solution due to its low cost of deployment and high flexibility. Please note that once the infrastructure for water-gauges remote metering is built it can be adopted also to other services, such as energy consumption metering etc.

4.4 P4 Discussion for Mankweng Township

As the technological aspects have been already discussed in other papers, e.g. in [13], let us briefly discuss the ways on how the P4 model can be applied. First, let us observe that the appropriate framework for realization of such concept has been already provided to the community by some of the countries in Southern African Developing Community (SADC) regions (please refer to Sect. 2). Second, the need for delivering of various services and facilities through easy and reliable Internet access has been also proved by the conducted experiments in Mankweng Township – most of the respondents expressed the importance of digital literacy. Also, the fact of the tests carried by Microsoft in some sense proves the potential interest of private companies in this activity. Thus, in the P4 model the missing nexus is the existence of private companies (e.g. village or town operators through the local government) that will deliver the above mentioned services to the users. Such a movement can be supported by local government by creating dedicated economical areas or providing dedicated programs for interested commercial bodies in favor of the communities.

5 Conclusion

In this work we have discussed the possibilities of township area development using Mankweng Township as a case. ICT infrastructure and the delivery of broadband Internet connectivity were discussed using three perspectives namely, regulatory issues, technological and economical aspects. This paper further demonstrated that the use of TVWSN in townships and rural settings is beneficial and can accelerate development. Additionally, ways in which to apply the P4 model were also discussed in the paper. The paper then concludes that in order to achieve community development which will improve quality of life in the townships and rural areas, the use of TVWSN for such purposes is highly beneficial.

Acknowledgment. A. Kliks has been funded by the Polish Ministry of Science and Higher Education for the status activity supporting development of young scientists and doctoral students in 2015 within task DS-MK-08/81/155. The first and second authors acknowledge the financial support by the South African Department of Science and Technology, University of Limpopo and Council for Scientific and Industrial Research.

References

1. Martadwiprani, H., Rahmawati, D.: Economic development as community resilience enhancement in Minapolis coastal settlement. Procedia-Soc. Behav. Sci. **135**, 106–111 (2014)
2. Lizarralde, G., Chmutina, K., Bosher, L., Dainty, A.: Sustainability and resilience in the built environment: the challenges of establishing a turquoise agenda in the UK. Sustain. Cities. Soc. **15**, 96–104 (2015)
3. Huang, Z., Wei, Y.D., He, C., Li, H.: Urban land expansion under economic transition in China: a multi-level modeling analysis. Habitat Int. **47**, 69–82 (2015)
4. Harrison, P., Todes, A.: Spatial transformations on a "loosening state": South Africa in a comparative perspective. Geoforum **61**, 148–162 (2015)
5. Criquei, L.: Infrastructure urbanism: roadmaps for servicing unplanned urbanisation in emerging cities. Habitat Int. **47**, 93–102 (2015)
6. Markham, F., Doran, B.: Equity, discrimination and remote policy: investigating the centralization of remote service delivery in the Northern territory. Appl. Geogr. **58**, 105–115 (2015)
7. Fehske, A., Fettweis, G., Malmodin, J., Biczok, G.: The global footprint of mobile communications: the ecological and economic perspective. IEEE Commun. Mag. **49**(8), 55–62 (2011)

8. Olwal, T., Masonta, M.T., Mfupe, L., Mzyece, M.: Broadband ICT policies in Southern Africa: initiatives and dynamic spectrum regulation. In: IST-Africa Conference, Kenya, May 2013
9. ETSI, White Space Devices (WSD); Wireless access systems operating in the 470 MHz to 790 MHz TV frequency band. EN 301 598 V1.0.9 (2014–02) (2014)
10. IEEE DySPAN: IEEE DySPAN standards committee (DySPAN-SC) (2015)
11. Ofcom: Implementing TV white spaces (2015). http://stakeholders.ofcom.org.uk/binaries/consultations/white-space-coexistence/statement/tvws-statement.pdf
12. Gruber, H.: Spectrum limits and competition in mobile markets: the role of licence fees. Telecommun. Policy **25**, 59–70 (2001)
13. Masonta, M.T., Kliks, A., Mzyece, M.: Framework for TV white space spectrum access in Southern African development community (SADC). In: 24th IEEE PIMRC, London (2013)
14. Masonta, M.T., Ramoroka, T.M., Lysko, A.A.: Using TV white spaces and e-Learning in South African rural schools. In: IST Africa, Malawi (2015)
15. Gumbo, S., Thinyane, H., Thinyane, M., Terzoli, A., Hansen, S.: Living lab methodology as an approach to innovation in ICT4D: the Siyakhula living lab experience. In: IST Africa (2013)
16. Masonta, M.T., Kola, L., Lysko, A.A., Pieterse, L., Mthulisi, V.: Network performance analysis of the Limpopo TV white space (TVWS) trial network. In: IEEE Africon, September 2015

Exploring TV White Spaces for Use in Campus Networks

Hope Mauwa[1(✉)], Antoine Bagula[1], and Marco Zennaro[2]

[1] ISAT Lab, Department of CS, University of the Western Cape,
Bellville 7535, South Africa
{mhope,bbagula}@uwc.ac.za
[2] ICT4D Lab, International Centre for Theoretical Physics, Trieste, Italy
mzennaro@ictp.it

Abstract. University campuses are busy places for wireless client traffic coming from Wi-Fi connections and other wireless devices that contend for the 2.4 GHz frequencies space that most campus Wi-Fi networks use currently. This is making the 2.4 GHz frequency unsuitable for Wi-Fi connection due to too much interference from other devices as well as from Wi-Fi connections themselves. TV white space could provide a suitable alternative to campus Wi-Fi networks because of its better signal propagation characteristics as compared to 5 GHz frequencies, which is currently being used as an alternative. As a first step towards white space management to prepare Africa's university campuses networks for the migration from analog to digital TV, this paper presents the results of an investigation that was conducted to look at the spatial distribution of white spaces frequencies around two university campuses in Cape Town-South Africa to assess if they are useful enough to be used for university campuses to complement Wi-Fi networks.

Keywords: Campus Wi-Fi · White-Fi · Loose spectrum identification · Coarse spectrum identification

1 Introduction

Without doubt, the 2.4 GHz radio frequencies contributed to the success of Wi-Fi. The success can be associated with the fact that the development and distribution of 2.4 GHz-based Wi-Fi products across nations is easier [1] as the 2.4 GHz radio frequencies are allowed for unlicensed use in almost all the regions of the world. But Wi-Fi devices are not the only ones operating in the 2.4 GHz band. Bluetooth devices, Zigbee, microwave ovens, cordless phones, wireless cameras, and many more devices also operate in the 2.4 GHz band. As a result, the band is congested in most places [2,3] making it more and more unsuitable for Wi-Fi connection due to interference from these devices. University campuses are such places where the 2.4 GHz band can be crowded or congested due to high demand for the 2.4 GHz frequency use. University campuses are busy places for wireless client traffic coming from Wi-Fi and other devices such as devices using

© ICST Institute for Computer Sciences, Social Informatics and Telecommunications Engineering 2016
R. Glitho et al. (Eds.): AFRICOMM 2015, LNICST 171, pp. 14–25, 2016.
DOI: 10.1007/978-3-319-43696-8_2

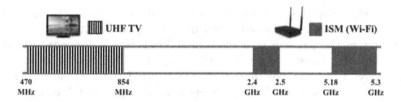

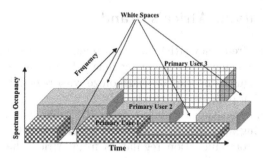

Fig. 1. White spaces: spatial characteristics

Fig. 2. White spaces: temporal characteristics

Bluetooth (keyboards, mice, trackpads, headsets, trackballs, speakers, docks), cordless phones, microwaves, wireless cameras and many more. Wi-Fi and these other devices contend for the same channel-constrained 2.4 GHz frequency spaces making it more crowded and unsuitable for Wi-Fi use due to too much interference from other devices and the Wi-Fi connections themselves.

With the advent of 5 GHz band as an alternative solution to the overcrowding problem in 2.4 GHz band for Wi-Fi networks, some universities are rebuilding campus Wi-Fi networks that are now designed for 5 GHz frequency band [4]. Much as the 5 GHz band provides some advantages like reduced interference, as there are no Bluetooth devices and other wireless peripherals operating in the band, its poor signal propagation characteristics may not be suitable for some Wi-Fi applications [5]. In addition, adopting the 5 GHz band means more associated cost due to the requirement to purchase more access points because the signals in 5 GHz band do not have better in-building penetration properties than in 2.4 GHz band. Lower frequencies with better signal propagation characteristics than 2.4 GHz frequencies are a suitable alternative. As revealed by Fig. 1, ultra-high frequency (UHF) TV broadcasting band is a lower frequency with such characteristics and white spaces found in the band could be ideal choice for university campus Wi-Fi networks. As shown by Fig. 2, when looking at their temporal characteristics, TV white spaces are unused frequency bands, which are availed by the primary users (the incumbents) to be used temporarily by secondary users subject to the protection of the incumbents' operation in the white space band. This paper presents the results of an investigation that was conducted to look at the spatial distribution of white spaces frequencies around two university campuses to assess if they are contiguous enough to be used for university campus networks to complement existing Wi-Fi networks.

The rest of the paper is structured as follows: Sect. 2 discusses regulatory status concerning the use of TVWS technology in Africa; Sect. 3 discusses the methodology of how the experiments were conducted and how the results were analysed; Sect. 4 discusses the experimental results and Sect. 5 concludes the paper.

2   WS Regulation: Africa's Stand

Generally, the radio frequency (RF) spectrum regulation in every country is the responsibility of particular government agencies. The agencies make sure that the RF spectrum regulations they set harmonize with regional, continental and world communication policies and regulations.

While the communication regulators from the other part of the world are currently formulating appropriate regulations to facilitate the deployment and access of TVWSs, communication regulators from African have not been left behind. Most African communication regulators have clearly seen the potential of using TVWS technology to accelerate the broadband connectivity of rural areas to the Internet [6, 7], and are busy working on policies and regulations that will make the use of this technology possible. For example, the communication regulator in Malawi, the Malawi Communications Regulatory Authority (MACRA), has drafted a set of rules and regulations that will govern the use of TVWS technology in the country and awaits review and comments from stake holders after which the regulations shall be gazetted for official use [8]. The communications regulator in South Africa, the Independent Communications Authority of South Africa (ICASA), published the terrestrial broadcasting frequency plan in 2013, which released some of the TV spectrum for non-broadcasting services such as TVWS technology, called the digital dividend spectrum [9]. The actual regulation and distribution of the digital dividend spectrum for non-broadcasting services was not specified in the plan.

3   Methodology

This section gives a detailed discussion of how the experiments were conducted. It also discussed how the results were analysed.

3.1   Measurement Campaign

We conducted long-time indoors spectrum-sensing experiments at two sites; higher campus of the University of Cape Town (UCT) located at the foot of Table Mountain and the Bellville campus of the University of the Western Cape (UWC). At UWC, the measurement location was a postgraduate computer laboratory on the ground floor of the Computer Science Department on latitude

33°56′04.2″S and longitude 18°37′47.4″E, and at UCT, it was Intelligent Systems and Advanced Telecommunications (ISAT) laboratory on the second floor of the Computer Science Department building on latitude 33°57′24.4″S and longitude 18°27′39.4″E. The choice of the experimental sites was sorely based on the fact that they are located in an area of high demand for TV service, and do not have any impact on the results apart from the mount of WSs found. Therefore, the results are extendible to other regions in Africa. If chunks of white spaces can be found in this area, places of low demand for TV services are expected to have plenty of white spaces.

The RF Explorer model WSUB1G was used in the measurement process. The model was fitted with a Nagoya NA-773 wideband telescopic antenna with vertical polarization and has wide band measurement capability of 240 MHz to 960 MHz. Its complete technical specifications can be found in [10]. The Windows PC Client tool was installed on a desktop computer before connecting the RF explorer to the computer to have additional functionality.

The main aim of the experiment was to look at the geographic distribution of white spaces frequencies in this band and eventually assess whether they are contiguous enough to be used for university campus Wi-Fi networks. Our objective was to (1) discover the spectrum occupancy in order to draw a spatial frequency map of white space bands in line with TV frequency assignments as allocated by ICASA and (2) find the channels occupancy patterns in order to find how correlated they are between the two sites.

3.2   Choice of the Detection Threshold

Deciding on the threshold to be used in spectrum sensing is a challenging issue that has been at the heart of debates concerning absolute value to be used; a higher threshold value might lead to a loose spectrum identification with many false negative resulting into interference to the primary users while a lower threshold value can cause a coarse spectrum identification leading to many false positives that results into spectrum wastage. Taking into account the fact that the signal detection threshold is a critical parameter, an adequate criterion had to be used to select the decision threshold to ensure maximum protection of primary users. Therefore, we looked at the Draft Terrestrial Broadcasting Plan 2013 document from ICASA [9] to see how the UHF TV channels are arranged in the band to come up with the signal detection threshold. According to ICASA [9], UHF TV frequency band $(470$ MHz and 854 MHz$)$ contains 48 channels of each 8 MHz bandwidth. The 48 channels are arranged into 12 groups of 4 channels each, which means that 4 channels are available for assignments at any transmitting site on a national basis. In areas of great demand, 7 to 11 channels are assigned to a particular area by either combining lattice node points or using both VHF and UHF channels [9]. The measurement sites are typical urban areas, and as such, we considered them as areas of great demand. This was confirmed when we examined the Tygerberg transmitting site in [9], which is the closest transmitting site to UWC, about 7.3 Km away from UWC. There are 6 UHF channels being used by different TV broadcasting station at the site. A close examination of how these channels are allocated in the band shows that each allocated channel is spaced by at least 4 channels before the next allocated channel, with channel 22 *(478* MHz *to 486* MHz*)* being the first allocated channel (see Fig. 3). We believe this allocation scheme was done to reduce interference coming from other transmitters at the same transmitting site. Based on this allocation scheme, we concluded that at least the first 24 channels on the frequency band could not be detected as white spaces at our measurement sites, i.e. the signal detection threshold was lower than any of the recorded signal values in these channels. The minimum signal strength value detected in the first 24 channels was −106 dBm. By trying −106.5 dBm as the detection threshold, we managed to get that protection level. Therefore, we decided to use −107 dBm as the final detection threshold to add an extra level of protection to the primary users.

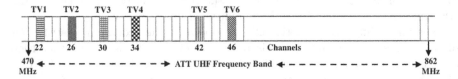

Fig. 3. Channel allocation at Tygerberg TV transmitting site

3.3   Performance Parameters

Two main experiments metrics were used in the analysis of data obtained:

1. The relative spectrum occupancy $O_{RS}(i)$ of channel i, defined by the three equations below.

$$O_{RS}(i) = 100 * O(i, T)/M(i, T) \tag{1}$$

$$O(i, T) = SS(i) - T \tag{2}$$

$$M(i, T) = max(O(i, T)) \tag{3}$$

where *SS(i)* is the signal strength collected in channel i, T is the spectrum sensing threshold below which a channel is considered unused, *O(i,T)* is the frequency occupancy of channel i and *M(i,T)* is the maximum frequency occupancy computed over channel i in the band.
2. The channels' statistics defined by averages, variances, and correlations.

4   Experimental Results

The spectrum measurements were taken continuously for a period of 5 days and periodically saved during that period. The data recorded for each channel were averaged and the mean value was taken as the absolute received signal strength *SS(i)* for that channel. At each location, we calculated the frequency occupancy

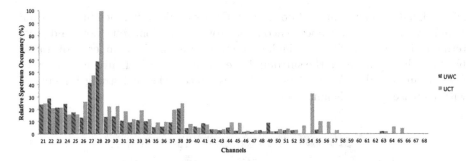

Fig. 4. Relative spectrum occupancy using detection threshold of $-107\,\mathrm{dBm}$

$O(i,T)$ for each channel and eventually calculated the relative spectrum occupancy $O_{RS}(i)$ for each channel using the equations in the previous section. The $M(i,T)$ that was greater out of the two $M(i,T)s$ from the two sites was used in the calculation of relative spectrum occupancy $O_{RT}(i)$ for each channel at both locations. Figure 4 shows relative spectrum occupancy for all the 48 channels in the band at the two sites.

4.1   Discussion

White spaces have been detected towards the end of the band at both locations. A total of 64 MHz spectra (8 channels) have been identified as white spaces at UCT white at UWC, 112 MHZ spectra (14 channels) have been identified. It is worthy to note that the white space spectrum identified is fragmented, i.e. it comprises of several non-contiguous TV channels of 8 MHz each, and as such, not all of it may be used for secondary usage. The use of a particular frequency spectrum by wireless devices is affected by how contiguous it is [2]. Although there are emerging technologies capable of exploiting such fragmented spectrum as a whole using carrier aggregation technology [11–13], currently widespread technologies such as Wi-Fi and WiMAX, which could be theoretically directly applicable for white space networking through adjustment in their radio frequency front-end in order to work in the TV frequency bands require a considerable amount of contiguous spectrum [3]. For example, an IEEE 802.11g network, which utilise a channel bandwidth of 20 MHz, will require three consecutive 8-MHz white space channels to operate. Based on our results, only consecutive white space channels from 58 to 62 and from 66 to 68 can be utilized for secondary usage by an IEEE 802.11g network.

The signal strengths are stronger in almost all the channels at UCT than at UWC and there are more white spaces at UWC than at UCT. Several factors may have contributed to this trend such as floor level difference where the measurements were conducted, difference in signal penetration properties of the building materials of walls of the two buildings, weather difference of the measurement locations, different effects of neighbouring buildings, difference in power of the transmitted signals arriving at each measurement point. Each of these factors affect signal propagation in its own way. For example, difference in floor level; signals arriving at lower floors encounter more diffraction, reflection, and scattering than signals arriving at higher floors [14] due to the number of obstacles blocking the signals from the surrounding environment, which are many at lower floors than at higher floors. Consequently, the received signal strength increases with increase in floor height [15].

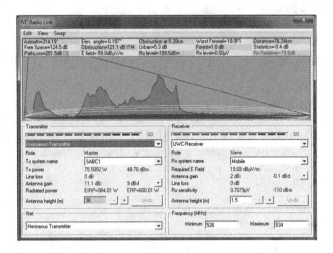

Fig. 5. Fresnel zone picture between Hermanus and UWC

The strongest signal was recorded in channel 28 both at UWC and UCT. The signal strength at UCT was stronger than at UWC on this channel. Therefore, the signal strength at UCT was used as the maximum frequency occupancy $M(i, T)$, which was used in the calculation of relative spectrum occupancy $O_{RS}(i)$ for each channel at both sites. From the sites, the closest analog television transmitter broadcasting in channel 28 is Hermanus, on latitude 34°24′48″S and longitude 19°13′18″E. It is about *116* Km from UCT and about *108* Km from UWC. Using Radio Mobile Network Planning tool [16], the shape of the Fresnel zones on the two radio links between Hermanus and UWC and Hermanus and UCT are depicted in Figs. 5 and 6 respectively. They reveal that there is no line-of-sight between the transmitters and the receivers and that they are totally blocked from each other to have the radio links possible. Therefore, a conclusion was drawn that the signal recorded in channel 28 at both campuses was not caused by analog TV broadcasting. A closer look at the Draft Terrestrial Broadcasting Frequency Plan 2013 document [9] shows that channel 28 is mostly used for digital mobile television broadcasting. It indicates that there is a digital mobile TV transmitter broadcasting from channel 28 at UCT, which is on latitude 33°57′21″S and longitude 18°27′38″E, about *100* m away from the measurement room. The document also shows that the closest digital mobile TV transmitter from UWC is on latitude 33°52′31″S and longitude 18°35′44″E, about *7.3* Km away from the

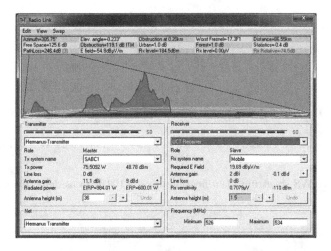

Fig. 6. Fresnel Zone picture between Hermanus and UCT

measurement room. Looking at how close the respective digital mobile TV transmitters are from their corresponding measurements sites, it is expected to have clear light-of-sights between them and their corresponding receivers. Therefore, a conclusion was made that the signal recorded in channel 28 at both sites is due to digital mobile television broadcasting and not analog television broadcasting.

Besides the results depicted by Fig. 4 where the signal detection threshold was chosen to ensure maximum protection of primary users, we conducted two other experiments to analyse spectrum occupancy under loose and coarse spectrum identification.

4.2   Loose Spectrum Identification

Loose spectrum identification means white space identification that results into false negatives where some channels are detected as white spaces but primary users are actually using them. In our case, choosing any signal strength value recorded in the first 24 channels results into loose spectrum identification (*refer to* Sect. 3 *and* Subsect. 3.2). Therefore, the signal strength value of −103 dBm was selected randomly and taken as the detection threshold for loose spectrum identification out of the signal strength values recorded in the first 24 channels. Figure 7 shows the results of white space identification when −103 dBm is used as the detection threshold. As it can be seen from the figure, many of the first 24 channels have been identified as white spaces but in reality they are not. For example, channel 31 has been identified as white space at UWC but using the analog television frequency assignment 2013 database from the Draft Terrestrial Broadcasting Frequency Plan 2013 document [9], channel 31 is being used by SABC3 with its closest transmitter from UWC at Aurora, latitude 33°49′39″S and longitude 18°38′29″S. Using the transmitter parameters provided in the database and the RF-Explorer technical parameters, the radio link between the

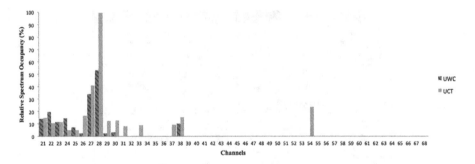

Fig. 7. Loose WS spectrum identification using −103 dBm as detection threshold

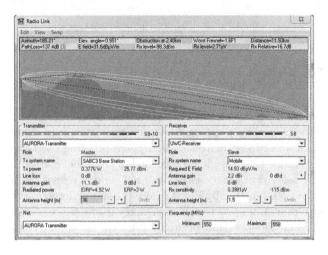

Fig. 8. Fresnel zone picture between Aurora transmitter and UWC

transmitter at Aurora and a receiver at UWC shows that the radio link is possible as shown in Fig. 8 rendered using Radio Mobile Network Planning too [16]. If channel 31 is used for secondary usage at UWC as it has been detected as white space under loose spectrum identification, it will results into interference of the TV broadcasting services of the SABC3 TV station.

4.3   Coarse Spectrum Identification

The FCC recommended white space detection threshold of −114 dBm was used, as it is considered conservative by many in the literature [17–20]. Using this detection threshold, there was no white space identified, i.e. all the channels were identified as occupied.

4.4   Translating Frequency Occupancy into Bandwidth Availability

Translation of frequency occupancy into secondary bandwidth availability is dependent on several factors as discussed in [3,21,22]. Some factors may be general while others may be specific to a country. In general, some factors that would affect translation of frequency occupancy into bandwidth availability are as follows: country or region's rules for protection of primary TV transmitters such as protection regions, adjacent TV channels that limit secondary operation; TV transmitter parameters such as transmit power, signal masks, modulation/coding used and interference sensitivity; secondary user transmitting parameters such as transmit power, signal masks, modulation/coding. A detailed exploration and mathematical analysis of the translation of frequency occupancy into secondary bandwidth availability is given in [21].

5   Conclusion and Future Work

In this paper, we investigated spatial distribution of TV white spaces around two university campuses to assess their suitability for use in university campus Wi-Fi networks. Indoor spectrum measurements were conducted at the upper campus of University of Cape Town and the Bellville campus of University of the Western Cape in South Africa. The results show that some white space bands exist towards the end of the frequency band, which can be useful enough to be used for university campus Wi-Fi networks.

Spectrum sensing is a first step towards efficient campus networks management by using white spaces to complement Wi-Fi frequencies. The management of networks to accurately share the available white spaces is another important process that may require redesigning existent network management techniques to manage white spaces. Multipath routing techniques such as presented in [23,24] will be redefined to use more paths upon secondary usage when white spaces are availed by the primary users. Cost-based traffic engineering techniques such as proposed in [25,26] will also be redesigned to include parameters that account for the white space availability under secondary usage. The design of market pricing mechanisms to protect primary users while managing white spaces to meet QoS agreements between the offered traffic and the available spectrum is another issue for future research. Assessing the impact of white space management on long distance sensor deployment as raised in [27,28] is another key issue that needs to be addressed as future research work. The design of low cost edge devices for white space deployment is another avenue for future research which can be addressed by using emerging embedded devices such as the Raspberry Pi and building around the flexibility and robustness principles proposed in [29].

References

1. Reiter, R.: Wireless connectivity for the Internet of Things, one size does not fit all. Tex. Instrum. (2014). http://www.ti.com.cn/cn/lit/wp/swry010/swry010.pdf
2. Brown, T.X., Pietrosemoli, E., Zennaro, M., Bagula, A., Mauwa, H., Nleya, S.M.: A survey of TV white space measurements. In: Nungu, A., Pehrson, B., Sansa-Otim, J. (eds.) AFRICOMM 2014. LNICSSITE, vol. 147, pp. 164–172. Springer, Heidelberg (2015). doi:10.1007/978-3-319-16886-9_17
3. Makris, D., Gardikis, G., Kourtis, A.: Quantifying TV white space capacity: a geolocation-based approach. IEEE Commun. Mag. **50**(9), 145 (2012). IEEE
4. Cox, J.: Wi-Fi devices crowd 2.4 GHz band; IT looks to 5 GHz. NETWORKWORLD (2011). http://www.networkworld.com/article/2182420/wireless/wi-fi-devices-crowd-2-4ghz-band--it-looks-to-5ghz.html
5. De Vries, G., De Vries, P.: The role of licence-exemption in spectrum reform. University of Washington (2007). http://mpra.ub.uni-muenchen.de/6847/
6. FCC: Third memorandum opinion and order, In the Matter of: Unlicensed Operation in the TV Broadcast Bands, ET Docket No. 12–36, United States, 05 April 2012
7. Ofcom: Digital dividend: cognitive access - statement on licence-exempting cognitive devices using interleaved spectrum, United Kingdom (2009)
8. Pinofolo, J., Rimer, S., Paul, B., Mikeka, C., Mlatho, J.: TV white spaces technical rules for Africa to enable efficient spectrum management. In: Proceedings and Report of the 7th UbuntuNet Alliance Annual Conference, pp. 355–364 (2014). http://www.ubuntunet.net/sites/default/files/uc2014/proceedings/pinifoloj2.pdf
9. Independent Communications Authority of South Africa: Draft Terrestrial Broadcasting Frequency Plan 2013. ICASA (2013)
10. RF Explorer: Handheld Spectrum Analyser. RF Explorer Combo Devices Specification Chart. Nuts About Nets. http://rfexplorer.com/combo-specs/
11. Iwamura, M., Etemad, K., Fong, M., Nory, R., Love, R.: Carrier aggregation framework in 3GPP LTE-advanced [WiMAX/LTE Update]. IEEE Commun. Mag. **48**(8), 60–67 (2010). IEEE
12. Pedersen, K.I., Frederiksen, F., Rosa, C., Nguyen, H., Garcia, L.G.U., Wang, Y.: Carrier aggregation for LTE-advanced: functionality and performance aspects. IEEE Commun. Mag. **49**(6), 89–95 (2011). IEEE
13. Yuan, G., Zhang, X., Wang, W., Yang, Y.: Carrier aggregation for LTE-advanced mobile communication systems. IEEE Commun. Mag. **48**(2), 88–93 (2010). IEEE
14. Martijn, E.F.T., Herben, M.: Characterization of radio wave propagation into buildings at 1800 MHz. IEEE Antennas Wirel. Propag. Lett. **2**(1), 122–125 (2003). IEEE
15. Elgannas, H., Kostanic, I.: Outdoor-to-indoor propagation characteristics of 850 MHz and 1900 MHz bands in macro cellular environments. In: World Congress on Engineering and Computer Science (WCECS-14). ACM (2014)
16. Coudé, R.: Radio Mobile - RF propagation simulation software (1988). http://radiomobile.pe1mew.nl/
17. Yin, L., Wu, K., Yin, S., Li, J., Li, S., Ni, L.M.: Digital dividend capacity in China: a developing country's case study. In: 2012 IEEE International Symposium on Dynamic Spectrum Access Networks (DYSPAN), pp. 121–130. IEEE (2012)
18. Zhang, T., Leng, N., Banerjee, S.: A vehicle-based measurement framework for enhancing whitespace spectrum databases. In: Proceedings of the 20th Annual International Conference on Mobile Computing and Networking, pp. 17–28. ACM (2014)

19. Naik, G., Singhal, S., Kumar, A., Karandikar, A.: Quantitative assessment of TV white space in India. In: 2014 Twentieth National Conference on Communications (NCC), pp. 1–6. IEEE (2014)
20. Mishra, S.M., Sahai, A.: How much white space has the FCC opened up? In: IEEE Communication Letters. IEEE (2010)
21. Hessar, F., Roy, S.: Capacity considerations for secondary networks in TV white space. IEEE Trans. Mob. Comput. 1(1), 1780–1793 (2014). IEEE
22. Harrison, K., Mishra, S.M., Saha, S.: How much white-space capacity is there? In: 2010 IEEE Symposium New Frontiers in Dynamic Spectrum, pp. 1–10. IEEE (2010)
23. Bagula, A.B.: Modelling and implementation of QoS in wireless sensor networks: a multi-constrained traffic engineering model. EURASIP J. Wireless Commun. Networking, 1 (2010)
24. Bagula, A.B.: Hybrid traffic engineering: the least path interference algorithm. In: Proceedings of the 2004 Annual Research Conference of the South African Institute of Computer Scientists and Information Technologists on IT Research in Developing Countries, pp. 89–96. South African Institute for Computer Scientists and Information Technologists (2004)
25. Bagula, A.B.: Hybrid routing in next generation IP networks. Comput. Commun. 29(7), 879–892 (2006)
26. Bagula, A.B.: On achieveing bandwidth-aware LSP//spl lambda/SP multiplexing/separation in multi-layer networks. J. Sel. Areas Commun. 25(5), 987–1000 (2007). IEEE
27. Zennaro, M., Bagula, A., Gascon, D., Noveleta, A.B.: Long distance wireless sensor networks: simulation vs reality. In: Proceedings of the 4th ACM Workshop on Networked Systems for Developing Regions. ACM (2012). no. 12
28. Bagula, A., Zennaro, M., Inggs, G., Scott, S., Gascon, D.: Ubiquitous sensor networking for development (USN4D): an application to pollution monitoring. Sensors 12(1), 391–414 (2012)
29. Zennaro, M., Bagula, A.B.: Design of a flexible and robust gateway to collect sensor data in intermittent power environments. Int. J. Sens. Networks 8(3–4), 172–181 (2010)

Impact of Small-World Effect on the IP-level Routing Dynamics

Frédéric Tounwendyam Ouédraogo[1(⊠)], Tegawendé Bissyandé[2],
Sawadogo Daouda[3], Didier Bassolé[2], Abdoulaye Séré[4], and Oumarou Sié[2]

[1] Université de Koudougou, BP 371, av. M. Yameogo,
Kdg, Koudougou, Burkina Faso
ouedraogo.tounwendyam@yahoo.fr
[2] Université de Ouagadougou, BP 7021, av. C.D.Gaulle, Ouaga, Burkina Faso
tegawende.bissyande@fasolabs.org, dbassole@gmail.com,
oumarou.sie@gmail.com
[3] Univeristé de La Rochelle, 23 av. A. Einstein, 17000 La Rochelle, France
daoudi5@gmail.com
[4] Université de Polytechnique de Bobo-Dioulasso, BP 1091, Bobo, Burkina Faso
abdoulayesere@gmail.com

Abstract. Running periodically TRACEROUTE-like measurements at
suite frequency from a given monitor towards a fixed set of destinations allows observing a dynamics of routing topology around the monitor. This observed dynamics has revealed two main characteristics: the
topology evolves at a pace much higher than expected and the occurrence of observed IP addresses provides a pattern of the IP-level routing
dynamics. In this paper, we aim to provide some explanation of these
characteristics through the small-world effect, observed on most complex
networks. We are able to reproduce the observed dynamics by modeling
the measurement on small-world graph. Thus, we show by simulation
the influence of the coefficient clustering and the average path lengths
on the dynamics.

Keywords: Internet · Dynamics · Modeling · Topology ·
Characterization

1 Introduction

Internet is world scale system that evolves over time. Some nodes and links
appear and disappear constantly on the measurement. This dynamics is due
to the routing, the load-balancing, physical dynamics, or some events like network failure. Understanding this dynamics is important for many applications. It
remains a challenge efficient tool to map the Internet. An efficient mapping tool
passes by take account the Internet dynamics features. Network protocols development and validation also require a good knowledge of underlying topology.
Some applications need to be tested on a model before real deploying.

© ICST Institute for Computer Sciences, Social Informatics and Telecommunications Engineering 2016
R. Glitho et al. (Eds.): AFRICOMM 2015, LNICST 171, pp. 26–35, 2016.
DOI: 10.1007/978-3-319-43696-8_3

Many works have been done in order to provide the most efficient and fast tool to map the Internet topology [4,6,8,10]. In this stream of studies, the TRACETREE tool has been proposed to measure the Internet dynamics. This tool performs an ego-centered view measurement periodically from a single monitor towards a set of destinations and provides a series of routing trees where the leaves are the destinations and the root is the monitor. The contribution of this work has brought a little more knowledge on the Internet dynamics measurement and characterization. The analysis of this dynamics has shown two properties that characterize the observed dynamics at IP-level topology [9,11].

Understanding these dynamics behaviors requires sufficient knowledge of the topology. We turn to the simulation to investigate the network properties that cause these dynamics behaviors. In the same goal, previous work has used power-law graph to modeling the IP-level topology of the Internet [11]. Our contribution goes further and studies the observed dynamics on small-world graph. The small-world effect is the fact that most pairs of vertices of the graph are connected by a short path. It may have implications for the network dynamics. For instance, the number of "hops" a packet must take to get from on computer to another on the Internet. The small-world graph has high coefficient clustering and short average path lengths. We address the issue of how to reproduce the observed dynamics on small-world graph. We find the appropriate setting by varying different parameter values.

We show that the small-world effect has a correlation with the observed dynamics of the Internet. This result represents an important step toward Internet dynamics characterization that lead to many applications, including realistic model designing, network routing protocols improvement regarding to some failure, especially for developing countries where the selective power cut makes often the Internet unreachable.

The rest of the paper is organized as follows. Section 2 presents the two properties observed on the dynamics of the IP-level routing topology. Section 3 presents the small-world graph model and shows how we simulate the dynamics on the model, the TRACETREE measurement and the topology evolution. We discuss the simulation results in Sect. 4. Section 5 surveys the related work. Section 6 ends the paper by the conclusion and future work.

2   Routing Dynamics Characteristics

Previous work has presented the TRACETREE tool [8] that collects the ego-centered view from a single monitor to a given set of destinations (chosen randomly in the Internet) by measuring the routes from this monitor to each destination. This view of the topology provides a routing tree, in which nodes are IP addresses, and a link exists between two nodes if they are connected.

Performing periodically TRACETREE measurement allows capturing the dynamics of ego-centered views of the routing topology. Many datasets were collected in this way from more than hundred monitors located at different places around the world: Burkina Faso, France, Japon, United States of America and mainly host provided by PlanetLab [5]. Each monitor performs TRACETREE measurement towards a set of 3 000 destinations during one month with a frequency of around 15 min at every round. These datasets are publicly available [5]. The analysis of these datasets revealed two main characteristics of the observed dynamics around a given monitor.

2.1   Sustained Discovery of IP Addresses

The number of IP addresses observed at each round measurement is roughly the same, as shown in Fig. 1. Note that this number may be different with other monitors. There are some downward peaks which indicate rounds with *less* IP addresses than usual. These peaks could indicate an event such as a major routing change or failure.[1]

Figure 2 shows the number of IP addresses observed since the beginning of one month measurement.

The unexpected behavior is the pace of the appearance of new IP addresses during the measurement. For measurements that lasted several month, new IP addresses still appears sustainably until the end. This characteristic of the Internet dynamics observed at IP-level topology has been presented in this work [9].

2.2   Parabolic Shape of the Dynamics Pattern

The pattern of occurrence of IP addresses follows a parabolic shape. The occurrence of IP addresses around a monitor may be defined by two quantities the number of occurrences and the number of block. The number of occurrences of an IP address represents the total of distinct rounds in which it appears. The number of blocks of an IP address is the number of groups of consecutive rounds in which it is observed. As an example, an IP address which was observed on rounds 1, 2, 3, 5, 6, 8, 9 has 7 occurrences and 3 blocks.

Figure 3 presents the correlation between these two quantities for a monitor. The plot exposes a clear parabolic shape, with a large number of points close to

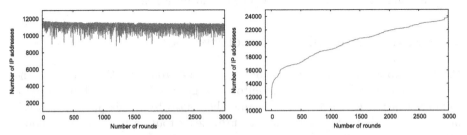

Fig. 1. Evolution of the number of IP addresses observed at each round measurement.

Fig. 2. Evolution of the number of IP addresses observed in the union of rounds.

---

[1] Studying these events is however out of the scope of this paper.

the x-axis and to the line $y = x/2$. The presence a large number of IP addresses close to the arc is due to the load-balancing routers. If a load-balancing router randomly spreads traffic among e paths, IP addresses belonging to any of these paths has a probability $p = 1/e$ of being observed at each round, leading to number of occurrences equal to rp approximately.

A given round is then the first of a consecutive blocks of occurrences for one of these routers with the probability p that this IP address was observed in this round, multiplied by the probability $1-p$ that it was not observed in the previous round. Multiplying this probability by r gives the expected number of blocks, which is then equal to $rp(1 - p)$ and is the equation of the parabola. In real case where an IP address may belong to paths used by several router performing load balancing. Therefore, an IP address belonging to paths with several load-balancing routers can have any probability p of being observed. This behavior of the dynamics has been presented in previous work by the authors of [11].

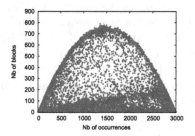

Fig. 3. Occurrences of IP addresses. Each point represent an IP address obtained by its number of occurrences on the x-axis and its number of blocks on the y-axis.

3   Modeling

The simulation model consists to reproduce the routing topology and dynamics (include routing change and load-balancing) and TRACETREE measurement on a given monitor to a set of destinations. Let us note that the model goal is explain the characteristics observed in previous work through the small-world networks properties.

3.1   IP-level Topology

We represent the Internet topology at IP-level by the undirected and connected graph $G = (V, E)$ where the set of vertices V represents IP addresses and each edge in the set E represents the links between IP addresses. The edges are not weighted.

3.2 TRACETREE Measurement

In real measurement the destinations are chosen randomly, and similarly the monitor location in the network. We made the same with the simulation. We randomly chose 3 000 destinations and the monitor among the set of vertices V. From the monitor, we perform a breadth-first search (BFS) on the graph G and obtain a tree. Afterwards, we remove recursively all the leaves of the tree which are not destinations. At the end, the leaves of the remaining tree are destinations, and the root represents the monitor.

3.3 Dynamics Modeling

We distinguish two dynamics in the model. The load-balancing and the routing change. We simulate the load-balancing when performing the BFS. Each vertex chooses at random the next vertex on a shortest path to the destination, therefore two BFS on the same graph G lead to different trees. The routing change corresponds to a modification of the topology new edges between vertices. We suppose that the number of news IP addresses is insignificant. We only consider the dynamics of edges between vertices in the model by swapping edges. Let (a, b) and (u, v) two edges of G chosen randomly. The swap consists to replace (a, b) and (u, v) by (a, u) and (b, v) in the graph G. We simulate two consecutive rounds TRACETREE measurement by performing a fixed number of swaps between two consecutive BFS.

3.4 Small-World Properties

The small-world network is mainly characterized by two quantities: a short average path lengths[2] and a high clustering coefficient[3] [1].

We used the Watts-Strogatz model to generate a small-world graph. Given the number of vertices n and the mean degree D (assumed $> \ln(n)$), the model constructs the graph in two steps:

- construct a ring network in which each node is connected to the same number D nearest neighbors, $D/2$ on each side.
- perform a rewiring on every edge with a probability p, $0 \leq p \leq 1$.

These two quantities decrease when the rewiring probability p increases but the path lengths decrease more quickly that the clustering coefficient. These properties of the ring network allow having an small-world network for small value of p, until some threshold. When p reaches the maximum value 1, all edges are rewired and the ring network becomes a random graph having a small clustering coefficient and a short average path lengths.

---

[2] If we denote $d(x, y)$, the distance (or shortest path) between the vertices x and y, the mean of distances of the vertex x to the other vertices of G is its average path lengths. The average path lengths of G is the mean of average path lengths of all vertices.

[3] Given a vertex x, the clustering coefficient is a measure of the probability to which two vertices connected to x tend to be connected.

4   Simulation

In this section we aim to find if it is possible, the appropriate settings of the small-world graph that will make possible to reproduce the dynamics with the characteristics presented in Sect. 2.

We are going further to investigate on the relation between the clustering and the average path with respect to the observed dynamics.

4.1   Appropriate Settings

In order to address the question of how to reproduce on small-world graph the observed dynamics. We perform simulations varying the values of the parameters. In this ways we found it is possible with suitable values to reproduce the dynamics with the characteristics describe in Sect. 2. The most meaningful parameters are the probability p of rewiring, the number s of swap and the number n of vertices of the graph. As we cannot have the sample as huge as the Internet, we make sure that the size of the sample is enough to leave invariant the parameters of the simulation. We vary the number of vertices n of the graph G. We simulate the measurement on a small-world graph with a size varying from 20 000 to 200 000 and the other parameters fixed $p = 0.15$, $d = 3000$, $s = 50$.

Firstly, we observe that it is possible to reproduce on the small-world graph the sustained discovery of IP addresses as observed with real data. Secondly, the number of vertices discovery increases with the size of sample until some threshold (around 150 000). Beyond this threshold the number of vertices discovery becomes invariants with respect to the size. Next, we choose to fix the size of sample beyond the threshold at 300 000 vertices.

Now, we focus on the evolution of the number of discovery vertices over time when varying the number s of swaps. The swaps simulate the dynamics of route changes on the topology. The number of swaps varies from 0 to 1 000 with the fixed parameters $n = 300\,000$, $p = 0.15$ and $d = 3\,000$.

Figure 4 presents the number of vertices observed at each and round. As observed with real measurement data, the number of vertices observed at each

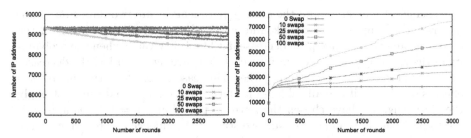

Fig. 4. Impact of the number of swaps on the number of vertices observed at each round.

Fig. 5. Impact of the number of swaps on the sustained discovery of vertices.

round is roughly the same with slight decrease at the end. When increasing the number of swaps, the slope of the curve becomes large.

Figure 5 shows the evolution of the cumulative number of vertices observed since the beginning of the measurement. We find a relation between the number of swaps and the speed of discovery new vertices. The curve of the high number of swaps is above and has a greater slope. This means that more swaps induce a faster discovery of new vertices. When there is no swap the number of discovered vertices remains stable. This means that only load-balancing cannot reproduce the sustained discovered of vertices as observed in Internet. Increasing beyond hundred the number of swaps lead to faster discovered of vertices than what observed on real measurement. We assume that the number of 50 swaps is relevant to fit simulation on the real data.

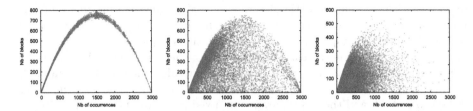

Fig. 6. Occurrences of IP addresses for different values of the number of swaps. Left: 0 swap. Middle: 50 swaps. Right: 500 swaps

We have the same result with the dynamics pattern. When there is no swap the load-balancing presents arc shape. The number of swaps spread the vertices under the arc. We obtain similar pattern of the Internet when the number of swaps is approximately between 25 and 100. The high number of swaps leads to faster discovery of the vertices and nearly all vertices that can be observed are discovered in short time. We suppose that the number of 50 swaps is appropriate to reproduce the observed dynamics of Internet topology.

4.2   Clustering vs Average Path Lengths

The coefficient clustering and the average path lengths are two important parameters of the complex networks like Internet. In the model of Watts-Strogatz, the clustering and the average path decrease until their low value when the probability of the rewiring p increases until reach 1. The average path lengths decreases faster than the coefficient clustering when p increases. Therefore, the small-world effect is obtained with small values of p which is not enough to decrease strongly the clustering. We have chosen the rewiring probability $p = 0.15$ as appropriate to perform the simulation. Now we study the influence the rewiring on the capacity to reproduce observed dynamics. We keep the other parameters fixed at their appropriate setting and we vary p from 0 to 1.

Figure 7 shows simulation result for three values of p. When $p = 0$, the graph is ring lattice with high coefficient clustering and the average path lengths is

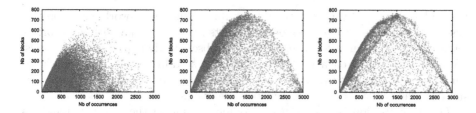

Fig. 7. Occurrences of IP addresses for different probabilities of rewiring p. Left: $p = 0$. Middle: $p = 0.25$. Right: $p = 1$.

at its maximal value. We do not see the arc shape representing the effect of the load-balancing. The points are concentrated on the left. Nearly all vertices in the graph are discovered before applying the first swaps. It is impossible to reproduce the sustained discovered of vertices and the dynamics pattern on the ring lattice.

When p increases a little bit more, for instance $p = 0.05$, the situation becomes different. Then, it is possible to reproduce the observed dynamics, until the probability p reaches 1. We notice that we are able to reproduce the observed dynamics only when the average path lengths becomes small. We are able to reproduce the observed dynamics only when the average path lengths becomes small. While the coefficient clustering seems to have weak influence on the observed dynamics.

5   Related Work

Many works on the Internet dynamics concern the measurement and characterisation [3,8,12–14,16,18]. The load-balancing has been identified as responsible of some observed dynamics on the internet and induces artefacts on the measurement [17]. The authors of [3] characterize the end-to-end paths dynamics with the presence of the load-balancing [3]. Recent work on the same topic provides a tool to predict and track Internet path changes [4].

The contributions on the Internet dynamics modeling concerns mostly the AS-level topology [2,7,15,19]. The work of these authors of [11] concerns the dynamics modeling at IP-level topology. Their main goal is not to obtain a realistic model but to analyze the impact of the power-law on the dynamics characteristics observed at IP-level topology. Our contribution is in the same stream of studies. We address the role of the small-world effect on the Internet dynamics observed at IP-level.

6   Conclusion and Perspectives

The Internet dynamics analysis at IP-level topology is at its beginning. Previous studies focused more the measurement. In this paper we provided a simulation results to explain some dynamics behaviors observed at IP-level of the topology.

Particularly our goal was to highlight the role of the Small-world effect on this observed dynamics. Using the model of Watts-Strogatz graph with appropriate setting we have been able to reproduce the observed dynamics characteristics. We used greedy approach in order to find the suitable values of the different parameters. It consisted to vary values of the target parameter until reach the suitable ones while the other parameters are fixed.

Our contribution is a step in the comprehension of the Internet dynamics and the results are useful for many applications, including new routing protocols development and modeling. In the continuation of this work, studying the correlation between other complex network properties and the observed dynamics of Internet is necessary for more comprehension of the network properties at the origin of the observed dynamics. Another future work should be the dynamics characterization. For instance, investigate whether the dynamics behaviors observed at IP-level topology is also the same at the AS-level.

Acknowledgment. This work is supported by the National Scientific Research Fund, MESS/BF/2014.

References

1. Barrat, A., Weight, M.: On the properties of small-word network models. Eur. Phys. J. B **13**(3), 547–560 (2000)
2. Chang, H., Jamin, S., Willinger, W.: Internet connectivity at the as-level: an optimization-driven modeling approach. In: ACM SIGCOMM MoMeTools Workshop (2003)
3. Cunha, Í., Teixeira, R., Diot, C.: Measuring and characterizing end-to-end route dynamics in the presence of load balancing. In: Spring, N., Riley, G.F. (eds.) PAM 2011. LNCS, vol. 6579, pp. 235–244. Springer, Heidelberg (2011). doi:10.1007/978-3-642-19260-9_24
4. Cunha, I., Teixeira, R., Veitch, D., Diot, C.: Dtrack: a system to predict and track internet path changes. IEEE/ACM Trans. Networking **22**(4), 1025–1038 (2014)
5. Radar data. http://data.complexnetworks.fr/Radar/
6. Donnet, B., Raoult, P., Friedman, T., Crovella, M.: Efficient algorithms for large-scale topology discovery. In: Eager, D.L., Williamson, C.L., Borst, S.C., Lui, J.C.S. (eds.) Proceedings of the International Conference on Measurements and Modeling of Computer Systems, SIGMETRICS, 6–10 June 2005, Banff, Alberta, Canada, pp. 327–338. ACM (2005)
7. Haddadi, H., Uhlig, S., Moore, A.W., Mortier, R., Rio, M.: Modeling internet topology dynamics. Comput. Commun. Rev. **38**(2), 65–68 (2008)
8. Latapy, M., Magnien, C., Ouédraogo, F.: A radar for the internet. In: Workshops Proceedings of the 8th IEEE International Conference on Data Mining (ICDM 2008), 15–19 December 2008, Pisa, Italy, pp. 901–908. IEEE Computer Society (2008)
9. Magnien, C., Ouedraogo, F., Valadon, G., Latapy, M.: Fast dynamics in internet topology: observations and first explanations. In: Proceedings of the 2009 Fourth International Conference on Internet Monitoring and Protection, ICIMP 2009, pp. 137–142. IEEE Computer Society, Washington, DC (2009)

10. Marchetta, P., Pescape, A.: Drago: detecting, quantifying and locating hidden routers in traceroute ip paths. In: 2013 IEEE Conference on Computer Communications Workshops (INFOCOM WKSHPS), pp. 109–114, April 2013

11. Medem, A., Magnien, C., Tarissan, F.: Impact of power-law topology on ip-level routing dynamics: simulation results. In: 2012 IEEE Conference on Computer Communications Workshops (INFOCOM WKSHPS), pp. 220–225, March 2012

12. Ni, J., Xie, H., Tatikonda, S., Yang, Y.R.: Efficient and dynamic routing topology inference from end-to-end measurements. IEEE/ACM Trans. Networking **18**(1), 123–135 (2010)

13. Oliveira, R.V., Zhang, B., Zhang, L.: Observing the evolution of internet as topology. SIGCOMM Comput. Commun. Rev. **37**(4), 313–324 (2007)

14. Pansiot, J.-J.: Local and dynamic analysis of internet multicast router topology. Ann. Telecommun. **62**(3–4), 408–425 (2007)

15. Park, S.-T., Pennock, D.M., Giles, C.L.: Comparing static and dynamic measurements and models of the internet's as topology. In: IEEE Infocom (2004)

16. Paxson, V.: End-to-end internet packet dynamics. IEEETON **7**(3), 277–292 (1999)

17. Viger, F., Augustin, B., Cuvellier, X., Orgogozo, B., Friedman, T., Latapy, M., Magnien, C., Teixeira, R.: Detection and prevention in internet graphs. Comput. Netw. **52**, 998–1018 (2008)

18. Wang, F., Mao, Z.M., Wang, J., Gao, L., Bush, R.: A measurement study on the impact of routing events on end-to-end internet path performance. SIGCOMM Comput. Commun. Rev. **36**(4), 375–386 (2006)

19. Wang, X., Loguinov, D.: Wealth-based evolution model for the internet as-level topology. In: IEEE INFOCOM (2006)

A Voice Over IP Deployment Solution for Public Social Institutions of Burkina Faso

Pasteur Poda$^{(\boxtimes)}$ and Tiguiane Yélémou

Ecole supérieure d'Informatique, Université polytechnique de Bobo-Dioulasso,
01 BP 1091, Bobo-Dioulasso 01, Burkina Faso
{pasteur.poda, tyelemou}@univ-bobo.bf

Abstract. Classically, social institutions are provided with a PABX-based unified and shared telephony service. With the mobile communications development, the organization of the telephony service is disrupted in favor of individual use. Mobile terminals capacities and usage development increase this trend. These terminals are more convenient in a social context which requires the ability to communicate anytime and anywhere. One non negligible perverse effect of this individual use of telephony service is the use of workers' private resources for their work. To face this practice, we analyzed Voice over Internet Protocol opportunity for low-budget institutions, designed a low-cost solution which offers a unified and shared access to GSM networks and made propositions about quality of service and security challenges.

Keywords: Voice over IP · SIP · Elastix · Softphone · IP phone · GSM

1 Introduction

The use of individual mobile terminal for accessing voice or data services has considerably increased in many countries of Sub-Saharan Africa [1]. In lot of social sectors of activities such as universities and hospitals, the workers often resort to their private individual mobile terminals for the public service. This is mainly the fact of the unsuitability of the classical PABX-based telephony. The extension and the maintenance of the classical PABX-based telephony infrastructure are expensive for social institutions. Though the classical PABX infrastructure could be replaced by an IPBX infrastructure, the available commercial products are often expensive and covered by licenses. Also, these telephony infrastructures do not natively well accommodate with the mobility requirement of the workers. However, leaning on computer networks which construction will remain a requirement for institutions, it is possible to build a voice service solution which meets the realities of social institutions. Designing a Voice over Internet Protocol (VoIP) deployment solution, of a low-cost institutional access to telephone service which could bring mobility is the main objective of this paper. A VoIP solution based on open software is built to interconnect a diversity of digital terminals (IP phones, PCs, smartphones and tablets) with interconnection to GSM networks. The proposed VoIP deployment solution is accompanied by propositions that address security and Quality of Service (QoS) management challenges.

© ICST Institute for Computer Sciences, Social Informatics and Telecommunications Engineering 2016
R. Glitho et al. (Eds.): AFRICOMM 2015, LNICST 171, pp. 36–41, 2016.
DOI: 10.1007/978-3-319-43696-8_4

2 Overview of VoIP Technology

VoIP [2] is based on the principle that the voice can be digitized and processed as any digital data. Unlike traditional circuit switching telephony, VoIP uses packet switching and IP protocol. In IP telephony, instead of a connection, a session is established between the source and the destination so that there is no dedicated channel. The digitized voice samples, in the form of IP packets, transit over the network by following different paths to the destination where they are processed to deliver an analog voice signal to the user.

Several protocols manage the communication in VoIP. There are usually grouped into communication management protocols and voice transport protocols. Regarding the communication management, ITU-T developed the recommendation H.323 [3]. H.323 takes into account signaling, codecs negotiation and information transmission. As for the signaling management, Internet Engineering Task Force worked on the standardization of Session Initiation Protocol (SIP) [4]. SIP has in charge the management of sessions establishment, release and modification. Each participant of a session has a unique identifier called SIP Uniform Resource Identifier (URI). The required entities for SIP protocol are: (i) a proxy server that receives and processes client requests and routes them to other servers; (ii) a redirect server that handles the translation of SIP addresses; (iii) a user agent that is a software on a user equipment or within an IP phone capable of transmitting and receiving SIP requests; (iv) and a registrar that maintains an SIP URI location database where each user is registered. Other protocols are grafted to SIP to provide additional services; e.g., the Media Gateway Control Protocol [5] used for the interconnection between IP networks and traditional telephony systems. For voice data transport, commonly used protocols are Real-Time Transport Protocol (RTP) [6], Secure RTP (SRTP) [7] developed to address security requirements, Real-Time Transport Control Protocol (RTCP) [8] for the control of the RTP stream and its secure version, Secure RTCP (SRTCP) [7].

The integration of voice data in a computer network is changing exponentially network load [9]. Compression algorithms are therefore essential to deal with the possible lack of resources to carry the large volume of data. The most used ITU compression algorithms (i.e.; codecs) for VoIP are G.711 (PCM), G.729, G.723.1 (MP-MLQ) and G.723.1 (ACELP) with respectively expected Mean Opinion Score (MOS) of 4.1, 3.92, 3.9 and 3.65 [10]. MOS is a metric that depends on the codecs and is useful for the measurement of the quality of VoIP connections. The choice of a codec is a trade-off to make between a desired QoS and available bandwidth.

3 VoIP Service Usages in Sub-saharan Africa

VoIP technology offers several types of services including the traditional and most used service of calls transmission and reception. If a favorable environment of electronic communications development was guaranteed, VoIP would contribute much in the reduction of the call service cost for the end-user. We would observe the development of local operators with the building of their private IP networks for commercial purpose. Unfortunately, VoIP technology, as an opportunity to reach at low cost the universal service for all, has suffered from insufficient and inadequate politics in Sub-Saharan Africa. Despite its advantages by providing telephony access at lower cost to providers and consumers, VoIP was prohibited in many African countries [11]. Until 2005 in South Africa, VoIP was reserved for Telkom, the second national operator and the under-serviced area licensees [12]. Fortunately, since February 2005, the lifting of the restrictions on VoIP opens up a vast number of opportunities and will reduce the costs of voice transmission for both network service providers and consumers [13]. In Burkina Faso, the business opportunity of VoIP technology is still not developed even if the legal environment is favorable [14]. The consumers generally use mobile operators' offers for their telephony needs. Only a privileged few resort to VoIP for international calls using software like Skype. As high rate Internet service is not always satisfactorily offered, this latter usage of VoIP call service remains very marginal and is locally unstructured. A more structured usage of VoIP is that oriented at destination of a group of persons linked by their professional or social activities. VoIP technology has been investigated as a solution to bridge the digital divide to service a specific need of a particular rural community in South Africa [12]. In Burkina Faso, the use of VoIP telephony service in an enterprise or public environment already occurred but is, as the classical traditional PABX, limited to utilization inside offices. In this paper, we propose an open and largely accessible VoIP deployment solution for a usage in a context of high populated social institutions such as universities and hospitals.

4 Proposed VoIP Deployment Solution

The proposed VoIP deployment solution is designed to connect both traditional VoIP terminals (PC, IP phone) and emerging mobile terminals (smartphone, tablet). Thus, users would be able to use their favorite terminal to access services. It also integrates an interconnection with any GSM network. So, the workers would benefit from a unified access to calls outside their network at the expense of their institution. It is designed with open technologies so that its cost is accessible to low budgets.

4.1 Technical Architecture, Services and Cost

A simplified technical architecture of the proposed VoIP deployment solution is depicted in Fig. 1. The network infrastructure is composed of wired Ethernet local area networks with extensions to WiFi components. At the core of the solution is Elastix [15], the server of VoIP services. Elastix is an open software selected for its multiple advantages: it operates with a diversity of protocols (SIP, H.323, IAX, RTP, RTCP) and codecs (G.711, G.729, G.722, G.723.1 …). If hosted on a server hardware with at least equal performance as HP Proliant DL120, 2.5 GHz Xeon, 8 GB of RAM, Elastix could allow 368 simultaneous communications and up to 3000 SIP accounts. Elastix can exchange services with Personal Computers (PC), IP phones, smartphones and tablets. Client software called softphones must be installed on PCs, smartphones and tablets. In Table 1, selected IP phones and softphones for the solution are given. The architecture integrates a firewall in order to filter accesses to the server. Additional

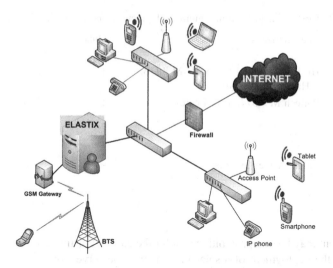

Fig. 1. A simplified technical architecture of the proposed VoIP deployment solution.

Table 1. Client software of the proposed VoIP server

Type of terminal	PC	IP phone	Smartphone/tablet
Softphones/IP phones	X-Lite, Ekiga	Snom 320, Snom 370	Csipsimple

security configurations that should be made are given in Sect. 4.2 together with QoS issue. The VoIP server is interconnected with a GSM network via a gateway like Portech MV-374, a device that can bear four SIM cards. The configuration of the gateway for Elastix is simple and a filtering can be made to authorize selected call numbers if needed.

The proposed solution has been implemented and several services successfully tested: visiophony, call transfer, audio-conference and instantaneous messages. To materialize it, a prior investment in the computer network construction is required. In Table 2, assuming no investment in IP phones and engineering, an estimation of how much could be a minimum deployment of the proposed VoIP solution is given.

4.2 Quality of Service Management and Security Challenges

Network availability and security are major constraints to the integration of VoIP in a computer network. To face these constraints, we recommend some measures for a satisfactory VoIP service. Firstly, we address the problem of the power grid instability. With the traditional circuit-switched telephone network, even when there is power outage, the service remains operational because the power supply is routed by the operator. Such a technique is possible with the IEEE 802.3af standard [16] that provides power to devices over the Ethernet cable. However, as this standard is not open,

Table 2. Cost estimate for a minimum deployment of the proposed VoIP solution

Product	Characteristics	Quantity	Unitary price	Total
Server hardware	HP Proliant DL 120 G5, RAM 8 GB, Hard disk 800 GB	1	660	660
GSM gateway	Portech MV-374, 4 SIM cards	1	1270	1270
Server software	Elastix	-	0	0
Softphones	Ekiga, X-lite, Csipsimple	-	0	0
Overall amount	-			1930 $US

its deployment may be of a prohibitive cost for the targeted institutions. For this reason, we propose the deployment of a solar kit to power the server room.

Secondly, we address the problem of the network bandwidth availability. VoIP is very sensitive to congestion. Low bandwidth is a source of network congestion and causes delays and packet losses. Delay is a critical parameter in VoIP. The phase jitter is caused by temporary network congestion and changes in packets routes. It can be damaging to QoS. To address this bandwidth resource constraint, we propose QoS management solutions, emergency plans and disaster recovery. The establishment of a QoS management policy includes the following three stages: characterization of traffic, classification of flows and definition of stream processing rules favoring voice stream. This last step will be to determine the routing priorities or minimum bandwidth levels for certain applications. With Diffserv (Differentiated Services) [17] architecture, every class of service is subjected to a special treatment. The emergency plan and disaster recovery aim at ensuring the flow of communication and especially the availability of phone equipment in case of network congestion or electrical failure.

Thirdly, VoIP is particularly susceptible to Deny of Service (DoS) attacks. As part of the proposed solution, the firewall will minimize the traffic entering the server and may limit DoS attacks. Also, we recommend the deployment of anti-hackers modules to protect Elastix and prevent hackers from attacking the main services.

Finally, to overcome communications confidentiality, we recommend encryption-based protocols such as SIPS [18] and SRTP respectively for signaling flow and voice flow encryption. SIPS also prevents from risks of identity theft.

5   Conclusion

This paper dealt with a low-cost VoIP deployment solution for social institutions such as universities and hospitals. The solution allows the users to use their smartphones or tablets to access VoIP services. An interconnection with GSM networks is made to offer a unified access to call services at the expense of the institution. The proposed VoIP solution could contribute significantly in the fight against poverty in institutions where the workers are constrained to use their own resources for the public service.

As perspectives, this study will be refined especially by sizing needs and capabilities of equipments. The impact of the integration of voice data in the computer network will be studied and possible extension of the proposed solution will be made.

Acknowledgments. The authors are grateful to Abdoul Razak Gansoré and Moumouni Sawadogo for their helpful contribution to the solution implementation.

References

1. Guy, Z., Christine, Z.-W.Q., Jenny, C.A., François-Xavier, R., Annie, C.-L., Samir, S., Tangui, B., Véronique, P., Guillaume, B.: La téléphonie mobile dans les pays en développement: quels impacts économiques et sociaux? Secteur Privé & Développement, Proparco, no. 4 (2009)
2. Black, U.: Voice Over IP. Prentice-Hall, Upper Saddle River (2000)
3. Liu, H., Mouchtaris, P.: Voice over IP signaling: H.323 and beyond. IEEE Commun. Mag. **38**(10), 142–148 (2000)
4. Rosenberg, J., Schulzrinne, H., Camarillo, G., Johnston, A., Peterson, J., Sparks, R., Handley, M., Schooler, E.: SIP: Session Initiation Protocol, RFC no 3261 (2002)
5. Anquetil, L.-P., Bouwen, J., Conte, A., Van Doorselaer, B.: Media gateway control protocol and voice over IP gateways. Alcatel Telecommun. Rev. **2**, 151–157 (1999)
6. Schulzrinne, H., Casner, S., Frederick, R., Jacobson, V.: RTP: a transport protocol for real-time applications, RFC no 3550 (2003)
7. Baugher, M., McGrew, D., Naslund, M., Carrara, E., Norrman, K.: The secure real-time transport protocol (SRTP), RFC 3711 (2004)
8. Ott, J., Wenger, S., Sato, N., Burmeister, C., Rey, J.: Extended RTP profile for real-time transport control protocol (RTCP)-based feedback (RTP/AVPF), RFC no 4585 (2006)
9. Nutt, G.J., Bayer, D.L.: Performance of CSMA/CD networks under combined voice and data loads. IEEE Trans. Commun. **30**(1), 6–11 (1982)
10. Mehta, P., Udani, S.: Voice over IP. IEEE Potentials **20**(4), 36–40 (2001)
11. Cohen, T., Southwood, R.: An Overview of VoIP Regulation in Africa: Policy Responses and Proposals, Commonwealth Telecommunications Organization (2004)
12. Chetty, M., Tucker, B., Blake, E.: Using voice over IP to bridge the digital divide - a critical action research approach. In: Southern African Telecommunications Networks & Applications Conference, South Africa (2003)
13. Chetty, M., Blake, E., McPhie, E.: VoIP deregulation in South Africa: implications for underserviced areas. Telecom Policy **30**(5–6), 332–344 (2006). Elsevier Ltd.
14. Autorité de Régulation des Communications électroniques, Déclaration de politique sectorielle des télécommunications de juillet (1999). http://www.arce.bf
15. Elastix official web site. http://www.elastix.org
16. Schindler, F.R.: U.S. Patent No. 7,930,568. Washington, DC: U.S. Patent and Trademark Office (2001)
17. Babiarz, J., Chan, K., Baker, F.: Configuration guidelines for DiffServ service classes, RFC 4594 (2006)
18. Salsano, S., Veltri, L., Papalilo, D.: SIP security issues: the SIP authentication procedure and its processing load. IEEE Network **16**(6), 38–44 (2002)

Access to Information

BJNet: Another Way to Build a NREN

Marc Lobelle[1(✉)], Norbert Hounkonnou[2], Firmin Donadje[3], and Victor Oyetola[4]

[1] Louvain School of Engineering, ICTEAM, Université catholique de Louvain,
Place Ste Barbe, 2, 1348 Louvain-la-Neuve, Belgium
marc.lobelle@uclouvain.b
[2] ICMPA, Université d'Abomey-Calavi, 072 BP50 Cotonou, Benin
norbert.hounkonnou@cipma.uac.bj
[3] Forces Armées Béninoises, Cotonou, Benin
cofindo@gmail.com
[4] SPTIC, Université d'Abomey-Calavi, Cotonou, Benin
victor.oyetola@uac.bj

Abstract. This paper presents the way a gigabit NREN (National Research and Education Network) covering the whole country of Benin and that will connect over twenty university centers is being built using mainly local unused infrastructures and local permanent staff already paid by the State of Benin (predominantly personnel from the Université d'Abomey-Calavi, UAC, in Benin and from Benin Armed Forces). The necessary additional equipments were provided by a relatively modest ACP (African, Caribbean and Pacific Group of States Organization) project mainly funded by the EU. The necessary expertise was mostly provided by a Belgian university, Université catholique de Louvain (UCL), a Beninese university, Université d'Abomey-Calavi (UAC), signal officers from Benin Armed Forces (FAB) and the Belgian NREN, Belnet.

Keywords: NREN · Internetworking · Network design and implementation · Development · Campus network · Civil-Military cooperation (CIMIC) · Development policy

1 Introduction

Every country should have a National Research and Education Network (NREN). These networks are much more than yet another internet service provider. Beside providing access to the internet at large, they are intended to connect with a wide bandwidth all universities and research centers in the world. They enable the use of MOOCS [5, 8] at low cost to higher education students and researchers worldwide. They enable sharing huge amounts of research data such as those of the CERN. Currently, developed countries have their NRENs. The situation is different in developing and emerging countries. Lucky ones have a NREN; some have nothing and others have still just a name, sometimes with a director or a steering committee, but neither infrastructure nor service.

When the first NRENs where created in developed countries, some 25 to 30 years ago, they were also just small organisations managing a few leased lines of a few tens of kbps, but they grew and are now managing, for their users, real information highways,

© ICST Institute for Computer Sciences, Social Informatics and Telecommunications Engineering 2016
R. Glitho et al. (Eds.): AFRICOMM 2015, LNICST 171, pp. 45–56, 2016.
DOI: 10.1007/978-3-319-43696-8_5

big data centers and many services such as authentication services, eduroam, clouds, software download mirrors etc. [2, 9]. They manage budgets in some cases of up to tens or even hundreds of millions of Euros a year for maintaining and developing the services and keeping up with the increasing demand [3].

Today, the needs for NRENs in developing countries are not different from those of developed countries but they cannot afford spending the same amount of money and, if they were using the same solutions, they would actually need more money because they do not just have to maintain the network and the services but they must build everything from scratch. Another approach is thus needed and has been demonstrated to be feasible by the BJNet project.

Section 2 will present the context of the BJNet project.
Section 3 will present the problem statement of building a NREN for Benin.
Section 4 will present the BJNet strategy to solve this problem.
Section 5 will discuss discuss synergies with the RERBénin project
Section 6 will discuss political issues.
Section 7 will summarize and conclude

2   Context of the BJNet Project

2.1   University Networking in Benin 2004-2010

In 2004, there were only two public universities in Benin, the Université d'Abomey-Calavi (UAC) close to Cotonou in the South and the Université de Parakou (UNIPAR), in the North. They had respectively some 30.000 and a few thousand students, but there was no campus network. On the campus of UAC there was (andthere still is) the Centre Numérique Francophone de Cotonou (CNFC), financed by the Agence Universitaire de la Francophonie (AUF), that was connected to internet and had a LAN with a few computer rooms. There were lines linking the CNFC to therectorate and a few faculties. In UNIPAR, only the rectorate was connected by radio to a local ISP, BorgouNet.

In 2006, the Belgian "Commission Universitaire pour le Développement" (CUD) financed a first extended campus network for the UAC under the coordination of prof. Hounkonnou and prof. Lobelle. This project was conditioned on the UAC subscribing at own cost to an internet connection (modest: 6 Mbps) and recruiting on the university payroll the staff to manage and operate the network. The CUD would bring the funding and the expertise to design and build the network.

Most buildings of the Abomey-Calavi Campus were connected to the the internet access point of the university through a shared radio network connecting all the buildings via outdoor 802.11a access points with sector antennas. Remote campuses in Dangbo (IMSP: Institut de Mathématiques et de Science Physique)), Porto-Novo (ENS: Ecole Normale Supérieure, FLASH: Faculté de Lettres, Arts et de Sciences Humaines), Cotonou (ENEAM: Ecole Nationale d'Economie Appliquée et de Management, FSS: Faculté des Sciences de la Santé) and Ouidah (IRSP: Institut Régional de Santé Publique) were connected through point-to-point 802.11a links with 30 dB antennas located on top of up to 40 m high guyed masts. The whole infrastructure provided a shared bandwidth of some 40 Mbps to the buildings of the main campus and 10 to 20 Mbps to each of the remote campuses, located at distances ranging from 10 to about 35 km. The quality of the long distance connections could be degraded by climatic conditions (heavy rain, thunderstorms).

In 2008 the ACP (African, Caribbean and Pacific) organization launched a call for projects to be funded mainly by Europe Aid in the framework of the @CP-ICT program. The authors submitted a project, called BJNet, aimed at reinforcing and extending the intercampus network under construction for UAC, in order to increase its capacity and also reach the campus of Lokossa, too far to be reached without relay from the nearest other site of UAC (IRSP-Ouidah), and the campus of the university of Parakou. The project was to build a network based on both the experience of building the intercampus network of UAC (based on radios with high gain antennas on 40 to 60 m high guyed masts) and the Belnet NREN in Belgium. The interesting particularity of Belnet is that it is not restricted to higher education and research institutions but that it is a State funded network open to all administrations, as long as they bear the additional costs induced by their use of the network. This use policy has three advantages: the first two are common to Belgium and Benin while the last one is specific to Benin.

1. The more administrations use the network the less the State will be prone to cutting in the budget of the network.
2. Because of savings due to the scale of the network and its large number of users, and the fact that traffic between sites in the country does not have to be routed through the internet at large, the use of this public network for connecting administrative sites is much more cost effective than renting leased lines or through private internet service providers.
3. By involving, in the network, other administrations than higher education, the number of possible sites for locating guyed masts for radio relay increases dramatically. Indeed, the reason why it had not been possible to connect Lokossa to the UAC network was the lack of a suitable site in the town of Comè, where the UAC does not own any premises. The maximum budget for these ACP projects was one million €, of which 85 % would be borne by the EU and 15 % by the partners. The BJNet partners were, in Belgium, Université catholique de Louvain (coordinator) and Belnet, and, in Benin, Université d'Abomey-Calavi (co-coordinator), Ministry of Higher Education and Research (MESRS), Ministry of Economy and Finances (MEF) and Ministry of Communications (MCTIC). The Beninese Armed Forces (FAB) also expressed interest in using the network and contributing to its implementation without being a formal partner.

For various reasons, the project was only accepted and allowed to start two years later, in September 2010. In the meantime huge changes had occurred in the Beninese higher education landscape: the number of campuses, called "Centres Universitaires" (CU) created or planned had been increased to 22, from Kandi and Nattitingou, in the North, to Savalou and Aplahoué in the West or Kétou and Adjara in the East: the new centers were spread all over the country. Many had little staff and thus needed facilities for distance learning. As it had been planned in 2008, the network would only have satisfied a small part of Benin's higher education needs.

2.2 Public Networking Resources in Benin at the Start of the Project

Networking resources in Benin are owned by the public operator Bénin Télécoms and its subsidiaries such as Kanakoo and by mobile operators (Bell Benin, Glo, Libercom, Moov and MTN). All have a long distance infrastructure based on microwave links (point-to-point radio links) between telecommunication towers. Bénin Télécoms also has optical fiber cables along 3 axes: one along the southern coast, from Togo to Nigeria, one South-North from Cotonou, on the coast where the SAT3 undersea cable lands in Benin, to the border with Niger in Malanville, via Bohicon, Parakou and Kandi. The third link is from Parakou to Porga on the border with Burkina-Faso, near Tanguiéta. This cables passes through the town of Nattitingou.

The short distance infrastructure used for data connections and internet access consists of one-to-many last mile radio links, adsl connections, and leased lines.

3 Problem Statement: A NREN for Benin

The NREN for Benin had to interconnect all University Centers (CU) in Benin. Other public sites could be connected if the concerned administration contributed at least enough to cover the cost of their connection. Indeed the European funding funding was dedicated to education and research institutions.

The most interested "administration" was Benin Armed Forces (FAB) which lacked a reliable territorial communication infrastructure, (as consequence, it could take up to a day for the headquarters in Cotonou to be warned on a border incident during the rainy season). The FAB were also interested by the possibilities offered in the field of tele-medecine between military hospitals: if the military hospitals could be connected through a suitable networking infrastructure, the FAB could get help in the field of telemedecine from the US army. Moreover, Benin Armed Forces have difficulties to deploy modern human resource management tools as they don't have access to a terri-torial communication infrastructure.

Regarding the University Centers, they could, broadly, be divided into two catego-ries: big campuses with thousands to tens of thousands of students and small campuses, with tens to hundreds of students. The first category counted fortunately only 3 members and the State of Benin was planning to connect two of them with optical fiber cable to the Bénin Télécoms exchange closest to their campus: Abomey-Calavi and Parakou. The third one is in Cotonou, namely the Faculty of Health Sciences. These three should be connected to BJNet with optical fiber cable; for the others, a 100 Mbps radio link is acceptable.

The BJNet backbone should be optical and at least 1 gigabit. One might argue why not more bandwidth? Janet, the UK NREN uses 40 Gbits links since 2007 [4]. The reasons are simple:

1. we want affordable technologies: cheap to buy, cheap to install, cheap and quick to replace in case of malfunction, easy to upgrade;
2. an earthen dam can hold huge amounts of water but as soon as a rivulet gets across through a rat hole or passes on top, the dam will be quickly destroyed. This is what

we want to do: get a significant rivulet of information across between higher education institutions and when it will not be enough anymore, it will be much easier to find funding to upgrade the network than to set it up initially, at least if it has been designed to be easily upgradable.

Another element to take into account was that several of the guyed masts built in 2006 had collapsed before 2010. Apparently some contractors of cooperation projects consider that the only purpose of a project is to provide some employment and some benefit in the target country, that nobody is interested any more in the results of a project after its implementation: the guyed masts were not adequately protected against corrosion. A closer analysis revealed that Benin has no hot zinc coating facility and thus locally built masts will rust at least at the weldings, without heavy maintenance work. Therefore imported masts, manufactured in a country where quality control matters, had to be used.

4   Resolution Strategy

The change in size of the problem to be solved, between the time the project was submitted and the time it had to be implemented imposed a choice between with 2 options:

1. implement the project according to the original plan: find a guyed masts manufacturer abroad and let a local contractor replace the old rotten masts and set up a chain of masts between Abomey-Calavi and Parakou and build a network serving only a few University Centers, and which soon would become obsolete.
2. Find available local resources (workforce, existing unused infrastructures), if possible at no cost, and use the european funding to buy what cannot be obtained that way and try to build a network corresponding to the current needs but, equally, easily upgradable.

The second option was selected.

4.1   Infrastructures

Fortunately for the project, many fiber pairs in the cables set up by Bénin Télécoms (BT) were found to be unused. The use of fiber pairs rather than single fibers was planned because, for bidirectional traffic, optical equipment was cheaper when using fiber pairs than when using single fibers, and because fiber pairs can obviously be upgraded later to twice the capacity of single fibers.

Allowing BJNet to use such "dark" (unused) fibers can make sense for Bénin Télécoms. Indeed, internet access is currently offered at reduced cost to universities by Bénin Télécoms and, if this traffic were moved to BJNet fibers, that bandwidth could be sold to other customers paying the full fare, at a higher profit for Bénin Télécoms. Besides, a renting tariff for the dark fibers can be negotiated later between Bénin Télécoms and the Government of Benin. The equipment to be added in each BT exchange in order to build the BJNet backbone from these dark fibers consists only of a box including a small router and fiber interfaces appropriate for the distance to the next exchange (plus whatever is needed to connect local user sites). When the exchange is just a relay for BJNet and the distances on both sides are short, a simple optical patch cable between the two cable heads is enough.

The active equipment uses only little power, typically a few tens of watts, and can be powered by the battery backed 48 VDC power supply that is standard in any telephone exchange. The total power used in the backbone including links to the user sites is only 1.2 KW. The cost of that power should be included in the renting agreement for using the dark fibers. Obviously, the equipment to be placed in the exchanges has to be bought by the project with European funding. It was selected to be cheap but offer all the functionalities needed in a high performance TCP/IP wide area network. MIKROTIK equipments were selected. Besides satisfying the above requirements all their devices use exactly the same software. This simplified the training of operational staff.

For the large University Centers of Abomey-Calavi and Parakou, the connection to the BJNet backbone can similarly use a pair of fibers in the cable planned to connect the campus to internet via the BT internet infrastructure.

For the smaller sites, with more limited needs, radio links are enough. Cheap radios allowing a bandwidth of 100 Mbps were selected (also MIKROTIK). They can be used for both small and long distances. If needed, some links may be upgraded later with higher bit rate radios. The radios are used with high gain (30 dB) wide band (covering the entire range of 5 Ghz) antennas. This allows the selection of cheap radios, mass produced for 802.11a links, which are tuned to a reserved military channel out of the standard 802/11a bands. Since high gain antennas reduce interferences with devices located out of the point-to-point link, it was decided to use the same radios and antennas for all the radio links. All these devices were bought using the EU funding.

5 Ghz radios need line of sight links with no obstacles close to the line of sight (the 1st Fresnel ellipsoid should be free [7]). This implies locating the radios and antennas higher than the obstacles taking into account the earth curvature for longer links. Thus, masts or towers are needed. Since the backbone fiber network of BJNet runs through BT exchanges, one of the ends of each radio link to a BJNet user site must be located above this exchange. This provides the opportunity to use other existing and often available resources. Indeed, optical fibers are relatively new in Benin (some 20 years). Before the availability of fibers, long distance links between exchanges were implemented with microwave links needing their antennas to be located, like ours, on communication towers, high above the BT exchanges. Therefore, there is a telecommunication tower above each BT exchange, sometimes almost empty, often moderately filled with antennas connecting Bénin Télécoms clients, such as bank branches etc. In most instances, there is enough free room on these towers to add a few radios and antennas to connect BJNet user sites. Again, the use of room on these towers may be included in the renting agreement to establish between the Beninese State and Bénin Télécoms.

Only the radios, the antennas and the cables to connect them are thus needed for the BJNet user links and must be bought, but, on the backbone side, the radios can be placed on the existing BT telecommunication towers.

On the user side, the same radios and antennas are used, and a small router is used indoors to isolate the user's local network from BJNet. Of course, here too, the radio must be higher than the obstacles, but because these sites are often not very far from the BT Exchange, rooftop masts are generally enough. These masts too were bought using the European funding. Apart from the sites discussed above, which are close to fiber fed BT exchanges, three other types of user sites must be considered

1. the big Cotonou site of the Faculty of Health Sciences,
2. the small sites which are too far to be connected using a rooftop mast but reachable if a guyed mast is erected in their premises,
3. the small sites that can only be reached through a chain of several radio relays.

For the Faculty of Heath Sciences (FSS) in Cotonou, either very high bandwidth radios such as the Ubiquity AirFiber [11] or fiber cables could have been used. Fiber cables were preferred because, in the Cotonou area, the radio spectrum is heavily polluted and the risk of interferences was high. Besides, this would have been the only link using such equipment. This would have involved training the staff and buying spares just for this link etc. On the other hand, building a fiber solution involved much more manpower, but in the specific case of the FSS, there was a way for the fiber cables to run almost entirely on "friendly ground" from the closest BT exchange to the FSS: the Benin Armed Forces headquarters that also needed to be connected to BJNet and to BT. The two cables could be buried in the same tube in the same trench and digging the trench itself was exercise for soldiers. So, this fiber solution was preferred in these circumstances although AirFiber could also have been preferred for this kind of site depending on the local street topology, distance, availability of manpower etc.

For the small sites unreachable from a BT exchange using rooftop masts, such as Adjara, Toffo, Dangbo, Aplahoué, a set of unassembled 55 m high bolted angled steel bars guyed masts with a thick zinc coating was imported. Bolted in order to be easily transportable and assembled on site; angled steel bars rather than hollow tubes to ease quality control of the zinc plating on all sides. Some telecommunication towers and guyed masts of the same source are in use in Benin for over 40 years, with very little maintenance, and they are still fine.

For the small sites needing several relays, towers located in BT exchanges that are not fed by fiber but by radio relays are used. Simply because all University Centers are close to towns that need communication (even if only plain old telephones), there is always such a way to reach them.

Unfortunately, there are many networks in need of reaching such places: banks, ISPs, mobile operators (although the largest have their own towers or guyed masts), and many of these networks were there before BJNet so that some of the communication towers of Bénin Télécoms are overloaded with radios and there is very little spare space to add more radios. Moreover, there are so many people climbing these towers that the risk of damage to radios is significant.

A typical case is Comè: one of the 55 m guyed masts had to be built on a site owned by the customs administration at a few hundreds of meters from the overloaded BT mast, with a short distance link from the top of he BJNet mast to half way up on the seaside leg of the BT mast, where nobody is interested. This BJNet mast is used as relay between the BT exchange in Comè, which is fed by fiber, and the town of Lokossa, where there is still no fiber. Currently, this link ends on a mast erected 9 years ago in IUT (Institut

Universitaire de Technologie) Lokossa. This mast was never used before by lack of a suitable relay in Comè, except for tests from the BT mast. This mast in IUT is corroded, and the radio will be moved to the BT tower in Lokossa and the University institutions in Lokossa, such as IUT, will be connected using rooftop masts. Another radio link will go from the BT Tower in Lokossa to the 55 m BJNet guyed mast to be built in the new CU of Aplahoué.

Similar relay systems will be used from Dassa to Savalou, from Bohikon to Ketou, etc.

4.2 Workforce

It was decided to use as much as possible the workforce of partners (mostly UAC and UCL) and "friends" interested in the projects (the FAB). This workforce was provided free of charge to the project. In return, the project took care (on EU funds) of training these people in the suitable technologies and the means for their transportation and subsistence when working away from their usual workplace.

The workforce was trained in optical fiber soldering (use of fiber soldering machine) and measuring (use of reflectometer), in FO cable termination in patch panels and jointing cables in the field by a Beninese officer, Capt Dossou who holds a PhD in fiberoptics and also teaches in EPAC (Ecole Polytechnique d'Abomey Calavi), the engineering school of UAC).

Two members of the team were trained to become themselves trainers in the setting up of Mikrotik devices (now, UAC is even a Mikrotik academy). They trained the others.

One of the FAB officers did his Master thesis in the Belgian Royal Military Academy (RMA) on microwave links modeling under the supervision of Major Gilles and prof. Lobelle. A group of Beninese Signal Corps and Engineering NCO and soldiers were trained to assemble and build the guyed masts as well as setting up radio links from their top.

The FAB officers and UAC ICT engineers were trained in network design and they themselves designed the campus networks of UAC-Calavi and Camp Guézo in Cotonou.

Most of the training costs were borne by EU funding or contributed without charge by members of the UCL, Belnet, the UAC, the RMA and the FAB. The training activities were performed during the two years of the European funding of the project.

An advantage of using staff of the partners as workforce for the project was that they were still available after the end of the European funding of the project and thus could proceed with the building of the network long after this end.

An inconvenience of using the staff of the partners is that they also have other activities. Organizing the missions to set up network nodes in BT exchanges or radio links from the towers above was a hard job because it requires simultaneously people from BT, the FAB and UAC and getting them available at the same time is not obvious.

The logistics of building the project were mainly borne by the EU funds as well. Two cars were bought for transportation purposes (two because, to set up a communication link, it is better to have people at both ends) as well as enough fuel vouchers to finish the complete set-up of the network. A call for tender was issued to feed the staff when they were in the field building the network.

However, delays in setting up the network made it necessary for the partners to also contribute to these logistic costs. And to train more staff members to build guyed masts (some of the military members of the staff had been sent on mission abroad).

5   Synergy with the RERBénin Project

Funded by the World Bank, the West And Central african Research and Education Network (WACREN), the Africa Universities Association (AUA), a Beninese NREN initiative, called RERBénin, was launched in July 2013 and aims to establish a national network dedicated to education and research. Said network aims to take into account research centers and public and private universities in Benin. The objectives of RERBénin are part of the objectives of BJNet. Moreover, BJNet has already established some interconnections between university centers. Thus for better efficiency and convergence of efforts in achieving the interconnection of academic centers, it is suggested to set up a virtual network for RERBénin over the BJNet infrastructure, using the MPLS protocol (Multi Protocol Label Switching). This way to carry several types of traffic, such as academic traffic, over BJNet had already been planned since the early phases of the design of the network.

RERBénin will then take care of the administrative management and applications over this virtual network that only connects universities and research centers. However, BJNet and RERBénin have to agree on an economic model and on the way RERBénin would be involved in the development and extension phases of BJNet.

6   Political Issues

The political context was excellent for BJNet because Benin had a clear objective to become the "quartier numérique de l'Afrique", as stated in the "Document de Politique et de Stratégie du secteur des Télécommunications, des TIC et de la Poste" [10]. The project was consistent with the "e-Gouvernement" project of the State of Benin [1].

Building a NREN requires good cooperation with political bodies that will have to finance the running costs of the network after its construction (ministry of Higher Education and Research and ministry of Telecommunications).

Building a NREN using existing available and unused hardware resources belonging to the State (optical fibers in inter-city cables and space on communication towers) requires an excellent cooperation with the ministry owning these resources (ministry of Telecommunications).

There are two kinds of obstacles to good cooperation with ministries.

1. Some ministers are frequently replaced and so is their staff and they know it. They are thus often focused on a few short term issues. But more important, each time the minister and its staff changes, contact must be re-established with the new people and one must re-brief them thoroughly on the project, taking into account that, when a minister and his staff leave, their files are often not properly transferred to their successors.

The new staff is usually very busy organizing itself and focusing on its top issues, thus time is lost.

2. While, in universities, projects originate from outside (calls for proposals by subsidizing organizations) or take a bottom up course (proposals by professors), in administrations, projects are organized following a top down in several steps (i) the president/minister/staff has an idea or consultants are asked to come up with ideas; (ii) funding is found for a feasibility study by more consultants who come up with technical specifications; (iii) funding is found to build the project or part of it according to the technical specification.

These budgets often include not only the direct cost of the project but also indirect costs such as the salaries or salary complements of the civil servants supervising the project.

BJNet absolutely did not follow this scheme. It originated from university professors; funding did not pass through administrations and all expenses were strictly controlled by university accountants in Belgium, according to EU and Belgian public markets rules.

When the project was originally proposed in 2008, the first reaction of some administration (fortunately, not all of them) was therefore more or less "Hu, only a million euro, ok, transfer it to us and it will help us finance part of the feasibility study". In other words, while some civil servants, particularly those with a fixed salary, (and the military authorities) saw clearly the advantage of the project and all the other future projects that it was enabling, other ones were reluctant to get involved because the indirect costs in the administration were not included and the organization of the project did not match their usual practice. Consequently they spread the opinion that the project was shady and it was safer not to be involved.

The above obstacles caused a lot of delay in the project and so did the presidential election of 2011 (all ministries and administrations were almost blind to anything else for a period of about six months).

However some ministers (e.g. D. Adadja), Directors of Cabinet in some ministries (e.g. W. Martin) and staff members at the presidency very quickly understood the benefits of the project for their country and actively supported the project even after they had been replaced in their former functions. They managed to get the needed endorsement of the project by the council of ministers [6].

Another political issue that interfered with the project was the possible privatization of the State owned Bénin Télécoms company, which owned the inter-city optical fiber cables and communication towers we planned to use. This uncertainty accentuated by the fact that decision makers in the company were replaced several times in the course of the project also caused delays.

On the other hand, many employees of Bénin Télécoms very well understood the advantage of the project for the country and for the company too, in particular, the innovating technologies used by the project and that could also benefit the company.

All this caused long delays but the project was never blocked and could always proceed, although slower than expected. These delays induced unexpected costs and, in September 2014, the project coordinators decided to return to the partners and

1. explain to them that an extra funding of about 5 % of the original EU funding was necessary because of the delays and the indirect costs in the ministries;
2. explain the urgent need to create and plan a budget for a permanent structure to operate the network.

Both requests have now been taken into account.

7   Conclusions

The BJNet project shows that all developing countries can build a NREN by using existing and available local resources, both material and human, with a limited amount of additional funding.

Originally, BJNet had not been planned to use this approach, but because of the big changes on the higher education landscape in Benin, this approach was more reasonable. Since the timeframe of the availability of EU funding for the project was short (2years), the BJNet team had to take the design decisions before convincing the authorities that it was the right thing to do. Now that the feasibility of the approach has been shown, other countries can follow it, but the different steps should preferably be performed in the following order.

1. Using the BJNet example, convince the highest possible authorities in the country of the adequacy of the approach.
2. Obtain the authorization to use available and unused passive telecommunication infrastructure: dark fibers in existing cables and antenna locations on communication towers. Such passive infrastructures are often available because activating them (i.e. installing the needed electronic equipment for the classical services) is expensive. Thus, in many instances cables with tens of fibers are installed (the total cost of buying and installing an optical fiber cable does not much depend on the number of fibers), but only a few fibers are actually used. Many telecommunication towers were built some years ago and except in vey densely populated areas, there is often plenty of available room for antennas on these towers.
3. Convince the future beneficiaries (e.g. universities) of the network to provide (at their own cost) the manpower to build it, even if they do not have trained staff (they usually have engineers that can esily be trained on the technologies to be used).
4. Evaluate the needed additional funding, i.e. the cost of the equipment to be purchased and the cost of the logistics for building the network: vehicle cost (borrowing, buying or renting plus maintenance costs and fuel costs), per diems of the staff when it is in the field, international travel, cost of tasks that have to be ousourced, training cost, etc.
5. Find a funding to cover this cost and start building the network keeping all the time the authorities and the beneficiaries informed of the progress.

And during all these steps, let the project be steered by a team of dynamic and committed people understanding all its technical and managerial aspects.

Acknowledgements. The authors and the whole BJNet team want to thank first the ACP organization and Europe-Aid for funding BJNet through grant contract external action of the EU FED/2010/250-288. The authors want also to thank the partners and other contributors to the implementation of the network: in Belgium, Belnet which provided help to set up an Eduroam service, the Ministry of Defense which provided transportation to Benin for part of the equipment, UCL which managed all the procurement process and the administrative tasks related to the grant contract; and, in Benin, the Ministries of Communications (MCTIC), Economy and Finances (MEF) and Higher Education and Research (MESRS) for all their contributions. Benin Armed Forces are also thanked for the constant support of the general staff and in particular the successive Chiefs of Staff, Gen. Boni, Gen.Okè, Gen. Akpona, Gen. Gbèssèmèhlan and Gen. Nangnimi. The military staff provided an important contribution to building the network. Finally, the Rector and Vice-Rector of Université d'Abomey-Calavi, prof. Sinsin and Farougou and their staff who where the other big contributors to building the network.

References

1. Ayoyo, C.: Etude de faisabilité du e-Gouvernement: Rapport Final, NLC Groupe, (Sept 2008), Cotonou, pp. 42–46 (2008)
2. Belnet: Belnet History (2014). https://www.belnet.be/en/about-us/history
3. Belnet: Belnet publications (2014). https://www.belnet.be/en/about-us/publications
4. Ciena: JANET Delivers Europe's First 40 Gbps Wavelength Service across National Research and Education Network with Ciena (2007). Ciena press release on www.ciena.com
5. Cormier, D., Siemens, G.: Through the open door: open courses as research, learning, and engagement. Educause Rev. **45**(4), 30–39 (2010)
6. Dossoumou E. : Communication gouvernementale 1298/12: relevé02 des décisions prises par le conseil des Ministres en sa séance du mercredi 30 Janvier 2013. Secrétariat du Gouvernement, Cotonou (2013)
7. ITU: Propagation by diffraction, ITU, recommendation ITU-R P.526–8 (1978)
8. Masters, K: A brief guide to understanding MOOCS. Internet J. Med. Educ. 1(2) (2011). doi: 10.5580/1f21, http://ispub.com/IJME/1/2/10995
9. Nowlan, M., Fosters, D., Reijs, V.,Rotkop, A., Wierenga, K., Witzig, C.: The Future Roles of NRENs, Aspire, September 2012. https://www.terena.org/activities/aspire/docs/ASPIRE-future-of-nrens.pdf
10. Présidence de la République du Bénin, 2011, Document de Politique et de Stratégie du secteur des Télécommunications, des Tics et de la Poste, April 2011
11. Ubiquity: Airfiber5. https://www.ubnt.com/airfiber/airfiber5/

Deployment of an e-Infrastructure for Academic Research

Collins N. Udanor[1(✉)], Florence I. Akaneme[2], Stephen Aneke[1], Blessing O. Ogbuokiri[1],
Assumpta O. Ezugwu[1], Chikaodili H. Ugwuishiwu[1],
Carl E.A. Okezie[2], and Benjamin Ogwo[3]

[1] Department of Computer Science, University of Nigeria Nsukka, Nsukka, Nigeria
{collins.udanor,stepehen.aneke,blessing.ogbuokiri,
assumpta.ezugwu,chikodili.uwguishiwu}@unn.edu.ng
[2] Department of Plant Science and Biotechnology,
University of Nigeria Nsukka, Nsukka, Nigeria
{florence.akaneme,carl.okezie}@unn.edu.ng
[3] Department of Vocational Teacher Preparation,
State University New York, Oswego, NY 13126, USA
Benjamin.ogwo@oswego.edu

Abstract. One of the greatest problems researchers in Africa face, according a 2007 UNESCO report is a chronic lack of investment in facilities for research and teaching. This has both affected the quality and quantity of research output from institutions of higher learning, with the ripple effect of stagnating industrialization and R&D processes. This paper presents the design and implementation of an e-infrastructure, which is made up of cloud and grid computing clusters domiciled in University of Nigeria Nsukka (UNN). The project has objectives, such as to deploy an Identity Provider (IdP) based on Simple Access Markup Language (SAML) that uses robot certificates to authenticate users on the cloud and grid infrastructures, deploy a Web 2.0 based Science Gateway application server that enables researchers have access to simulation, and modeling applications in their research domains on the infrastructure. As well as implement a Virtualized cluster for big data analytics. Results from one of the applications developed and deployed on the infrastructure show over 60 % predication accuracy while participation database in the infrastructure has reached up to 350 users.

Keywords: Cloud computing · Science gateway · e-Infrastructure · IdP · Clusters · Robot certificates

1 Introduction

One of the greatest problems researchers in Africa face, according a 2007 UNESCO report is a chronic lack of investment in facilities for research and teaching [1]. According to Thomson Reuters National Science Indicators database, between 1999 and 2008 the quantity of papers published in the three highest publishing countries in Africa stands as follows; Egypt in the North, 30,000; Nigeria in the middle, 10,000; and South Africa in the South, 47,000. Yet, Netherlands alone produces over 27,000 every year. Researchers, who would want to publish papers with impact factors like Thomson

© ICST Institute for Computer Sciences, Social Informatics and Telecommunications Engineering 2016
R. Glitho et al. (Eds.): AFRICOMM 2015, LNICST 171, pp. 57–65, 2016.
DOI: 10.1007/978-3-319-43696-8_6

Reuters, would usually travel to countries where the facilities exist. Research in the 21st century requires skills in the area of the 4Cs (critical thinking and problem solving, communication, collaboration, and creativity and innovation), all which are addressed by Grid and Cloud Computing. Most research tools today are soft tools. And most research works done today are based on the use of software simulation, modeling or analytic tools. High Performance Computing (HPC) comes with multi-cores of processing power, petabytes of storage and myriad of software tools that range from the modeling of bridges to protein synthesis, etc.

E-Infrastructures can be defined as networked tools, data and resources that support a community of researchers, broadly including all those who participate in and benefit from research [2]. According to [2], the term e-Infrastructure comprises very heterogeneous projects and institutions within the scientific community. E-Infrastructures include services as diverse as the physical supply of backbone connectivity, single- or multi-purpose grids, supercomputer infrastructure, data grids and repositories, tools for visualization, simulation, data management, storage, analysis and collection, tools for support in relation to methods or analysis, as well as remote access to research instruments and very large research facilities.

In 2011 the University of Nigeria Brain Gain Initiative (BGI) project successfully set up the first ever Grid Computing Infrastructure in Nigeria (The Lion Grid), under the funding of UNESCO and HP [3, 4]. The Grid computing infrastructure enables researchers to run jobs remotely from their PCs, monitor the job and receive results. Because of this success UNESCO granted the UNN BGI further sustainability funding from June till December, 2013 when the project ended. The BGI project organized several seminars and workshops within and outside the university, including one workshop at Federal University Ndufu-Alike (FUNIA) Ebonyi state, Nigeria in July 2013 which had over 150 academics in attendance, a presentation at the West and Central Africa Research and Education Network (WACREN) conference in 2013 at the National Universities Commission (NUC) Abuja Nigeria, eI4Africa International Thematic Workshop in March 2014 at the University of Lagos (UNILAG) [5], two workshops in UNN for academics and researchers in which staff of the Centre for Atmospheric Research Ayingba (CAR), a unit of the National Space Research and Development Agency (NASRDA) attended in July 2014, and a presentation at UNESCO headquarters, Paris in September, 2013.

Since the establishment of the High performance Computing (HPC) infrastructure (the Lion Grid), a number of research applications have been deployed and put to use by researchers, including the OpenFoam application for fluid dynamics used by some PhD research students in Mechanical Engineering, UNN, Plantisc, a Plant Tissue Culture micro propagation simulation software, which achieved over 60 % predication accuracy [6] developed locally by the UNN BGI team, etc. Active research on the project continued even after the end of the BGI project. The team has continued to work hard on sustaining the project by deploying more applications for researchers and extending the infrastructure to include the science gateway cloud and big data cluster components. The Lion Grid was established to meet the challenges faced by researchers as well as limit brain drain. In view of recent changes in technologies it has become expedient to upgrade the infrastructure.

In mid-2012, a new approach to grid computing was introduced by the eI4Africa FP7 project funded by the European Commission (DG CONNECT). The aim of the eI4Africa project was to boost the Research, Technological Development and Innovation (RTDI) potential of African e-Infrastructures and to support policy dialogues and EuroAfrican cooperation in the framework of the joint Africa-EU Strategic Partnership [7]. The eI4Africa project developed the grid Science Gateway (SGW) for Africa [8], a cloud based infrastructure for research application repository. This new infrastructure brings the grid closer to individuals as against the Virtual Organization method that involved the use of Digital Certificates that were difficult to obtain. The Science Gateway uses robot certificates issued by Identity providers (IdPs), which can now be located at individual institutions, rather than Certificate Authorities (CAs).

2 The Proposed Infrastructure

It is against this background that we proposed to develop an institutional based Cloud computing infrastructure that has both an IdP and a Grid Science Gateway, a repository for simulation, modeling and analytic applications. Simulation helps a scientist test his ideas before practice, detect problems in workflows and enables one increase business productivity as well as minimize the number of experimental trials in the laboratory, where applicable. This infrastructure could be adopted by ngREN as a service provider (SP) in the recently commissioned ngREN network of interconnected universities in Nigeria, which till now has no services running on it. This project will bring e-infrastructures such as the grid and SGW with a repository of simulation and analytic software tools like R, GATES, Octave, OpenFoam, Clustalw, etc. closer to the researchers in Nigeria by limiting network latency and improve response time. It can also be used by other NRENs within and beyond the WACREN region.

The processes of implementing this project includes the following tasks:

1. Upgrade the current infrastructure for the Lion Grid by adding a Cloud computing component made up of additional high performance servers with Redundant Arrays of Independent Disks (RAIDs) and virtual machines. The Cloud will offer Infrastructure as a Service (IaaS), Platform as a Service (PaaS), and Software as a Service (SaaS) based on multi-tenant approach.

2. Add Solar panels to the existing power backup infrastructure currently made up of a 5KVA inverter and 8 nos of 400 AHr deep cycle batteries. The addition of the solar unit will ensure additional 18–20 h backup, in addition to that of the inverter, generator and public electricity supplies. If this is achieved, there will be a guaranty of 99.9 % server availability (uptime) comparable to most other Grid and Cloud infrastructures and ISPs based in the US and Europe.

3. Develop a Cloud Computing portal with IdP authentication interface that authenticates users of the Grid Science Gateway, and grant them access to a repository of research applications for simulation, modeling, forecasting, analytics, etc.

4. Develop sample simulation applications for researchers as well as port existing ones not readily available to the proposed Cloud infrastructure, in collaboration with our colleagues in the eI4Africa project.

5. Conduct training for support staff and advocacy to the university community.

3 Design and Implementation

The Architecture of the proposed Cloud Infrastructure for Lion Grid UNN is shown in Fig. 1. The implementation strategies are in two phases, systems deployment & configuration and software development.

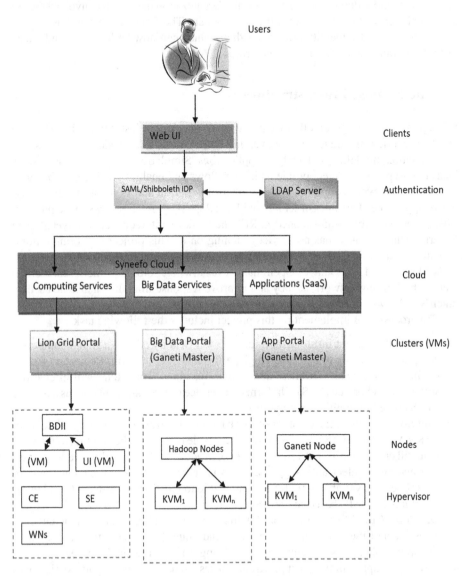

Fig. 1. The architecture of the proposed cloud infrastructure for lion grid UNN

3.1 System Deployment and Configuration

While work is completed on the Grid computing services, which is already configured and running, work is still in progress on the other components of the infrastructure. Due to the challenges of low computing resources, we have built a number of virtual machines using KVM, a kernel virtualization hypervisor in Linux platforms. The VMs are used to build computing clusters, such as the Hadoop cluster. The VMs will also increase the number of available machines to users for computing and running user applications and storages. While Scientific Linux, SL 5.5-64bit is installed on the physical machines for the Grid middleware (gLite 3.2), the Debian 6.5, 64bit distribution of Linux is installed on all the virtual machines. The clusters will be managed by the Ganeti Manager. Ganeti is a cluster management system developed by Google [9]. Each of the machines have a dedicated public IP address, since we have already acquired a/24 bundle of IP-v4 addresses, enough for all our machines. Table 1 summarizes the machine configurations.

Table 1. Machine configuration details

S/N	Machine SPEC	Host name	VMs
1.	IDP HP PROLIANT ML 110 G6 SERVER, 2.8GHZ, core i3, 2BG RAM, 250 GB HDD, VT-x	idp.grid.unn.edu.ng	Nil
2.	LDAP SERVER ML 110 G6 SERVER, 2.8GHZ, core i3, 2BG RAM, 250 GB HDD, VT-x	ldap.grid.unn.edu.ng	1. VM (APP)
3.	BDII HP PROLIANT GL360, G5 SERVER, 2.4GHZ XEON, 4 GB RAM, 1 TB HDD	bdii.grid.unn.edu.ng	1. (UI) Grid.unn.edu.ng 2. VM2
4.	WN HP PROLIANT GL360, G5 SERVER, 2.4GHZ XEON, 4 GB RAM, 1 TB HDD	wn01.grid.unn.edu.ng	1. VM1(Hadoop) 2. VM2(Hadoop)
5.	CE HP Workstations	ce.grid.unn.edu.ng	1. VM1(Hadoop)
6.	SE HP Workstations	se1.grid.unn.edu.ng	

One physical server is dedicated for use as the IdP machine, another for the SGW, and another for storage using RAID-5. At present we have two HP Proliant 360 GL 6 servers with 8 CPU cores each, 1 TB of storage, and 4 GB RAM each, as well as two HP Proliant ML 110 G5 servers with 2 CPU cores each, 250 GB storage and 2 GB RAM each, in addition to two HP Z-workstations.

Installation and configuration of the services like the IdP, SGW will be done remotely by using repositories from cloud clusters like Ansible playbooks. The Simple Access Markup Language (SAML) and Shibboleth will be the principal tools to be used in configuring the IdP and SGW. Figure 2 shows a screen shot of the Lion Grid portal.

Fig. 2. Lion grid UNN portal

Figure 3 shows the micro-propagation of plant tissue culture experiment laboratory, while Figs. 4 and 5 show the input and results screen shots of the plant tissue culture prediction software (Plantisc), respectively.

Fig. 3. Tissue culture experiments in the lab

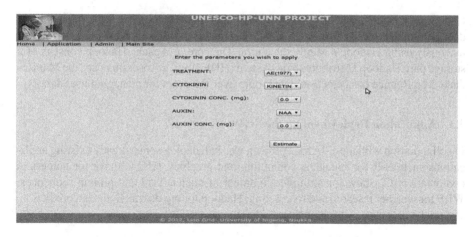

Fig. 4. Plantisc software showing auxin combinations input

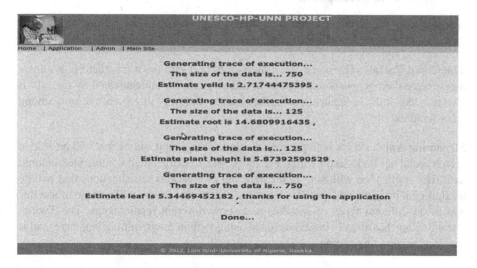

Fig. 5. The result page of the Plantisc application

3.2   Big Data Analytic Application Deployment

Big data can be processed faster and more efficiently than it would be in the more conventional supercomputer architecture in enterprise settings that relies on parallel file system where computation and data are connected to high speed networks. This can be achieved by creating a cluster of distributed computer nodes on which Apache Hadoop tool is installed. Hadoop is an open source framework written in Java for distributed storage and distributed processing on very large datasets on distributed clusters [10]. Hadoop is useful for pre-processing data to identify macro trends or find nuggets of information, such as out-of-range values. It enables businesses to unlock potential value from new data using inexpensive commodity servers. Organizations primarily use

Hadoop as a precursor to advanced forms of analytics. Hadoop can scale down a large data into smaller pieces distributed among computers in a cluster to be processed simultaneously using Hadoop's MapReduce tool. The core of Apache Hadoop consists of a storage part, Hadoop Distributed File System (HDFS) and a processing part, the MapReduce. MapReduce has been used by Google over the years for managing user data.

3.3 Application Deployment on the SGW

In collaboration with the eI4Africa project, we shall deploy some already existing applications such as R for statistical computing and graphics, GNU Octave for numerical computation, Clustalw for multiple alignment of nucleic acid and protein sequences, WRF for weather research and forecasting, Hadoop for big data analytic and prediction, etc. on the proposed e-infrastructure.

3.4 Application Development

Having set up the physical hardware systems and configured the various services on them, the next phase is to develop a number of applications. These will include:

The Cloud Portal: The portal is a single entry port into the infrastructure. It allows users create their accounts and sign in into the system for authenticated by the IdP. It also provides links to applications in the Science Gateway that users can run, among other features.

Streaming Apps: Work is in progress on developing applications that will be able to search social networks like Twitter, Facebook, etc. to extract high volume unstructured data. The application will analyze the data and plot various visualizations that will be used to gain insights into specific areas of user interests. Users will be able to use this app to do different types of searches and show different relationships. The Twitter streaming app has already been developed using Python programming language, and is currently undergoing testing.

3.5 Training

As reported earlier, a number of trainings have been conducted, yet more are scheduled, which will include: Training of researchers on the use of the cloud infrastructure and demonstration of the applications. This will also include how to use our application to extract data from social networks and analyze them.

Training of developers: We shall identify young promising programmers within the university and invite them to be trained on how to develop applications for the SGW. This will ensure sustainability of the project.

4   Conclusion

The impact of e-infrastructures on academic research is huge. According to a survey carried out by [2], more than 85 % of e-Infrastructure users classify e-Infrastructure as important or very important to their work. Most would also see their research work or programmes impaired if the e-Infrastructure did not exist. E-infrastructure opens doors for collaboration, innovation and communication among researchers in virtual communities. The impact of e-infrastructure also brings about the integration or separation of e-Infrastructures at national and disciplinary levels, different organizational and business models, considerations of research communities' needs and practices in the services provided by e-Infrastructures. The research community is in dire need of the innovative tools promised by the e-infrastructure. Over and again we have seen the enthusiasm and eagerness with which the workshops are received and we are certain that this infrastructure is not only timely but a must-have for all institutions that promote credible and cutting-edge research in this 21st century.

Acknowledgment.   We acknowledge the support from the United Nations Education Scientific and Cultural Organization (UNESCO), for providing the funds for this research project and Hewlett Packard (HP) for providing the equipment for the deployment of the grid infrastructure. And also University of Nigeria for providing the enabling ground and other forms of support.

References

1. Adams, J., King, C., Hook, D.: Global Research Report Africa. Thomson Reuters publishers, Philadelphia (2010)
2. The Role of e-Infrastructures in the Creation of Global Virtual Research Communities. European Communities (2010)
3. Lion Grid. http://grid.unn.edu.ng
4. Brain Gain Initiative. http://www.unesco.org/new/en/education/themes/strengthening-educationsystems/higher-education/reform-and-innovation/brain-gain-initiative/
5. The 3rd eI4Africa Thematic Workshop. http://ei4africa.eu/wp-content/plugins/alcyonis-eventagenda//files/Training_experience_in_Nigeria_with_the_NgREN_Identity_Provider.pdf
6. Akaneme, F.I., Udanor, C.N., Nwachukwu, J., Ugwuoke, C., Okezie, C.E.A., Ogwo, B.: A grid enabled application for the simulation of plant tissue culture experiments. Int. J. Adv. Comput. Sci. Inf. Technol. **3**(3), 227–242 (2014)
7. ei4Africa. http://ei4africa.eu/
8. Africa Grid Science Gateway. http://sgw-africa.grid.org
9. Apache Hadoop. http://en.wikipedia.org/wiki/Apache_Hadoop
10. Ganeti. http://docs.ganeti.org/ganeti/2.13/html/

Possible Challenges of Integrating ICTs into the Public Transportation System in the Free State Province, South Africa

Ndakhona Bashingi[1]([✉]), M. Mostafa Hassan[2], and Muthoni Masinde[3]

[1] SURT Research Group, Central University of Technology,
Bloemfontein, Free State, South Africa
nbashingi@gmail.com
[2] Department of Civil Engineering, Central University of Technology,
Bloemfontein, Free State, South Africa
mmostafa@cut.ac
[3] Department of Information Technology, Central University of Technology,
Bloemfontein, Free State, South Africa
emasinde@cut.ac

Abstract. There is need for ICT in the Free State public transportation system and for its implementation to be successful, information is needed on the needs of the various stakeholders and assessment of whether those needs are possible to fulfill using ICT solutions. The conventional and traditional poor quality transportation system needs to be improved. ICTs have shown to be the ultimate solution to most public transport problems. For successful ICT integration, implementation and operation of these ICT solutions to improve the public transportation system challenges may be encountered which has to be addressed. This study investigates the challenges which are likely to be faced by the different stakeholders at the different levels of the integration process.

Keywords: ICT · Integration · Public transportation system · Challenges

1 Introduction

Information Communication Technologies (ICTs) are becoming a huge part of the public transportation systems all over the world. ICTs in public transportation, also known as Intelligent Transportation Systems are relatively new in South Africa and even unheard of in some parts of the Free State province of South Africa. These technologies, which include electronic fare payments, Variable Message Signs, Automatic Vehicle Location, CCTV surveillance, mobile applications and the internet are yet to be implemented in the Free State province. The uptake of ICT solutions in public transportation in other countries was based on assumptions that it will improve public transportation through these technological developments. It was thought that technology will improve service delivery, therefore reducing the existing barriers towards public transportation and resulting in the public being more patriotic to public transportation systems (Nelson and Mulley 2013).

© ICST Institute for Computer Sciences, Social Informatics and Telecommunications Engineering 2016
R. Glitho et al. (Eds.): AFRICOMM 2015, LNICST 171, pp. 66–69, 2016.
DOI: 10.1007/978-3-319-43696-8_7

Challenges are likely to be encountered when integrating ICTs into the public transportation at all stages of the process, from planning how to use the solutions to the functional stage of the fully integrated public transportation system. Therefore, before deploying these technologies, these possible challenges should be considered, taking into consideration the current state of public transportation, its management, commuters, operators and drivers.

2 Motivation

Public transportation systems all over the world and in South Africa are improving because of ICT while the Free State's public transportation system is still very much conventional and inefficient with no ICT integration. Considering how ICTs have improved transportation in other areas, implementation should be considered in the Free State. Stakeholders may not all be positively affected by ICT solutions in the public transportation system and even though ICTs may lead to good results, challenges and negative impacts may be encountered when integrating ICTs into the public transportation system at all stages of the integration process, i.e. from planning stages to the final stage where the public transportation is fully integrated with ICT.

3 Research Question

What challenges are likely to be faced by stakeholders in integrating ICT solutions into the public transportation system? The public transportation system has many stakeholders who may encounter varying challenges at the different stages of integration.

4 Methodology

Qualitative data gathering through questionnaires and interviews were used. Stratified random sampling was used for fair representation of all stakeholders. Data was gathered between June 2015 and August 2015. Both questionnaires and interviews respondents were passengers, operators, drivers, transportation planners, IT professionals and academics in order to provide a heterogeneous overview of challenges from all the stakeholders perspectives.

5 Results

The challenges (Fig. 2) are influenced by other findings on the study regarding the types of ICT stakeholders were willing to use and those operators were willing to provide in future (Fig. 1). Operators willing to install buzzers, map and route display screens, tracking devices and online platforms for booking tickets should consider financial implications, literacy and user's willingness to use the technologies.

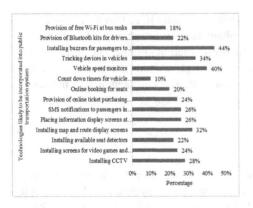

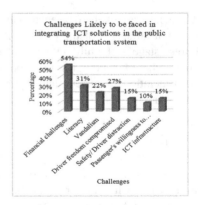

Fig. 1. ICTs operators are willing to provide   **Fig. 2.** Possible challenges

6   Discussion

As the public transportation system is a government controlled but run by private companies and individuals, politics plays an integral part in any major decision making that involves public transportation. Skills and competence are needed for the integration process to be fully operational. Resistance to these technologies and applications by stakeholders may also be encountered. The public should have the ability and knowledge to use the applications and devices once they are in place and be willing to use them. Education and awareness of ICT solutions should be promoted to the public because these are some of the may lead to resistance of the system. Results further showed that most stakeholders may face financial challenges that my substantially curtail successful integration of ICTs into the public transportation system. Another major challenge is the infrastructure; even though some ICT solutions can work within the current infra-structure, it needs to be expanded to support other technologies and as well as ensure efficiency.

References

Maritz, J., Maponya, G.: Development, use and potential contribution of appropriate ICT–based service systems to address rural transport related accessibility constraints–Emerging lessons from case studies in South Africa. In: 29th Annual Southern African Transport Conference, "walk Together", CSIR International Convention Centre, Pretoria, South Africa, p. 13, 16–19 August 2010

Nelson, J., Mulley, C.: The impact of the application of new technology on public transport service provision and the passenger experience: a focus on implementation in Australia. Res. Transp. Econ. **39**(1), 300–308 (2013)

Nair, R.M., Devi, L.S.: Sanskrit Informatics: Informatics for Sanskrit Studies and Research, pp. 113–114. Centre for informatics research and development, Kerala (2011)

Toba, L., Campbell, M., Schoeman, D., Lesia, P.: A critical examination of public transport: a case study of mangaung metropolitan municipality, South Africa. In: 48th ISOCARP Congress 2012. MLM Public Transport (2012)

Wilkinson, P.: Integrated planning at the local level? the problematic intersection of integrated development planning and integrated transport planning in contemporary South Africa. In: Planning Africa 2002: Regenerating Africa Through Planning, pp. 1–9. School of Architecture and Planning, University of Cape Town (2002

On the Internet Connectivity in Africa

Assane Gueye[1]([✉]), Peter Mell[2], Desire Banse[2], and Faical Y. Congo[2]

[1] University of Maryland, College Park, USA
agueye@umd.edu
[2] National Institute of Standards and Technology, Gaithersburg, USA
{peter.mell,desire.banse,faical.congo}@nist.gov

Abstract. This study measures growth of Internet connectivity in Africa from 2010 to 2014 with a focus on inter-country relationships. An initial analysis reveals a modest increase in the number of participating countries but an explosive increase in the number of routers and network links. We then form the first country level topology maps of the African Internet and evaluate the robustness of the network. We study raw connectivity, pairwise shortest paths, and betweeness centrality, suggesting how improvements can be made to the inter-country African connectivity to enhance its robustness without reliance on paths traversing multiple continents.

Keywords: Africa · Internet · Connectivity · Measurement

1 Introduction

As recently as 2007, more than 70 % of internal African Internet traffic was routed to other continents (generally Europe) before reaching its final African destination [1]. This statistic suggests that internal African Internet connectivity was composed of non-communicating isolated clusters, despite the existence of fiber optic submarine cables circling the entire continent [2]. In this study we measure and document the growth of the African Internet with respect to connectivity from 2010 to 2014. We show how the African Internet is losing its fractured nature and is strengthening in its robustness to connectivity disruptions. We first focus our measurements on router to router connectivity and observe a consistent imbalance in the density of Internet infrastructures between different countries. Supporting this is a 2013 observation that 80 % of the hosts in Africa were in the country of South Africa [3]. To avoid biasing our analysis toward countries with this high density, we create a novel country-to-country connectivity map of Africa. With this approach, we evaluate the connectivity of individual countries to each other and thereby measure more uniform growth.

Our study is based on traceroute data provided by the Cooperative Association for Internet Data Analysis (CAIDA) [4]. The data contains router level topological maps of the Internet with embedded geolocation information obtained by recoding IP addresses of routers between sources chosen from a set of worldwide distributed 94 monitors and destinations chosen randomly within each/24 subnet in the IPv4 address space. With this approach, over time, each subnet is accessed from many different parts of the world,

© ICST Institute for Computer Sciences, Social Informatics and Telecommunications Engineering 2016
R. Glitho et al. (Eds.): AFRICOMM 2015, LNICST 171, pp. 70–77, 2016.
DOI: 10.1007/978-3-319-43696-8_8

revealing the primary pathways through the Internet. Thus, we have confidence that we are discovering the major pathways through Africa. However, this approach has known limitations (only preferred paths can be discovered) and, because of that, our resulting connectivity analyses should be considered as worst case bounds. Using the geo-location data files provided by CAIDA, we label each router with its country. Unfortunately, this data is incomplete and a large fraction of routers miss the geolocation information. To circumvent this limitation, we use a majority vote heuristic to complete the geo-location information. For each router for which a country label is not available, we label it with the country label that is most common among its neighbors (using a random assignment whenever there is a tie). With this procedure, almost all nodes (except a tiny fraction ~0.0001 %) were assigned a geo-location. We lastly form a country level topology map from the router level topology map by merging nodes with identical country labels. Lastly, we represent the non-African continents as single nodes by merging all non-African country nodes into nodes representing their respective continents. The end result is communication interconnectivity graphs for Africa from 2010 to 2014 showing each country as a separate node and each non-African continent as a node (all multi-edges are removed). We then study country connectivity within Africa by evaluating raw connectivity, pairwise shortest paths, and betweenness centrality.

2 Data Analysis

Figure 1 shows the number of routers observed within Africa during the measurement period. The 'A-Nodes' line represents the number of routing nodes in Africa, the 'AA-Links' line the number of intra-Africa links, and the 'AW-Links' line the number of links between African routers and the rest of the world. The plots show a steady growth in the number of routers and links, indicating the growth in the overall infrastructure of the African Internet. From 2011 to 2014 there is growth factor of 35 in the number of routers observed in Africa. The number of observed links to other continents has also increased, but less significantly. The number of observed countries rises from 54 in 2010 to 57 in 2013 (all countries in the mainland). For the inter-country African links, we see a growth factor of 5 from 2010 to 2014, showing significant growth. However in 2014, these links accounted for only 0.3 % of the links where both routers reside within Africa. Thus, the number of these critical inter-country links is relatively small but growing rapidly. In 2014, the African routers represent about 1.6 % of the world's routers (and 1.2 % of the world's links). Africa's share of worldwide routers and links modestly increases over the period of investigation while the fraction of world links that connect Africa to the other continents has stayed steady (not shown). In summary, the data indicates that most of the effort to improve Africa's connectivity has been spent to connect nodes inside Africa. However, the countries with the greatest share of routing infrastructure have seen the most growth while the countries with the smallest share have experienced much smaller growth. Table 1 shows this disparity. The 'top 3 countries' (South Africa, Egypt, and Morocco) are those with the greatest number of nodes/links in 2014 while the 'bottom 24 countries' are those with the fewest nodes/links in 2014.

Similar observations were made in reference [3] for the period 2004–2007 showing that this is a long term trend.

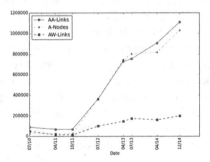

Fig. 1. Number of nodes and number links within Africa and between Africa and the rest of the world.

Table 1. Improvement in the number of links and nodes in Africa from 2010 to 2014.

	Continent	Top 3	Bottom 24	Rest of Africa
Nodes	35x	46x	6x	17x
Links	12x	15x	6x	7x

To avoid biases involving countries with more infrastructures we now evaluate the country level interconnectivity maps. Figure 2 shows the number of country-level links within Africa and between Africa and the rest of the world. Figures 3, 4, 5 and 6 show a graphic representation of the country-level connectivity for part of the investigation period. As was already seen at the router level, the number of country level links within Africa is increasing but it is always smaller than the number of country-level links to the rest of the world. This indicates that even though Africa is improving its connectivity at the country level, it largely depends on the other continents (or satellite) for Internet connectivity. In 2010 and 2011, a number of African countries (24 %) did not have any direct link to other African countries. This was mostly the case for inland countries whereas coastal countries are almost all directly connected to the Internet. In 2014, the

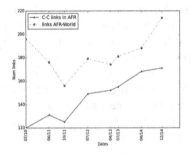

Fig. 2. Number of country-level links within Africa and between Africa and the rest of the world.

African country-level graph is connected (except for some island countries), implying that (*in principle*) any African country can now communicate with any other African country using only links within the continent.

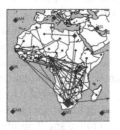

Fig. 3. 2010–07

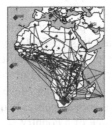

Fig. 4. 2012–07

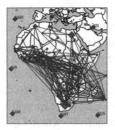

Fig. 5. 2013–07

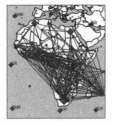

Fig. 6. 2014–12

We now study the characteristics of the country level connectivity graph. We first analyze the degree distribution of the country level map (for year 2014) and observe that most countries (always more than 25) have low degree, while a few countries (mostly South Africa) have high degree (greater than 20). The many low degree nodes and few high degree nodes is a characteristic of many engineered networks [5] and is usually referred as 'scale-free'. Furthermore, we observed that nodes with low degrees tend to connect with nodes with high degree, and vice versa. This is another previously observed property of engineered networks and is referred as 'dissassortativity' [6]. Another metric of interest is the 'betweenness' centrality of individual countries, the fraction of shortest paths that go through that country (among pairs of African countries). By analyzing this metric, we observe that the majority of countries have very low betweenness centrality (carrying very little "relay" traffic). Only a small number of countries have a significant betweenness centrality. This indicates that if inter-country traffic is routed using shortest path, only a few African countries will play a role of big hubs, while most countries will carry only traffic which they have generated or which is destined to them. Also, the average number of hops between any pair of countries is always greater than 1 during the measurement period (in contrast, it is 0.5 for Europe). This means that, in average, communication between any pair of African countries has to transit through a third African country (while, in average, countries in Europe have direct link to each other).

We next study the robustness of the country-level Africa graph to node and link failures. There exist several graph theoretic metrics to quantify the importance of a node (or link) in a network: (a) the degree of a country ($Deg(c)$), (b) the betweenness of a country ($Bet(c)$) which quantifies how often a country lies in the shortest path between other countries that represent the source and destination of a communication, and (c) the eigenvector centrality of the country ($Eig(c)$) which measures how connected the country is to well-connected countries (the higher it is, the more connected the country is to well-connected countries). Since all these features are important in the connectivity of a given country, we combine them with the formula $Conn(c) = (Deg(c) + Bet(c))e^{Eig(c)}$ to define the connectivity of a country. We define the connectivity of the continent as the sum of the connectivity of its countries. We then use this metric to study the robustness of the Africa network to node and link failures by asking the following question: what is the maximum drop in connectivity when 1 (2, 3, 4, ...) node (resp. link) of the network fails? Figure 7 shows the evolution of the continent connectivity when we allow up to 5 countries to fail. For each of the number of nodes (allowed) to fail, we sequentially

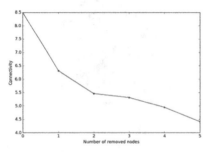

Fig. 7. Robustness to node failures.

remove the node with largest drop in connectivity. We observe a very sharp decline for the first two countries and then the connectivity decreases at a slower rate. This suggests that the first two countries are very important for the connectivity of the continent as a whole. Similar analysis for link failures shows an almost linear drop in connectivity as more links fail (not shown).

Finally, we propose an improvement of Africa's connectivity by adding new links to the country-level graph. For each additional link, we ask the question: where in the continent (i.e., between which pairs of countries) to put the link to obtain the maximum increase in connectivity. We assume that there are 19 links to be added sequentially. For each new link, we use the connectivity metric defined above to compute its best placement (i.e., which has a maximum increase in connectivity). Figure 8 shows the improvement in the continent connectivity after the addition of each optimally placed link. We can see that the connectivity improves as more links are being added. However, the curve has a few plateaus (between 5 and 8 additional links, between 10 and 12, and after 15) between which its increases. One interpretation is that after having added 5 (resp. 10) links in the continent, one does not gain much by adding more links except if one can add at least 3 (2) additional nodes. This pattern of flat region-increasing region repeats even beyond 20 links (not shown). We also see that connecting nodes that already have many connections results in a smaller payoff while connecting nodes with small number of connections results in large payoff. In other words, in order to improve Africa's connectivity, we need to build links between countries with less Internet infrastructure.

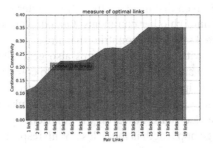

Fig. 8. Improving by adding links.

3   Related Work

Several studies are available showing African Internet accessibility (see [2, 7]). The African Economic Outlook [7] provides and analyzes data on telecommunication investments, access to information technology, technology penetration, and connectivity in Africa. They have reported 16 undersea cables connecting Africa to the Americas, Europe and Asia (e.g., SAT3/WASC, EASSy, Seacom, TEAMS, RCIP, GL01, MaIN, ACE). With the exception of Eritrea and Western Sahara, all coastline countries have a cable landing on their shore. This has helped triple the Africa Internet access in the last decade. On the other hand, landlocked countries were (up to 2010) mainly connected via satellite (VSAT). However, our data shows that this is changing with inland countries connecting to the undersea cable via fiber optic cables traversing neighboring coastline countries. Most of the observations in [7] are also made in this paper, although it is based on (different) topological data set. Our paper, however, goes one step further by introducing a novel country-level connectivity graph of Africa and studies its properties. We also investigate improvement to the current country-level connectivity. [8] provides an analysis of the distribution of Internet infrastructure in Africa for the years prior to our study (with some of the same trends being found with respect to a few countries dominating African network growth). The ping end-to-end reporting (PingER) project is, like CAIDA, an Internet End-to-end Performance Measurement (IEPM) project that monitors end-to-end performance of Internet links [9] using the simple and common "ping" test. [10] uses PingER to shown the low presence of Africa in the world Internet, a steady improvement of Africa connectivity since late 2010, and the disparity in improvement among the African countries. Our study, although based on a different data set, confirms such observation. Their paper, however, does not study country-level connectivity nor does it consider the robustness and improvement analyses carried in our study.

4   Conclusion

This study has shown that Africa's Internet connectivity has significantly improved during the period from 2010 to 2014. Both the fraction of worldwide Internet backbone routers attributable to Africa and the number of intra-Africa links have risen substantially. This is important given that much of the African inter-country connectivity had been previously routed through other continents. On a downside, we note that most of the router growth occurred in African countries that already had a robust infrastructure. That said, the countries with less infrastructures also generally experienced Internet infrastructure growth. The analysis of a novel country to country connectivity map has shown an increasing participation of African countries over the time period of study. We also see a significant increase in the number of direct links between African countries. Even with these added links, however, the connectivity is still not as robust as Europe where the average hop length is much less. With respect to the rest of the world, we see an increase in links from African to other continents. At a deeper level, our connectivity metrics also reveal a highly *scale-free* nature in the country to country Africa connectivity graph. Most countries have low degree and a few have high degree. There is a *negative assortativity* whereby low degree nodes tend to connect to high degree nodes and not to each other. The problem with this current architecture is that it is susceptible to node failure. The majority of African countries are dependent upon just a few other African countries for their intra-continental Internet access. However, judicious placement of additional links (i.e., links among the low degree nodes) can reduce the fragility induced by the scale free nature. This translates in the need for direct Internet links between countries with less Internet infrastructure in order to make that African Internet stronger as a whole.

Acknowledgements. This research was sponsored by the National Institute of Standards and Technology (NIST) and partially accomplished under NIST Cooperative Agreement No. 70NANB13H012 with the University of Maryland. The views and conclusions contained in this document should not be interpreted as representing the official policies, either expressed or implied of NIST or the U.S. Government. The U.S. Government is authorized to reproduce and distribute reprints for Government purposes, notwithstanding any copyright notation hereon.

References

1. Africa Waiting for Net Revolution: BBC News. http://news.bbc.co.uk/2/hi/technology/7063682.stm. Accessed 13 July 2015
2. ITU: Telecommunication/ICT Markets and Trends in Africa (2007). http://www.itu.int/ITU-D/ict/statistics/material/af_report07.pdf. Accessed 13 July 2015
3. Livraghi, G.: Data on Internet Activity in Africa (Hostcount). http://www.gandalf.it/data/africeng.htm. Accessed 13 July 2015
4. CAIDA: Macroscopic Internet Topology Data Kit. http://www.caida.org/data/internet-topology-data-kit/. Accessed 13 July 2015
5. Barabási, A.-L., Albert, R.: Emergence of scaling in random networks. Science **286**, 509–512 (1999)
6. Newman, M.E.J.: Mixing patterns in networks. Phy. Rev. **67**(2), 026126 (2003)
7. African Economic Outlook: Technology Infrastructure and Services in Africa. http://www.africaneconomicoutlook.org/en/theme/ict-africa/technology-infrastructure-and-services-in-africa/
8. Data on Internet Activity in Africa (Hostcount). http://www.gandalf.it/data/africeng.htm. Accessed 13 July 2015
9. Ping End-to-End Reporting (PingER). Project http://www-iepm.slac.stanford.edu/pinger/
10. Les Cottrell, R.: How bad is Africa's Internet? IEEE Spectrum. http://spectrum.ieee.org/telecom/internet/how-bad-is-africas-internet

Proof of Concept of the Online Neighbourhood Watch System

Stacey Omeleze[1]([✉]) and Hein S. Venter[2]

[1] ICSA Research Group, Computer Science Department,
University of Pretoria, Pretoria, South Africa
someleze@cs.up.ac.za
[2] Computer Science Dept.,
University of Pretoria, Pretoria, South Africa
hventer@cs.up.ac.za

Abstract. Potential digital evidence captured by an onlooker at a crime scene when stored in a repository can be used during criminal investigations, or as admissible evidence in a court of law. However, to employ the captured and stored potential digital evidence (PDE) some challenges are required to be dealt with, such as, retaining the forensic soundness of the captured PDE, adequate measures to secure the PDE and measures to protect the privacy rights of the PDE uploader (citizens).

In previous work, the authors proposed a conceptual model termed online neighbourhood watch (ONW). The ONW model allows community members to use their mobile devices in capturing PDE, store the captured PDE to a repository to be used in neighbourhood crime investigation in South Africa. But, the focus of this paper is to present a proof of concept of the ONW model. The proof of concept outlines the functional and architectural requirements specifications of the ONW system and evaluates the performance of the underlying functional requirements using mathematical proofs in testing the forensic soundness of the captured and stored PDE. Furthermore, using the information security services mechanisms, the forensic soundness indicators (FSI) are generated. The FSI ensures originality, authenticity and admissibility of PDE from the ONW system.

Keywords: PDE · Forensic soundness · ONW system · Digital evidence · Information security services · Repository

1 Introduction

The high rate of crime in South Africa demands a proactive community response to tackling the menace of these crime. Mobile devices are among the most used electronic devices [1], mobile devices can therefore be used as crime fighting, monitoring or prevention device when its camera, voice-recording and image-capturing functions are employed as a real-time potential digital evidence (PDE) capturing tool. In previous work, the authors modelled the online neighbourhood watch (ONW) conceptual model [8,9], that enables community members

© ICST Institute for Computer Sciences, Social Informatics and Telecommunications Engineering 2016
R. Glitho et al. (Eds.): AFRICOMM 2015, LNICST 171, pp. 78–93, 2016.
DOI: 10.1007/978-3-319-43696-8_9

in South Africa to use their mobile devices in capturing potential digital evidence (PDE) of crime. The mobile devices capture images, audio and video recordings of criminal activities in their neighbourhoods stored to be used that can be used to convict the criminals.

The purpose of this paper is to provide a proof of concept for the ONW model. This is to identify the practical aspects of the conceptual model, determine the challenges that are not readily seen during the conceptual modelling and explain the design and development process of the ONW system. The proof of concept entails the development of an application termed uWatch. uWatch is a crowd-sourcing medium that involves community members to use their mobile devices to in generating potential digital evidence (PDE) of crime. It also includes a web application termed neighbourhood watch system. The ONW system utilised by the law enforcement agents (LEA), digital forensic investigators (DFI) or the judiciary to access and download the stored PDE during neighbourhood crime investigation or prosecution. The ONW system employs the information security services mechanisms to maintain confidentiality, integrity, authentication, authorisation and non-repudiations (CIAAN) of captured and stored PDE [15]. The CIAAN mechanisms are used in conjunction with the forensic soundness indicators (FSI) properties to verify the forensic soundness of PDE captured with the ONW system, while maintaining chain of custody, chain of evidence, and protecting the privacy rights of the uploader (citizen).

2   Digital Forensics

Digital forensics is drawn from the field of forensic science which has been developed in conjunction with the biological sciences. It is used to determine the path of digital data during a digital forensic investigation, whether for criminal or civil proceedings in a court of law or private inquiries in order to re-construct incidents to establish what happened.

Cohen [2] defines digital forensics as a subject that started between art and craft containing a scientific body of knowledge with an underlying scientific methodology and consisting of four basic elements. These elements are the study of previous and current theories and methods, conducting experiments to prove the theories, identification of inconsistencies between theories and the repeatability of these experiments in correlation with expert witnesses. Evidence determines the flow of major decisions, in criminal or civil investigations. It establishes that an incident occurred to initiate any form of investigation. Hargreaves [4] defines digital evidence as a reliable object that can uphold or refute a hypothesis in legal or civil proceedings. That means, for the admissibility of digital evidence, its integrity must be proven with a certain degree of reliability

For electronic data to be used as evidence, it must be in its originally uncontaminated state and maintain evidential weight. Using the information security service mechanisms [15] and upholding legal standards of evidential weight [3,14], the forensic soundness of digital data can be achieved. Forensic soundness of digital data is ensured when confidentiality, integrity, authentication, authorisation and non-repudiation are in place using the information security services mechanisms of cryptography, digital signatures, cryptographic hash functions and access control [11,13,15].

In order to legally employ the captured potential digital evidence (PDE) to either commence investigations or be used as 'real' evidence in a criminal or civil proceeding, the stipulations and guidelines from various acts must be adhered to. These acts include the Electronic Communications and Transactions (ECT) Act, Act 25 of 2002 [3], the Privacy of Personal Information (POPI) Act, Act 4 of 2013 [12] and the Regulation of Interception of Communications and Provision of Communication-Related Information (RICA) Act, Act 70 of 2002. These acts deal with the protection of an individuals privacy but also spells out when individuals and criminals lose those rights when national security is at stake. This has major implications for the ONW system and how PDE can be used.

3   Methodology

In developing the proof of concept of the ONW system, the methods employed include: *(i)* The use of set theory to formulate a proof of forensic reliability of PDE captured and stored in the ONW repository, which is then implemented using programming languages. *(ii)* The use of programming languages framework, APIs, and IDEs in the implementation of the ONW system which consists of the uWatch application and neighbourhood watch system. The languages include PHP web socket for a dynamic lightweight and high efficiency server-end, JavaEE, Python-Django framework, and Bootstrap framework that allows the authorised PDE downloader the use of any device ranging from mobile device to table or desktop computers. The bootstrap framework allows for a responsible web front design and performs usability functions. *(iii)* The use of Android development platform for the uploader's application-side. *(iv)* MySQL and SQLite databases are used for the uploader's application-side and downloader's-side respectively. The database storage are in forms, converted to JASON objects.

4   The ONW System Design

In designing the ONW system, the benefit of implementing the ONW conceptual model as well as the quality of captured PDE is portrayed using the functional and non functional (architectural) requirements and the constraints mapped out to achieve the ONW system's objectives. Part A of the ONW system is designed as a mobile device application. Part B is designed as a web application to be used by the downloader. Part B also deals with the retention of confidentiality, integrity, maintaining access management of the authorised users, and the verification of PDE authenticity in order to determine its admissibility.

4.1   Functional Requirements

Functional requirements focuses on the behaviour and capabilities that describe the use cases, capturing the roles of the various users of the system [7]. The use cases are mapped to roles describing the functions that each role holder performs - see Fig. 1. The primary actors of the ONW system are the PDE uploader, the LEA/DFI, judiciary and the system manager. Each role performs a functions of a case as follows: *(i)* Capture potential digital evidence; *(ii)* Verify the forensic soundness of the captured potential digital evidence; *(iii)* Store potential digital evidence, while making it available to the authorised users (i.e. LEA, DFI and judiciary); *(iv)* Maintain access management to the stored PDE, in order to protect the privacy of the citizens and abide by the rule of law [14].

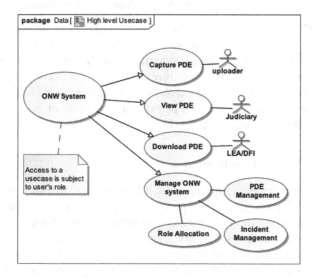

Fig. 1. High-level use case of the ONW system

Uploader: The uploader role is attributed to a human user (citizen). The citizen uses a mobile device to capture PDE which is uploaded to the ONW repository and then receives notifications. The notifications are meant to update uploaders on PDE-sourcing efforts to motivate citizens in neighbourhood crime minimisation. The notifications are provided by the ONW system as usage statistics and citizens status such as, when an uploaded PDE passes the forensic soundness checks, and when a citizen's uploaded PDE is utilised as real evidence during crime investigation or in a court of law.

The Judiciary: The judiciary role is carried out by any member of the judiciary such as the court clerk or legal counsel to the plaintiff or defendant, especially in situations where stored PDE is to be utilised as real evidence to shed light on a case before the court. The Judiciary may require to view the PDE, which is then made available to all parties involved. For the ONW system to attain its set goals of usefulness and admissibility in any court of law, the role of the judiciary is essential as it ensures that all processes operate within legal boundaries.

The Law Enforcement Agent and Digital Forensic Investigator: As depicted in Fig. 1, the actor role of the Law Enforcement Agent (LEA) is bound to that of the Digital Forensic Investigator (DFI) who may assume both roles when required. The function of the LEA is to download PDE from the ONW repository to corroborate the first respondent's report, the physical crime scene and possible eye-witness testimony of the alleged incident. The LEA uses the date, time, location or incident type to determine whether PDE is valid or applicable to a case under investigation. The LEA also manages the ONW system along with the system administrator. For example, PDE retrieved to investigate a case relating to an assault crime must be focused on assault related crime search criteria using date, time, and location to correlate the incident to other assault crimes.

Manage the ONW System: Manage the ONW System functions includes incident record management and role allocations. These functions are shared responsibilities between the LEA and the system administrator. The ONW system validates PDE, returns exception, success or failure of transaction notifications, performs PDE forensic soundness check, controls access management, adds or removes roles, and audits log maintenance. The system management ensures that PDE is accessed by the LEA according to the attributes of the case.

4.2   Architectural Requirements

Architectural requirements provide the infrastructure within which the system components can realise the functional requirements [7]. The ONW system's architectural requirements include the system access channel requirements, architectural responsibilities, quality requirements and the architectural constraints. Each of which is used in correlation to the architectural patterns and strategies to promote the quality requirements of the system. The ONW system's access channels are via web - i.e. HTTPS using RESTful with secure message channels and mobile application interface for the uploader (citizen).

ONW System's Architectural Responsibilities. The ONW system's architectural responsibilities are the architectural requirements that the system must support through which the system is evaluated. The ONW system is based on a layered architectural pattern, supported by other architectural patterns such as, model view controller (MVC), microkernel architectural patterns, pipes and filters architectural patterns and decorator patterns. The MVC is used at the access layer to ensure separation of concerns, while pipes and filters and microkernel architectural patterns are used to support the business logic layer and the persistence layer to ensure security, reliability and stability of the system. Furthermore, these ensure that the functional requirements (i.e., capture PDE; ensure confidentiality, integrity, authentication, authorisation and non-repudiation (CIAAN); store captured PDE; manage access of stored PDE) are realised using architectural requirements. These architectural requirements include the use the following features: *(i)* Web interface which is employed to separate the business logic from the access layer, this is in order to avoid direct access to the content of the back-end system. It maintains control of events from the business logic (I/O) to the persistence layer. *(ii)* The persistence layer supports Object Relational Mapper. *(iii)* Transactional processes associate components or users to activities within the system using interceptor patterns. *(iv)* The microkernel adapters enable the addition of external systems and flexible communication channels between the access layer, business logic and the persistence layer. *(v)* Ensuring confidentiality, integrity, authorisation, authentication and non repudiation (CIAAN) of captured PDE. *(vi)* Ensuring that the ONW quality requirements (i.e., security, auditability, usability, auditability and pluggability) are realised.

5 Explaining the ONW System

In developing the ONW system, two aspects were the focus: the uploader's part (mobile application-side) which is termed uWatch application and the downloader part called Neighbourhood watch system. The uWatch application is developed using the Android development platform. The neighbourhood watch system, which is a web application is developed using Python Django framework with BootStrap framework, and JavaEE. The choice is based on the architectural responsibilities of the system. For example, the Django framework accommodates databases, such as MySQL, and reference architecture framework like JavaEE and PHP server, thereby allowing for easy storage of audio, video or images.

5.1   uWatch Application

uWatch uses the existing functions of Android devices (i.e. camera and microphone) in the PDE capturing processes. It enables members of a community to capture images, videos and audios of criminal behaviour within their neighbourhood and upload the captured PDE to the ONW repository. The uploaded PDE is analysed by the law enforcement agents and other authorised users during neighbourhood crime investigations.

As shown in Fig. 2, at the launch of uWatch, the user is prompted to select which form of PDE they wish to capture (i.e., photo image, video or audio) of the alleged criminal activity. At the selection of any of the option buttons in Fig. 3 the built-in camera or audio features of the Android device is activated to commence PDE capturing. PDE can be captured by an eye-witness with or without WIFI or cellular network data connectivity. This is achieved using the queue service event where offline captured PDE is posted to a remote url using ThreadPoolExecutor. The remote url also provides similar services of capture-to-upload-later, when there is a slow or unsuccessful transaction to the ONW repository. The type of incident and the location where the incident occurred is selected by the citizen (see Fig. 3). The location selection is used by the LEA

Fig. 2. User interface of the uWatch application

Fig. 3. Audio-capturing Process using uWatch application

to cross-reference geographical locations. The location selection enhances PDE originality checks. However, to upload the captured PDE, the citizen is required to log-in, meanwhile, authentication is not required to capture PDE, it is only required at PDE upload to the ONW repository. Finally, the stored output is stored as $\{Z\} = (E_{ncrypt} \wedge (DGsign) \wedge (Geolocation, timestamp) \wedge (\#PDE_p)$. An acknowledgment feedback mechanism is in place to notify uploader and components at successful or failed forensic soundness checks, when PDE uploaded by the citizen is download for investigation, or used as real evidence.

5.2 Neighbourhood Watch System

The neighbourhood watch system is the downloader-side of the ONW system. It's users are the system administrator, LEA, DFI, the judiciary or other authorised users who utilise sourced PDE during crimes or civil investigations or as real evidence in a court of law. Meanwhile, only an authorised user with access credentials is able to download PDE from the ONW repository by creating a caseName, caseNumber and caseType.

The neighbourhood watch system is developed with the Django framework which is used due to the framework's abstraction level in web development using Bootstrap framework to absorb Hypertext Mark-up Language (HTML), Cascading Style Sheets (CSS) and Javascript at the usability design process [5]. On the transactions between the uWatch application and the neighbourhood watch system, servlets initialise a call function from the access layer to the persistence layer through the business logic layer. It converts forms to JSON schema parse through the HTML using RESTful Web service and PHP cluster. The JSON objects format is used because it is faster to parse, lighter, flexible with PHP, and it presents data in a more readable format over the XML message transfer protocol.

5.3   Usability

The usability of the ONW system is realised using a decorators pattern and the Bootstrap framework to enhance better user experience, easy operation with little to no training required for downloaders or citizens to utilise the system. Figure 4 shows images, videos and audios captured and stored as PDE in the ONW repository. Each captured PDE holds location co-ordinates, the provinces (for example Eastern cape - see Fig. 4), time and date, type of alleged crime and the checksum value of the PDE. While on the uWatch application (Android side) SQLite is used to send PDE both online or offline to a queue that is synchronised as JSON objects via HTTPS.

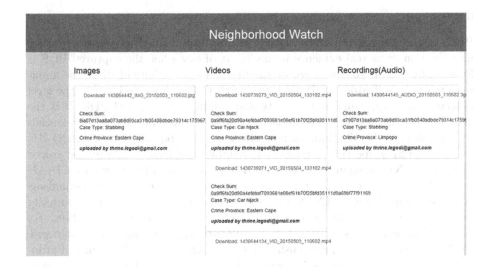

Fig. 4. Stored PDE with metadata in the ONW repository

5.4   Auditability

The auditability functions of the ONW system is maintained using MySQL trigger, PDE validation and global interception. Trigger automates the audit-log, while rules are created by the rule engine and specified at system's configuration to allow traceability of authorised user's actions.

5.5   PDE Storage

For PDE storage, the neighbourhood watch system uses MySQL and PHP to enable the insertion of binary data to database tables, and specifying the required PDE using rules based on the case under investigation [9]. The platform and scalable functionalities of MySQL enable the ONW system to handle concurrent user base, while captured PDE is stored as a JSON object. At any given state, the uploaded optimised PDE object is in the form of: $\mathcal{Z} = \{N\} \wedge \{M\} \wedge \{x_j\}$ (i.e., Encryption ($E_{ncrypt} \wedge (Cryptographichash - (\#)) \wedge$ (Digital signature) $\wedge (PDE_p) \wedge$ (Geo location) $\wedge$ (Date/timestamp) $\wedge$ (Device type) $\wedge$ (Wifi connection identifier)). The upload and stored PDE data includes the AES encrypted version of the checksum value of the PDE, which is digitally signed in collaboration with the timestamp, to determine the time of PDE acquisition, and the geo-location showing where PDE was acquired in correlation with other metadata like the device type, wifi connection or GSM data connection. This process ensure consistency with the chain of evidence and the chain of custody, so as to ascertain what operations were performed during the acquisition and storage process.

5.6   Security - Forensic Soundness Indicators

PDE captured using the ONW system is only useful for neighbourhood crime investigation or as real evidence in any court of law when the captured PDE is forensically sound. To ensure the originality and authenticity of PDE, the forensic soundness indicators (FSI) are introduced. FSI are used to indicate the level of soundness (originality, authenticity and validity) of captured PDE. It is the process that merges information security services mechanisms of confidentiality, integrity, authentication, authorisation and non-repudiation (CIAAN) [15] with PDE FSI properties to ensure the reliability of PDE captured and stored using the ONW system. Throughout this paper, the FSIs refers to CIAAN mechanisms and the PDE properties of forensic soundness. The mechanisms employed to implement CIAAN are: *(a)* Confidentiality - which is realised using *encryption. (b)* Integrity is realised using *cryptographic hash function. (c)* Authentication is realised using *session authentication, username and password. (d)* Non-repudiation is achieved using *digital signature.* While the PDE FSI properties used to address forensics soundness in conjunction with the CIAAN mechanisms are: *(a)* Timestamp *(b)* Geographical location tag. *(c)* Device type. *(d)* International mobile equipment identifier (IMEI). *(e)* Wifi connection identifier. *(f)* GSM data connection.

Testing Forensic Soundness of PDE using Mathematical Illustration To ascertain the reliability and forensic soundness of captured and stored PDE, a test is carried out using set theory and elementary logic algebra [6, 10]. The conducted test is focusing on identifying the *minimal-state* of forensic soundness of any captured and stored PDE is denoted as set $\{\mathcal{W}\}$ and the *optimal-state* is set $\{\mathcal{Z}\}$ as depicted in Figs. 5 and 6 respectively.

Figures 5 and 6 is described as follows: The elements of PDE is defined as the set of $X\epsilon$ {video, audio, and photo}, where video, audio or photo is referred to as $\{x_1\}$ or $\{x_2\}$ or $\{x_3\}$ respectively. For clarity, $\{x_1\}$ is video, $\{x_2\}$ is audio and $\{x_3\}$ is photo. The FSIs are represented as the set of $\{Y\}$, which consist of $Y\epsilon$ {encryption, cryptographic hash, digital signature, geo-location, timestamp, device type, IMEI identifier, wifi connection identifier or GSM data connection}. Where set $\{Y\}$ is further decomposed to consist of sets $\{N\}$ and $\{M\}$ i.e., $\{Y\} = \{N\} \wedge \{M\}$. Where set $\{N\}$ represents the FSIs focusing on

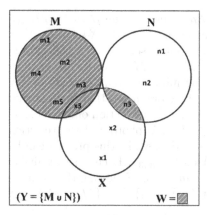

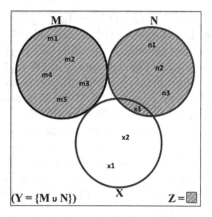

Fig. 5. Is set $\mathcal{W} = \{\{\}(n_3 \cap x_3) \cup \mathcal{M}\}$

Fig. 6. Is the set of $\mathcal{Z} = \{\{\}(\mathcal{M} \cup \mathcal{N}) \cap x_3\}$

CIAAN mechanisms - $\{N\}$ consists of $\{n_1\}$ or $\{n_2\}$ or $\{n_3\}$ where $\{n_1\}$ represent encryptions, $\{n_2\}$ cryptography hash and $\{n_3\}$ digital signature respectively. Set $\{M\}$ consists of geo-location, timestamp, device type, IMEI identifier, wifi connection identifier or GSM data connection which represents $\{m_1\}$, $\{m_2\}$, $\{m_3\}$, $\{m_4\}$ and $\{m_5\}$ respectively, where $\{m_5\}$ can be either wifi connection identifier or GSM data connection at any given set of $\{M\}$. Therefore the set $M = \{m_1, m_2, m_3, m_4, m_5\}$.

To test for the forensic soundness of the captured PDE, the shaded portions of sets $\{\mathcal{W}\}$ and $\{\mathcal{Z}\}$ as depicted in Figs. 5 and 6 is used. Where set $\{\mathcal{W}\}$ consists of exactly one element of $\{X\}$ i.e., either $\{x_1\}$ or $\{x_2\}$ or $\{x_3\}$, this is so because at any given PDE capturing process, the captured PDE data object is either a video, or an audio or a photo image (see Figs. 5 and 6) because the PDE cannot be more than one of these elements at the same time. For example, the illustration in Figure 5 shows that $\{x_3\}$ i.e., photo is used. The selection of at least one or more elements of set $\{N\}$ i.e., $\{n_1\}$ and/or $\{n_2\}$ and/or $\{n_3\}$ and the selection of a complete set of $\{M\}$ is necessary to obtain the set $\{\mathcal{W}\}$. For example in the illustration of Fig. 5 the whole elements of set $\{M\}$ is include, recall that the set $\{M\}$ is $\{m_1, m_2, m_3, m_4, m_5\}$ and the selection of $\{n_3\}$ i.e., digital signature is employed to generate set $\{\mathcal{W}\}$. An illustration that shows the processes employed to determine the validity of PDE captured in its most minimal-state of forensic soundness of any given PDE is denoted as set $\{\mathcal{W}\}$ - is as follow:

Proof. - to Illustrate - the processes of obtaining the minimal - state of PDE $\{\mathcal{W}\}$. Let set $X = \{x_1 \vee x_2 \vee x_3\}$ - that is, select a video, or audio or photo. Let set $N = \{n_1 \vee n_2 \vee n_3\}$ - that is, select at least one of cryptographic hash and/or encryption, and/or digital signature. Let set $M = \{m_1 \wedge m_2 \wedge m_3 \wedge m_4 \wedge m_5\}$ that is, the product of geo-location, timestamp, device type, IMEI identifier, wifi connection (i.e., select all elements of $\{M\}$).

Therefore the set $\mathcal{W} = \{x_1 \vee x_2 \vee x_3\} \wedge \{m_1 \wedge m_2 \wedge m_3 \wedge m_4 \wedge m_5\} \wedge \{n_1 \vee n_2 \vee n_3\}$ - which means set $\{\mathcal{W}\}$ is the collection of one element of set $\{X\}$ i.e. $\{x_3\}$, at least one element of set $\{N\}$ i.e., $\{n_3\}$ and a complete set of $\{M\}$ - substituted as shown in Fig. 5 resulting in $\mathcal{W} = (M_{x1n1} \vee M_{x2n2} \vee Mx3n3)$.

- Recall that the illustration is to show the minimum requirements of any PDE to be stored in the ONW repository, this therefore means that the first case scenario of forensically sound PDE is $\{M_{x1n1}\}$ that is, a selection of all elements of set of $\{M\}$, selection of one element $\{x_1\}$ which is photo and the selection of one element $\{n_1\}$ that is cryptographic hash. Meanwhile, this process can be the selection of any of $\{M_{x1n1}\}$ or $\{M_{x2n2}\}$ or $\{M_{x3n3}\}$. Each case results in the lowest minimal-forensic soundness-state of any PDE. Following the example of set $\mathcal{W}$ in Fig. 5, $\{\mathcal{W}\}$ is the selection of $\{x_3\}$, $\{n_3\}$ and $\{M\}$, $\{\mathcal{W}\}$ is $\therefore$ $\mathcal{W} = \{M_{x3n3}\}$.

The next possible value of $\{\mathcal{W}\}$ is realised by increasing the number of elements of $\{N\}$ to exceed more than one. Equating the value of $\{n_1\}$, $\{n_2\}$, $\{n_3\}$ to be i, therefore i can be defined as $i = \{n_1, n_2\}$ or $i = \{n_1, n_2, n_3\}$. While set $\{X\}$ can be defined as j, so that, at any given PDE capturing process, j represents video, audio or photo. This is because a citizen can either capture a video or an audio or photo image at any circumstance - $\therefore$ $j = \{x_1\}$ or $j = \{x_2\}$ or $j = \{x_3\}$ which means the selection of either video $\{x_1\}$ or audio $\{x_2\}$ or photo $\{x_3\}$ is equated to j - Therefore, the in-between (mid-level) forensic soundness state of PDE is derived to be - $\mathcal{W} = \{M_{xj} \wedge M_{ni}\}$ where $\{M\}$ is the FSI properties that ascertain the forensic soundness, x_j is the captured PDE and $\{n_i\}$ is the selection of more than one elements of set $\{N\}$.

$\therefore$ $\forall \mathcal{W} \exists \{M_{xjni}\}$ - meaning for all $\{\mathcal{W}\}$ there exist exactly one captured PDE (video or audio or photo), a complete set of $\{M\}$ (geo-location, timestamp, wifi, device description, etc.) and at least one or more elements of set $\{N\}$ (i.e., encryption, cryptographic hash function and digital signature).

In summary the minimal-forensic soundness-state of any given PDE object is $\mathcal{W} = \{M_{x3n3}\}$, while there is an in-between level which is higher than minimal-state, but less than in-between-state of forensic soundness $\mathcal{W} = \{M_{xjni}\}$, while the optimal-state of forensic soundness is $\{\mathcal{Z}\}$. Therefore there are three state of forensic soundness of PDE captured with the ONW system - minimal-state $<$ mid-level-state $<$ optimal-state of forensic soundness - With the Equation $\{\mathcal{W}\} < \{M_{xjni}\} < \{\mathcal{Z}\}$ is the various states of PDE forensic soundness. Recall that the illustration above is focused on showing the minimal-state $\{\mathcal{W}\}$ of PDE, which also derived the in-between-state (mid-level-state) $\{M_{xjni}\}$ of PDE forensic soundness. Next paragraph is the proof to show the optimal-forensic-soundness-state of PDE $\{\mathcal{Z}\}$.

Proof. - to Illustrate the processes of obtaining the optimal-state of PDE $\{\mathcal{Z}\}$. Let set $X = \{x_1 \vee x_2 \vee x_3\}$ - that is, select a video, or audio or photo. Let set $N = \{n_1 \wedge n_2 \wedge n_3\}$ - that is, select all elements $\{N\}$ (i.e., cryptographic hash and encryption, and digital signature).

Let set $M = \{m_1 \wedge m_2 \wedge m_3 \wedge m_4 \wedge m_5\}$ - select all elements of $\{M\}$ (i.e., geo-location, timestamp, device type, IMEI identifier, wifi connection identifier).

. Therefore the set of $\mathcal{Z} = (x_1 \vee x_2 \vee x_3) \wedge (m_1 \wedge m_2 \wedge m_3 \wedge m_4 \wedge m_5) \wedge (n_1 \wedge n_2 \wedge n_3)$ - That is the set $\mathcal{Z}$ is the collection of one element of set $\{X\}$ i.e. $\{x_3\}$, all element of set $\{M\}$ and all elements of set $\{N\}$.

$\therefore \mathcal{Z} = \{N\} \wedge \{M\} \wedge \{x_3\}$, which is $\mathcal{Z} = \{MN_{x3}\}$. The elements of set $\{X\}$ can be video, or audio or photo, however, in reference to the example in Fig. 5, the element $\{x_3\}$ is selected. Therefore alternatively the set $\mathcal{Z}$ can be represented as $\mathcal{Z} = \{MN_{xj}\}$ where $\{x_j\}$ can be any selection of video, audio or photo.

Forensic Soundness Validations. The goal is to establish the forensic soundness validation of PDE captured with the ONW system, using the three states of PDE forensic soundness i.e., the optimal-state of PDE $\mathcal{Z} = \{MN_{xj}\}$, the mid-level state $\mathcal{W} = \{M_{xjni}\}$ and the minimal-state $\mathcal{W} = \{M_{x3n3}\}$ of forensic soundness of any PDE. These are used to formulate equations to show the validation process for PDE captured using the ONW system. The elements of $\mathcal{W}$ and $\mathcal{Z}$ are substituted at each case that is, optimal-state, mid-level state and minimal-state of forensic soundness. Taking the first derived illustration of $\mathcal{W}$ (i.e., $\{M_{x3n3}\}$) the substitution is presented as Eq. (1).

$$\mathcal{W} = \{M_{x3n3}\} \tag{1}$$

The predicate of Eq. (1) is the minimal requirements, because only one element of the set of $\{N\}$ that is, $\{n_3\}$ is considered at FSI checking. For example using Eq. (1) to validate photo PDE - set $\mathcal{W}$ becomes: $\mathcal{W} = \{M_{x3n3}\}$ where $\{M\}$ is (Geo location, Timestamp, device type, IMEI identifier and wifi connections), $\{x_3\}$ is the captured photo (PDE_p) and $\{n_3\}$ is the cryptographic hash ($\#$). The output becomes the checksum of the photo PDE ($\# PDE_p$) and the embedded FSI properties ($\{M\}$ (i.e. Geo location, Timestamp, device type, IMEI identifier and wifi connections) - $\#(PDE_p \wedge M)$ is the final output of Eq. (1). However, to increase the forensic soundness of PDE, using only cryptographic hash ($\#$) with the embedded PDE FSI properties $\{M\}$ may require additional factors, thereby enhancing the forensic soundness of the photo PDE (PDE_p). To realise the high strength forensic soundness, Eq. (2) replaces (1) in the forensic soundness validation check.

$$\mathcal{W} = \{M_{xjni}\} \tag{2}$$

The predicates of Eq. (2) is derived by adding encryption to the output of Eq. (1), therefore realising the in-between (mid-level) forensic soundness state of captured PDE. Set $\mathcal{W}$ becomes: $\mathcal{W} = \{M_{xjni}\}$ where $\{\mathcal{M}\}$ is the FSIs properties, $\{x_j\}$ is either video, audio or the photo PDE (PDE_p) (Photo PDE is used as in Fig. 5 example), and $\{n_i\}$ is cryptographic hashing of photo PDE and the addition of encryption. By using $\{n_i\}$, the predicate of Eq. (2) enhances the forensic soundness of captured PDE. Where $i = \{n_1, n_2\}$ or $i = \{n_1, n_2, n_3\}$, that is, cryptographic hash is $\{n_1\}$, encryption $\{n_2\}$ and digital signature $\{n_3\}$). The substitution for $\mathcal{W} = \{M_{xjni}\}$ becomes ((Geo location, timestamp, device type, IMEI identifier and wifi connections - M), x_j is the photo PDE - (PDE_p) with cryptographic hash - (#) and encryption (E_{ncrypt})) - The output becomes $E_{ncrypt}(\#(PDE_p \wedge M))$. Meanwhile Eq. (2) upholds two of the CIAAN mechanisms and all the PDE FSI properties, however there is room for stronger forensic soundness implementation to ascertain photo PDE (PDE_p) validity. Eq. (3) therefore insert all elements of set $\{N\}$ to achieve an optimal-state of the photo PDE (PDE_p) forensic soundness.

$$\mathcal{Z} = \{MN_{xj}\} \tag{3}$$

Equation (3) uses all the elements of set $\{N\}$ and that of set $\{M\}$, therefore Eq. (3) is the most efficient forensically sound process to ensure authenticity and originality of PDE stored in the ONW repository. This makes set $\{\mathcal{Z}\}$ the strongest predicate compared to set $\{\mathcal{W}\}$. For example to employ Eq. (3) i.e. $\mathcal{Z} = \{M\} \wedge \{N\} \wedge \{x_j\}$ the expression becomes adding digital signature $(DGsign)$ to the encrypted (E_{ncrypt}) PDE $\{x_j\}$ (photo PDE - (PDE_p)) and $\{M\}$ (Geo location, timestamp, device type, IMEI identifier and wifi connections) and $\{N\}$ (cryptographic hash - (#). That is $DGsign(E_{ncrypt}(\#(PDE_p \wedge M)))$.

Equation (3) however makes it possible to add digital signature in conjunction with cryptographic hash and encryption to the photo PDE to enhance its admissibility and ensure its forensic soundness, which is not possible with Eqs. (1) and (2). However, for Eq. (3) to hold, there are trade-offs to efficiency and high cost of resource implementation such as, processing time, architectural requirements specifications that encompasses the requirements of meeting the demands of Eq. (3). Meanwhile, to reduce cost while retaining the forensic soundness of the Photo-PDE, Eq. (2) may be employed. This notwithstanding, for the proof of concept of the ONW system, Eq. (3) is used. This is because using all elements of sets $\{\mathcal{M}\}$ and $\{\mathcal{N}\}$ is the most efficient method to retain forensic soundness, ensures chain of custody and chain of evidence of any PDE captured using the ONW system.

5.7   Measures to Ensure Users Privacy

For citizens to participate in the PDE sourcing process, or utilise the sourced PDE in criminal/civil investigations or in any court of law, their privacy rights of must be preserved as far as possible. Therefore adequate measures are put in place to uphold legal requirements regarding evidential weight, hearsay, rule of relevance and completeness, especially when the individual or witness wishes to invoke the non-compellable clause, as in Sect. 203 of the CPA Act, Act 51 of 1977 [14]. The ONW system is designed to eliminate the need to request uploader's information. However, when such a situation presents itself, the authorised downloader has to adhere to the validation rules put in place. To this effect, the ONW system uses four methods for privacy protection:

(i) The use of the public and private key pair for encryption and decryption of citizen's information like device metadata to ensure confidentiality while protecting privacy. For example, an authorised downloader requires a corresponding public key to obtain citizen's details or device metadata when needed to corroborate an crime scene documentation or first respondents report during neighbourhood crime investigation.

(ii) The downloader must obtain a formal and legal authorisation, such as a warrant, to obtain the user's information or device metadata.

(iii) The non-compellable witness clause of the Criminal Procedures Act (CPA), Act 51 of 1977, Sect. 203 [14] makes possible for an uploader to choose when to testify or provide his or her personal information.

(iv) The use of a traditional username and password applying password rules to increase user's awareness of the need to use unique username and password. Furthermore, citizen's log-in details are stored on their device, while their details stored in the back-end of the ONW system are encrypted using the public-private key system.

In summary, the profile information provided by the user is encrypted using the PKI system. Moreover, in a situation where an investigator requires the identity of an uploader to verify certain details of an uploaded PDE, the authorised user is then required to go through the legal process for obtaining authority (i.e. warrant) in order to access uploader's information. When the warrant has been obtained, the authorised user is then required to provide a matching key that corresponds to the uploader's encryption key.

6   Discussion

The requirements for privacy rights sometimes conflict with the methods devised to eradicate neighbourhood crime. However, technological innovations and the prevalence of the World Wide Web has made it viable to achieve neighbourhood crime watch using mobile devices' built-in technology like camera and audio functionalities. Using mobile devices as a tool in neighbourhood crime watch is motivated by the rise in neighbourhood crime across South Africa, which demands a proactive means to encourage community members to take part in neighbourhood security. The mathematical proofs are used to illustrate the forensic soundness of PDE captured using the ONW system. It showed the processes employed to determine the reliability of captured and stored PDE $\{X\}$.

The ONW system is required to protect the privacy of the uploader, however, anonymity is not completely guaranteed in the ONW system. This is because, a sourced PDE that has complete anonymity loses its completeness and evidential weight therefore rendering the PDE invalid [3]. According to the ECT Act, evidential weight is determined by establishing a clear origin of any digital evidence. Untraceable PDE loses evidential weight and therefore is inadmissible.

However, to the protect the privacy of citizens, the use of the public private key encryption (PKI) system [11] is employed where the downloader matches a decryption key to obtain access to uploader's information. It adds a third layer of security to the already existing cryptographic hash (first layer) and digital signature (second layer). The legal requirements of obtaining a warrant is an additional constraint when an uploader's details are necessary. Although according to the Criminal Procedures Act (CPA), Act 51 of 1977 Sect. 203 [14] an uploader may plea the non-compellable witness clause, thereby exempting the witness from testifying.

One assumption of the ONW system is that the uploader is able to capture PDE at a safe distance from the crime scene to avoid self-endangerment. It also assumes an uploader can identify what constitutes a crime. However, the psychological state of mind of the uploader, as well as what constitutes a potential crime, fall outside the of scope of this paper.

7   Conclusion

The ONW system's proof of concept shows the processes employed to ensure that stored PDE retains forensic soundness from the time of PDE capturing to storage and final usage. The various states of forensic soundness made prevision to ascertain the validity of captured PDE. Opting for the optimal-state of PDE forensic soundness, the ONW system provides admissible potential digital evidence of neighbourhood crime.

Acknowledgment. This work is based on the research supported wholly or in part by the National Research Foundation of South Africa (Grant Numbers 88211, 89143 and TP13081227420).

References

1. Aker, J.C., Fafchamps, M.: Mobile phone coverage, producer markets: evidence from west africa. World Bank Econ. Rev. lhu006 (2014)
2. Cohen, F.A.: Digital Forensic Evidence Examination. Fred Cohen and Associates Out of Livermore, 3rd edn. (2009). 9781878109446
3. Government Gazette: Electronic Communications and Transactions Act, Act 25 of 2002. Technical report, PDF Scanned by Sabinet. Accessed 08 February 2014. South Africa Government Gazette - Legislation- South Africa - National/Acts and Regulations/E/Electronic Communications and Transactions Act No. 25 Of 2002/The Act, August 2002
4. Hargreaves, C.J.: Assessing the reliability of digital evidence from live investigations involving encryption. Ph.D. thesis, Deartment of Informatics and Sensors, Cranfield University, UK (2009)
5. Holovaty, A., Kaplan-Moss, J.: The Definitive Guide to Django: Web Development Done Right. Apress (2009)
6. Klir, G., Yuan, B.: Fuzzy Sets and Fuzzy Logic, vol. 4. Prentice Hall, New Jersey (1995)
7. Bass, R.K.L., Clements, P.: Software Architecture in Practice. Part of the SEI Series in Software Engineering Series, 3rd edn. Addison-wesley Professional, USA (2012). ISBN -13: 000-0321815734, ISBN-10: 0321815734
8. Omeleze, S., Venter, H.S.: Towards a model for acquiring digital evidence using mobile devices. In: Tenth International Network Conference (INC 2014) and WDFIA 2014 Plymouth University, UK, pp. 1–14 (2014)

9. Omeleze, S., Venter, S.H.: A model for access management of potential digital evidence. In: 10th International Conference on Cyber Warfare and Security (ICCWS), pp. 491–501. CSIR, University of Vender and Academic Conferences Limited (2015)

10. Pawlak, Z.: Rough set theory and its applications to data analysis. Cybern. Syst. **29**(7), 661–688 (1998)

11. Charles Pfleeger, P., Pfleeger, S.L.: Security in Computing, 4th edn, pp. 35–43. Prentice Hall Publication, Upper Saddle Rivers (2006). ISBN:0132390779

12. Government-Gazette POPI-Act: Privacy and data protection - discussion paper 109 (project 124) - South African law reform commission (2005–2010). Technical report, Accessed 08 August 2014. South Africa Government Gazette - Legislation - South Africa - National/Acts - Privacy and data protection Act No. 4, August 2013

13. Saleem, S., Popov, O., Dahman, R.: Evaluation of security methods for ensuring the integrity of digital evidence. Institute of Electrical Electronics Engineers (IEEE Xplore Digital Library) (2011)

14. Schwikkard, P.-J., Van der Merwe, S.E.: Principles of Evidence. Juta and Company Ltd. (2009). ISBN:978 0 7021 79501

15. Susanto, H., Almunawar, M.N., Tuan, Y.C.: Information security manage-ment system standards: a comparative study of the big five (2011)

Optimal Advertisement Strategies for Small and Big Companies

Tossou Aristide$^{(\boxtimes)}$ and Christos Dimitrakakis

Chalmers University of Technology, Gothenburg, Sweden
`aristide@chalmers.se`

Abstract. Many small and big companies in developing countries struggle to make their products or services known to the public. This is especially the case when there are new or have a new product. Most of them use publicity through radio, tv, social networks, billboard, SMS... Moreover, they also need to decide at what time to display their publicity for maximal effects. The companies which have more money typically used a simple strategy which consists in doing the publicity at many sources at different time or at a time such as to maximize the number of viewers. The smaller ones typically target the best popular programs.

However, this strategy is not the best as many users listening to your publicity might not be interested in it. So, you are more likely to miss the interested readers. Moreover, there will be many other competing publicities.

We propose a strategy by using the Multi-Armed bandit problem to optimally solve this problem under realistic assumptions. We further extend the model to deal with many competing companies by proposing the use of a time-division sharing algorithm.

Keywords: Bandit algorithm · Advertisement · Developing countries

1 Introduction

Advertisement is one of the most important component of the development of any company. This is especially true in developing countries where people tend to buy what their friends are buying. By choosing correctly when and where to make publicity, a company can then boost its profit significantly.

However, many companies in developing countries do not put too much effort in designing a strategy for where and when to make advertisements. They simply target the program which they believe is the most popular hoping that the more people see their publicity the more clients they will get.

This is not always the case, as the most potential interested users might not be available when a publicity is delivered. Or their publicity will be hidden by many other similar ones.

This problem is related to the budget allocation in marketing which has received a lot of attention. In [1], they modeled it as a bipartite graph where

© ICST Institute for Computer Sciences, Social Informatics and Telecommunications Engineering 2016
R. Glitho et al. (Eds.): AFRICOMM 2015, LNICST 171, pp. 94–98, 2016.
DOI: 10.1007/978-3-319-43696-8_10

on one side are the customers and the other the medias. They then formulate it as a knapsack problem and solve the resulting maximization. This approach is further extended in [8] who proposes more efficient algorithms. However, their model only deal with a single advertiser. In [7], the problem is modeled in a game theoretic setting where advertisers are the players wishing to maximize their own utility. They solved it using a best response strategy. In our case, we solved this problem using the more natural multi-armed bandit (MAB) setting. All of the previous approach, only care about the budget to allocate to each media and not when is the appropriate time to advertise.

The MAB setting has previously being used for advertisement in [9]. But they solved the problem of which advertisement a search engine or media should display.

2 Modelisation

2.1 Problem Description

We assume that a company has at its disposal K spaces (combination of medias and time-slot) for publicity. For every new product, the company wants to make T publicities. The company incurs a cost of c_i for each publicity and expects in return to have many new clients giving him a profit of b_i. The overall goal of the company is to maximize its expected earnings after making T publicities.

We mapped this problem to the classical issue of exploration/exploitation which arises in many domains. Indeed, if a given publicity space leads to an immediate high reward, the company needs to keep choosing it to maximize its short term revenue. However, the company needs also to choose other spaces to check if its long-term revenue will not improve. This issue has been formally studied as the multi-armed bandit problem.

We first give the formal definition of multi-armed bandit and then detailed its mapping to our setting.

2.2 Multi-armed Bandit Problem

The K-armed bandit problem [5] involves an agent sequentially choosing among a set of K arms $\mathcal{A}$. At each time step t, the agent selects an action $a_t = i \in \mathcal{A}$ and obtains a reward r_t. The goal of the agent is to draw arms so as to maximize the total reward obtained after T interactions. An equivalent notion is to minimize the total regret against an agent who knew the best sequence of arms to play before the game starts. This is defined by:

$$\mathcal{R} \triangleq \mathbb{E}^{\pi_*} \sum_{t=1}^{T} r_t - \mathbb{E}^{\pi} \sum_{t=1}^{T} r_t. \tag{1}$$

where π_* is the optimal policy and π the one of the learning agent.

When the reward is drawn from some fixed unknown distribution, it leads to a stochastic MAB, otherwise it leads to an adversarial MAB. The stochastic MAB can be efficiently solved using the *UCB* algorithm [2] whereas the adversarial can be efficiently solved using the *EXP3* algorithm [3].

We now described the mapping from our setting to MAB. The set of K arms $\mathcal{A}$ is the set of spaces available for publicity. A reward is received for all previously played spaces at each *aggregation period* which can be taken to be a day for simplicity. We defined the reward as $r_t = \frac{p_s}{p_m \cdot c_s}$ with p_m the maximum profit possible for a *period*, c_s the percentage of costs incurred when choosing space s and p_s the profit due to space s for the *period*. We played a space at the end of each *period* when the budget allocated to publicity allowed it.

2.3   Dealing with Competition

In practice, however, the company is not the only one looking for publicity space. And they might be many other companies willing to advertise similar products. To deal with it, we consider the distributed multiple-player multi-armed bandit setting [6].

The multiple-player multi-armed bandit involves M players who have to choose between the same set of arms. They play simultaneously and whenever any two of them pick the same arm there is a collision. Two collision models are considered. When a collision happens, only one of the player receives the full reward and the other receive 0. The second collision model assumes that each player equally share the reward. The collision are observed by all players when it happens and the goal of each agent is to strategically maximize its own expected utility.

The mapping to the multiple-player multi-armed bandit to our setting is direct. And we can note that each player/company can observe collision by monitoring other publicities presented in the same slot as theirs or simply by asking the publicity provider.

To solve the distributed multi-armed bandits problem, we used the time division sharing technique [6]. In the first time step, the first player will target the best arm, and the k-th player target the k-th best arm. In the second time step, the first player will target the second best arm, etc. This idea can be modeled by associating an offset o to each player p. At each time step t, player p will target the $(t - 1 + o - 1) \mod M + 1$ best action. The offset used by each player is generated randomly. When a collision happens after a number of times, each player involved in the collision change its offset with probability 0.5 and keeps it old offset with the same probability (See [6]).

It is shown in [6] that if all players used this strategy they will get the same expected utility.

2.4   Determining Which Publicity Space Generate Which Customer

Our mapping to MAB requires that we are able to determine the exact publicity that a customer has followed.

This information can be obtained by asking customers to fill a survey where they are simply ask to tell which publicity push them to the company. However, customers might not be willing to tell us this information and when they do they could lie.

To solve this issue, we proposed to use the robust Bayesian truth serum (RBTS) [10]. We first described what is RBTS and then we described how it can be used in our setup.

The description of this RBTS is as follows:

– There are $n \geq 2$ agents who observe some signal about the same phenomenon and report it. Depending on the quality of the report, the agents receive a score or money. The goal of the agents is to maximize their expected score after multiple interaction with the system.
– It is assumed that all agents have the same prior belief about the outcome of the phenomenon and after observing the signal they all update their posterior similarly.

In [10], the score received by each agent is described by the following two steps:

1. Each agent i is asked to provide two reports:
   – Information report x_i which represents agent i's reported signal.
   – Prediction report y_i which represents agent i's prediction about the frequencies of signal values in the overall population.
2. Each agent i is linked with her peer agent $j = i + 1$ (mod n) and is rewarded with a score:

$$\frac{1}{y_j(x_i)} \cdot \mathbb{1}_{x_j=x_i} + R(y_i, x_j)$$

with the first term the information score, the second the prediction score, where R is a strictly proper scoring rule and $\mathbb{1}_{x_j=x_i}$ is the indicator variable.

The mapping of this setting in our system is as follows:

– The agents here are our customers. We assume that the client who viewed the same publicity share the same common belief a about the quality of our services. Then, after becoming our customers, they update their prior belief accordingly.
– We map the phenomenon to observe as the quality of our product/service.
– The signal is the publicity about the product/service.
– We will ask each customer three questions: The first is where/when he has heard about us, the second is the rating about the quality of our service/product (QOS) he guessed after viewing the publicity (x_i) and the last is the rating about our QOS when he interacts with us (y_i).
– We then assign a score to each of our client by choosing R as the Brier Score [4].

If each agent goal is to maximize its score, then the previous mechanism is Bayes-Nash incentive-compatible [10]. That is, all agents will report their true signals. If they don't, then their expected score will be lower.

To make the customers willing to increase their score, we can give them a monetary reward proportional to their score. For a supermarket, it could mean giving reduction on overall purchase which is proportional to the score of the customer. This could also be a discount in other stores or in the form of Internet, mobile credits bonus.

3   Conclusion and Outlook

We have presented an algorithm which will allow companies to optimally advertise their product. For that we observe that this problem is a standard exploration/exploitation issue which allows us to convert it to a Multi-Armed bandit problem. We also defined the reward sequence to be used. Furthermore, we extend the model to deal with competing companies by using the distributed multiple players multi-armed bandit which is solved using a time fair division sharing algorithm.

Finally, we present an incentivizing mechanism that will help companies to know where their customer heard about them. The Mechanism is a truthful one and encourage customers not only to participate but not to lie.

As future work, we would like to experiment this model with a company in Benin and check if the theory guarantees are observed in practice.

References

1. Alon, N., Gamzu, I., Tennenholtz, M.: Optimizing budget allocation among channels and influencers. In: Proceedings of the 21st International Conference on World Wide Web, WWW 2012, pp. 381–388 (2012)
2. Auer, P., Cesa-Bianchi, N., Fischer, P.: Finite time analysis of the multiarmed bandit problem. Mach. Learn. **47**(2/3), 235–256 (2002)
3. Auer, P., Cesa-Bianchi, N., Freund, Y., Schapire, R.E.: The nonstochastic multi-armed bandit problem. SIAM J. Comput. **32**(1), 48–77 (2003)
4. Brier, G.W.: Verification of forecasts expressed in terms of probability. Mon. Weather Rev. **78**(1), 1–3 (1950). 30 Sept 2015
5. Lai, T.L., Robbins, H.: Asymptotically efficient adaptive allocation rules. Adv. Appl. Math. **6**(1), 4–22 (1985)
6. Liu, K., Zhao, Q.: Distributed learning in multi-armed bandit with multiple players. IEEE Trans. Signal Process. **58**(11), 5667–5681 (2010)
7. Maehara, T., Yabe, A., Kawarabayashi, K.: Budget allocation problem with multiple advertisers: a game theoretic view. In: ICML 32, JMLR Proceedings, vol. 37, pp. 428–437. JMLR.org (2015)
8. Miyauchi, A., Iwamasa, Y., Fukunaga, T., Kakimura, N.: Threshold influence model for allocating advertising budgets. In: ICML 32, JMLR Proceedings, vol. 37, pp. 1395–1404. JMLR.org (2015)
9. Pandey, S., Olston, C.: Handling advertisements of unknown quality in search advertising. In: NIPS 20, pp. 1065–1072. MIT Press (2006)
10. Radanovic, G., Faltings, B.: A robust Bayesian truth serum for non-binary signals. In: AAAI 27, pp. 833–839 (2013)

Innovation Factory: An Innovative Collaboration and Management Scenario

Paolo Ceravolo, Ernesto Damiani, Fulvio Frati$^{(\boxtimes)}$, Jonatan Maggesi,
Riccardo Mainardi, and Francesco Zavatarelli

Computer Science Department, Università degli Studi di Milano,
via Bramante 65, 26013 Crema, Italy
{paolo.ceravolo,ernesto.damiani,fulvio.frati,jonatan.maggesi,
riccardo.mainardi,francesco.zavatarelli}@unimi.it

Abstract. The Open Innovation model has its foundations on a very basic theoretical ideas: it is necessity to combine ideas internal to your enterprise and, at the same time, draw information and resources from the outside, i.e. from users, competitors, partners or others, who belong to the same market segment. This approach is well established and widely supported globally. However, in recent years, the technological solutions proposed have tried to provide cutting-edge solutions, which are able to channel resources from disparate sources to our businesses. But Open Innovation is not only this: its challenge is to break barriers, even if located within a single organisation hierarchy or geographical locations. Our work goes in this direction, introducing the concept of the Innovation Factory, where various new collaborative features are merged together into a consistent innovation management process.

1 Introduction

In the essay "The wisdom of crowds" the journalist James Surowiecki [1] argues that, under certain conditions, the collective intelligence of a large number of people is more important than the advice of a small group of experts. The Web evolution along its first twenty years of history [2] has largely demonstrated the effectiveness of these ideas. This revolution has taken place thanks to services such as wikis, blogs and social bookmarking, and with the formation of social networks, new forms of collective intelligence became a source for the creation of new business opportunities. In recent years, social networks have redesigned the look of the Web by introducing tools that have fostered collaboration, sharing and relationships between people. Facebook, Twitter, Google+, LinkedIn, Instagram and all the online services based on these models are included in the term Web 2.0, and in fact they represent today the most advanced technologies, monopolising the ranking of the most visited Internet sites. This new frontier has been able to penetrate even within companies overcoming organisational and geographical barriers. In the old business model the research and development (R&D) department was confined within the walls of an enterprise, and was limited to a small number of people. In the modern business this scheme is finally

© ICST Institute for Computer Sciences, Social Informatics and Telecommunications Engineering 2016
R. Glitho et al. (Eds.): AFRICOMM 2015, LNICST 171, pp. 99–105, 2016.
DOI: 10.1007/978-3-319-43696-8_11

overcome. The principle behind this revolution lies in the possibility that each individual can make a contribution for the benefit of the whole community, be it a group of friends or a research team. In this context we introduce the notion of the *Innovation Factory*, the platform at the center of our work. In particular we point out that such a tool is not only usable in a developing economy, but it is also useful and even necessary in a context where a multinational company has outsourced some activities to a branch office in a developing country since this platform improves the communication between the main office and the subsidiaries.

The paper is organised as follow. Section 2 starts the discussion with the related work. Section 3 gives motivations and reasons for which it is useful to introduce the Innovation Factory in a commercial business. Section 4 provides a description of the main components of the platform, and provides the technological context in which the Innovation Factory stands. Section 5 recalls the outcomes of the tests performed for our initial deployment. Section 6 proposes our conclusions.

2   Related Work

Along the years many articles were published about collaborative venues, community forums, electronic meeting systems, collaborative working environments, enterprise social software, enterprise social networks. All these terms refer to the concept of collaboration platform.

Since the development of modern organisational studies, the understanding and operativeness of collaboration environments has been considered a relevant research topic [3]. Even if, most of the studies conducted fall in the area of social science [4], in the last years contributions adopting quantitative approaches are emerging in different contexts, such as multimodal support of group dynamics [5,6] or automatic recognition of social and task-oriented functional roles [7,8].

In recent years, technology triggered a large number of new products. In [9–12] the authors present the results of qualitative analyses on the impact that collaboration platforms have on organisations. In [13] commercial products and research prototypes in the domain of collaborative computing are examined.

3   Motivations

It is not surprising that a recent research involving several multi-national companies, conducted by Mimecast [14] found that on an average basis, company staff spends on average 13 h a week for managing email, each employee loses 5.3 h per week due to inefficient processes, and 67 % of the information available in the company are not found due to poor organisation of the data.

This lead us to consider that the traditional intranet model is obsolete. When then investigated an approach capable of supporting the maturation of team knowledge by (i) increasing the awareness of the ideas transiting through phases of collaboration [15], and by consequence (ii) accelerating the convergence of team members in tackling with common tasks and in adopting a shared terminology [16].

4   Structure and Components for the Innovation Factory

In this section we will present the platform with some details about the individual components. After defining the environment as a whole we will also evaluate the limits that have led us to study the new features recently introduced.

4.1   Liferay Basic Components and the Innovation Factory Customisation

We now provide a very short overview of Liferay and propose the reasons that led us to choose this tool as the basis of our project. Liferay is an open source product written in Java and consists of three basic parts: a kernel (*Liferay Portal*), which serves as the core for applications and contents, a content management system (*CMS Liferay*) and a suite of applications to achieve collaboration and social networks (*Liferay Collaboration*). Liferay is based on a service-oriented architecture (SOA). Thanks to this modularity we consider a flexible tool well suited to the integration of new features and the expansion of existing ones. The reasons why we chose Liferay can summarised in the following points. *Open source policy and Low cost*: all software within the IF is open source; this choice allows anyone to create new features or to expand existing ones starting from the experience of a very large community of developers. Also, being free of license fees Liferay is highly competitive compared to all other commercial solutions. *Integration*: thanks to its modular platform, Liferay allows integration with third party software, the Web and easily permits the introduction of new components that can enhance the product's capabilities. *Time To Market*: Liferay provides a number of built-in functionality of existing applications and templates that make it easy and fast implementing new *portlet* and the start of production of a new portal. In this way, Innovation Factory, our customisation of Liferay, provides users with a all-in-one platform where the innovative elements we added can be an advantage over competing products. Our solution is developed from *Liferay Portal*, while *Social Office* [17] is the tool that provides the basic functionalities of sharing and collaboration. Then we chose *Etherpad Lite* [18] as open source editor for the creation and the processing of documents that must be shared among multiple users. An Etherpad text is synchronised as you type, so that everyone is viewing the same text. This allows you to collaborate seamlessly on documents[1]. *Apache Stanbol* is the core of the platform: its semantic engine can analyse resources, correlate and enriche content for the users. By leveraging the capabilities of Stanbol we developed the core component of the Innovation Factory, i.e. a *Recommender System* [19], which an extended collaborative environment supporting participatory design. [20]. The RS, through a tag cloud system, provides suggestions to stimulate the collaborative process and offers all the resources correlated to a specific area of discussion. Through Stanbol, any Etherpad file written by the users is parsed and compared to the dictionary. Any

---

[1] First launched in November 2008, Etherpad software was acquired by Google in December 2009 and released as open source later that month.

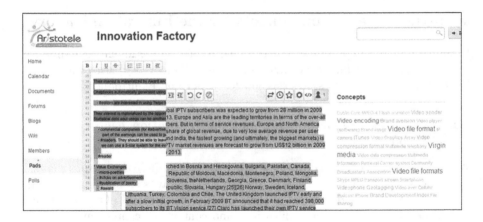

Fig. 1. Innovation factory (IF).

dictionary contents related to that document appear on the right hand side (for example other files with similar content, concepts and people related, etc.), as shown in Fig. 1. Documents that are linked can be either stored internally in a file system, or in the internet. In the latter case documents are retrieved by a web crawler. The open source *Crawler4j* [21] was chosen and used for parsing and managing external resources. In this way IF facilitates the handling of collaborative tasks by facilitating coordination activities and making important resources detectable. A Knowledge Base (KB) is finally created to store and manage documents. The key contributions of the IF are *(i)* the integration of the different open source modules and *(ii)* a the tag cloud system, which visualises the recommendations computed by the RS and provides team members with tags linked to relevant documents in the KB. As discussed in [22], the RS reacts to three particular kinds of inputs: *(i)* a stimulus, describing a task to be performed or a set of goals to be achieved, *(ii)* a target, defining the set of employees over which suggestions must be applied, and *(iii)* a set of local configurations defining, e.g., the type and the similarity measures. The RS computes the concept adequacy, between the targets and stimulus, and returns recommendations on concepts connected to the stimulus.

4.2 Limits of the Innovation Factory First Version and the New Features

The scenario presented in the previous paragraph is the starting point of our next updates. The Innovation Factory was already a complete, extensible environment that adapts quickly and easily to different kind of company.

However, in order to straighten its capability in accordance to the objective presented in Sect. 3, we set some new requirements for a new version of the IF, in particular we want to make the creation of the dictionary contextual with the development of the discussion. When editing a new pad users may perceive new entities became relevant and consequently add them in the dictionary. In this way the system will track the use of that element in next interactions. Later on, users may access the administration tab of the dictionary to enrich definitions by creating relationships among entities or to attach documents and link as of these entities.

More specifically the new features extending the IF are the following:

- Fast creation of dictionary entities using hashtags directly in textual documents.
- Contextually update recommendations matching dictionary entities to data generated by interactions.

5   Tests performed on the IF features

A preliminary version of the IF is deployed during EC-funded ARISTOTELE project, which sought to raise awareness about the importance of collaboration aspects for understanding variations in team processes which, in turn, impact team outcomes. At the end of the project pre- and post-questionnaire data was gathered from 27 professionals of a medium-sized company operating in the knowledge-intensive sector of telecommunication. Test outcomes are found in [23]. Test results indicated that teams working in highly integrated computer-supported collaboration environments had higher team innovation, better agreement, better coordination, and less dominance than in traditional settings.

More recently we adopted the IF environment to test the impact of recommender systems on team processes [24]. We observed that teams using recommendations spent less effort on information handling, engaged more in communication, shared their work more equally than teams without recommendations. Finding initial supports to the idea that our tool effectively accelerate the convergence of team to common tasks.

6   Conclusion

In this article we highlighted the concepts of Open Innovation and Collaboration Platform to enhance innovation in a community through technological support. Initial experimental studies has demonstrated that our platform can develop the collaborative capacity of a team, building new relationships and accelerating the convergence of ideas. Future works will test the platform using industrial datasets and will address the issues raised in the initial test phase.[2]

[2] This work was partly funded by EU-funded ARISTOTELE project (EU call: FP7-ICT-2009-5, Topic: ICT-2009.4.2 - Technology-enhanced learning).

References

1. Surowiecki, J.: The Wisdom of Crowds. Google books (2005)
2. Ceravolo, P., Damiani, E.: Knowledge representation progress in the brief webhistory. In: Proceedings of the European Computing and Philosophy Conference on Computing, Philosophy and Cognition (ECAP 2004) (2005)
3. Doyle, M., Straus, D.: How to Make Meetings Work. Jove Books, New York (1976)
4. Rickards, T., Moger, S.: Creative leaders: a decade of contributions from creativity and innovation management journal. Creat. Innov. Manag. **15**(1), 4–18 (2006)
5. Pianesi, F., Zancanaro, M., Not, E., Leonardi, C., Falcon, V., Lepri, B.: Multimodal support to group dynamics. Pers. Ubiquit. Comput. **12**(3), 181–195 (2008)
6. Kim, T., Chang, A., Holland, L., Pentland, A.S.: Meeting mediator: enhancing-group collaborationusing sociometric feedback. In: Proceedings of the 2008 ACM Conference on Computer Supported Cooperative Work, pp. 457–466. ACM (2008)
7. Dong, W., Lepri, B., Pianesi, F., Pentland, A.: Modeling functional roles dynamics in small group interactions. IEEE Trans. Multimed. **15**(1), 83–95 (2013)
8. Pentland, A., Choudhury, T., Eagle, N., Singh, P.: Human dynamics: computation for organizations. Pattern Recogn. Lett. **26**(4), 503–511 (2005)
9. Foster-Fishman, P.G., et al.: Building collaborative capacity incommunity coalitions: a review and integrative framework. Am. J. Commun. Psychol. **29**(2), 241–261 (2001)
10. Chin, C.P.-Y., Evans, N., Choo, K.-K.R.: Exploring factors influencing the use of enterprise social networks in multinational professional service firms. J. Organ. Comput. Electron. Commer. **25**(3), 289–315 (2015)
11. Wang, X., Love, P.E., Kim, M.J., Wang, W.: Mutual awareness in collaborative design: an augmented reality integrated telepresence system. Comput. Ind. **65**(2), 314–324 (2014)
12. Hong, H.-Y., Chang, Y.-H., Chai, C.S.: Fostering a collaborative and creative climate in a college class through idea-centered knowledge-building. Instr. Sci. **42**(3), 389–407 (2014)
13. Bafoutsou, G., et al.: Review and functional classification of collaborative systems. Int. J. Inf. Manage. **22**(2002), 281–305 (2002)
14. Mimecast: Mimecast unified email management. https://www.mimecast.com
15. Seeber, I., Maier, R., Ceravolo, P., Frati, F.: Tracing the development of ideas in distributed, it-supported teams during synchronous collaboration (2014)
16. Bellandi, V., Ceravolo, P., Damiani, E., Frati, F., Cota, G.L., Maggesi, J.: Boosting the innovation process in collaborative environments. In: 2013 IEEE International Conference on Systems, Man, and Cybernetics (SMC), pp. 1432–1437. IEEE (2013)
17. Liferay: an open source sharepoint alternative. http://www.liferay.com/products/liferay-social-office
18. Etherpad.org: Etherpad customizable open source online editor (2015). http://etherpad.org
19. Resnick, P., Varian, H.: Recommender systems (guest editors) (1997). http://delivery.acm.org/
20. Bellandi, V., Ceravolo, P., Damiani, E., Frati, F., Maggesi, J., Zhu, L.: Exploiting participatory design in open innovation factories. In: Eighth International Conference on Signal Image Technology and Internet Based Systems (SITIS), pp. 937–943 (2012). doi:10.1109/SITIS.2012.139
21. Google: yasserg/crawler4j. https://github.com/yasserg/crawler4j

22. Bellandi, V., Ceravolo, P., Frati, F., Maggesi, J., Waldhart, G., Seeber, I.: Design principles for competence-based recommender systems. In: Proceedings of 2012 IEEE International Conference on Digital Ecosystem Technologies (DEST), pp. 1–6 (2012)
23. Seeber, I., et al.: Computer-supported collaboration environments andthe emergence of collaboration aspects. In: Proceedings of the Pre-ICIS2013, SIG-Organizational Systems Research Association (OSRA) Workshop, Milan, Italy, 15 December 2013 (2013)
24. Ceravolo, P., Damiani, E., Frati, F., Bellandi, V., Maier, R., Seeber, I.: Applying recommender systems in collaboration environments. Comput. Hum. Behav. **51**, 1124–1133 (2015)

A Framework for Accurate Drought Forecasting System Using Semantics-Based Data Integration Middleware

Adeyinka K. Akanbi[(✉)] and Muthoni Masinde

Department of Information Technology, Central University of Technology,
Bloemfontein, Free State, South Africa
{aakanbi,emasinde}@cut.ac.za

Abstract. Technological advancement in Wireless Sensor Networks (WSN) has made it become an invaluable component of a reliable environmental monitoring system; they form the 'digital skin' through which to 'sense' and collect the context of the surroundings and provides information on the process leading to complex events such as drought. However, these environmental properties are measured by various heterogeneous sensors of different modalities in distributed locations making up the WSN, using different abstruse terms and vocabulary in most cases to denote the same observed property, causing data heterogeneity. Adding semantics and understanding the relationships that exist between the observed properties, and augmenting it with local indigenous knowledge is necessary for an accurate drought forecasting system. In this paper, we propose the framework for the semantic representation of sensor data and integration with indigenous knowledge on drought using a middleware for an efficient drought forecasting system.

Keywords: Middleware · Internet of things · Drought forecasting · Semantic integration · Ontology · Interoperability · Semantic technology

1 Introduction

The application of Semantic Technology for drought forecasting is a growing research area. Our work investigates the semantic representation and integration of measured environmental entities with the local Indigenous knowledge (IK) using an ontology to allow reasoning and generate inference based on their interrelationship. We present a proposed model which outline our research directions, [7] provides a further overview of the framework towards an accurate drought forecasting system.

In terms of negative impacts, droughts are currently ranked[1] number one (CRED 2012). Compared to other natural disasters such as floods, hurricanes,

---

[1] The ranking is based on severity, length of event, total area affected, total loss of life, total economic loss, social effect, long-term impacts, suddenness and frequency [1].

© ICST Institute for Computer Sciences, Social Informatics and Telecommunications Engineering 2016
R. Glitho et al. (Eds.): AFRICOMM 2015, LNICST 171, pp. 106–110, 2016.
DOI: 10.1007/978-3-319-43696-8_12

earthquakes and epidemics, droughts are very difficult to predict; they creep slowly and last longest. The complex nature of droughts onset-termination has made it acquire the title "the creeping disaster" [2]. The greatest challenge is designing a framework which can track information about the 'what', 'where' and 'when' of environmental phenomena and the representation of the various dynamic aspects of the phenomena [3]. The representation of such phenomena requires better understanding of the 'process' that leads to the 'event'. For example, a *soil moisture sensor* provides sets of values for the observed property *soil moisture*. The measured property can also be influenced by the *temperature heat index* measured over the observed period. This makes accurate prediction based on these sensor values almost impossible without understanding the semantics and relationships that exist between this various properties. Hypothetically, drought prediction tools could be used to establish precise drought development patterns as early as possible and provide sufficient information to decision-makers to prepare for the droughts long before they happen. This way, the prediction can be used to mitigate effects of droughts.

The technological advancement in Wireless Sensor Networks (WSN) has facilitated its use in monitoring environmental properties irrespective of the geographical location. In their (WSNs) current implementation, these properties are measured using heterogeneous sensors that are mostly distributed in different locations. Further, different abstruse terms and vocabulary in most cases are used to denote the same observed property, thereby leading to data heterogeneity. Moreover, research [4,5] on indigenous knowledge (IK) on droughts has pointed to the fact that IK on living and non-living things e.g., *sifennefene worms, peulwane birds, lehota frogs* and plants like *mutiga tree, mothokolo tree* etc. can indicate drier or wetter conditions, which can imply likely occurrence of drought event over time [6]. This scenario shows that environmental events can be inferred from sensors data augmented with IK, if proper semantic is attached to it based on some set of indicators. Therefore, a semantics-based data integration middleware is required to bridge the gap between heterogeneous sensor data and IK for an accurate drought forecasting and prediction system.

2   Problem Statements

The following problems were identified as a major bottleneck for the utilization of semantic technologies for drought forecasting:

The current lack of ontology based middleware for the semantic representation of environmental process: Ontological modeling of key concepts of environmental phenomena such as object, state, process and event, ensures the drawing of accurate inference from the sequence of processes that lead to an event. Presently, what is currently missing is an environmental ontology with well-defined vocabularies that allow explicit representation of the process, events and also attach semantics to the participants in the environmental domain.

Lack of semantic integration of heterogeneous data sources with indigenous knowledge for an accurate environmental forecasting: Studies reveal that over

80 % of farmers in some parts of Kenya, Zambia, Zimbabwe and South Africa rely on Indigenous knowledge forecasts (IKF) for their agricultural practices [5]. An IoT-based environmental monitoring system made up of interconnected heterogeneous weather information sources such as sensors, mobile phones, conventional weather stations, and indigenous knowledge could improve the accuracy of environmental forecasting.

Lack of IoT-based drought forecasts communication and dissemination channels: There is a lack of effective dissemination channels for drought forecasting information. For example, the absence of smart billboards placed at strategic location and smart phones. The output channels would ensure farmers have access to drought forecasting information know the spatial distribution of a *drought vulnerability index.*

3   Research Questions

To what extent does the adoption of knowledge representation and semantic technology in the development of a middleware enable seamless sharing and exchange of data among heterogeneous IoT entities?

Several standards have been created to cope with the data heterogeneities. Examples are the Sensor Markup Language (SensorML)[2], WaterML, and American Federal Geographic Data (FGDC) Standard[3]. However, these standards provide sensor data to a predefined application in a standardized format, and hence do not generally solve data heterogeneity. Semantic technology solves this by representing data in a machine readable language such as Resource Description Framework (RDF) and Ontology Web Language (OWL), for seamless data sharing irrespective of the domain.

What are the main components of an implementation framework/architecture that employs the middleware to implement an IoT-based Drought Early Warning Systems (DEWS)?

The existence of ontology with well-defined vocabularies that allows an explicit representation of process and events; the representation and integration of the inputs in machine-readable formats, the availability of a reasoning engine (*CEP Engine*) that generates inference based on input parameters.

4   Methodology

The proposed semantic middleware is a software layer composed of a set of various sub-layers interposed between the application layer and the physical layer. It incorporates interface protocols, which liaise with the storage database in the cloud for downloading the semi-processed sensory reading to be represented based on the ontology through a mediator device as shown in Fig. 3 [7].

---

[2] http://www.opengeospatial.org/standards.
[3] https://www.fgdc.gov/metadata.

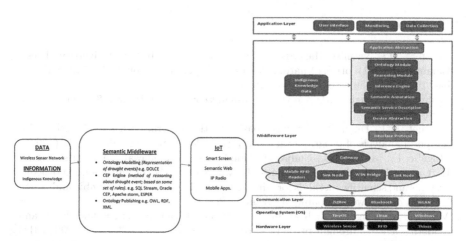

Fig. 1. The semantic middleware integration framework

Fig. 2. Overview of the middleware architecture

An environmental process-based ontology is required to overcome the problems associated with the dynamic nature of environmental data and the data heterogeneities. The study proposes to use DOLCE top-level ontology for the modelling of the foundational entities needed to represent the dynamic phenomena. Information from the sensor data streams is integrated with indigenous knowledge using a Complex Events Processing (*CEP*) engine as proposed in Fig. 1. This will serve as the reasoning engine for inferring patterns leading to drought, based on a set of rules derived from indigenous knowledge of the local people on drought. Figure 2 depicts the overview of the middleware architecture. The domain of this particular case study is Free State Province, South Africa - an ongoing research project by AfriCRID[4], Department of Information Technology, Central University of Technology, Free State.

5   Results and Discussion

The study is expected to produce a semantic based data integration middleware that semantically represents and integrates heterogeneous data sources with indigenous knowledge based on a unified ontology for an accurate IoT-based drought forecasting system. With more integrated comprehensive services that are based on semantic interoperability, our approach makes a unique contribution towards improving the accuracy of drought prediction and forecasting systems.

---

[4] http://africrid.com/.

References

1. Chester, D.: Natural Hazards by ea Bryant. Cambridge University Press, Cambridge (1991). price:40(hardback); 14.95 (paperback). isbn 0 521 37295 x (hardback); 0 521 37889 3 (paperback), (1993)
2. Mishra, A.K., Singh, V.P.: A review of drought concepts. J. Hydrol. **391**(1), 202–216 (2010)
3. Peuquet, D.J., Duan, N.: An event-based spatiotemporal data model (estdm) for temporal analysis of geographical data. Int. J. Geogr. Inf. Syst. **9**(1), 7–24 (1995)
4. Mugabe, F., Mubaya, C., Nanja, D., Gondwe, P., Munodawafa, A., Mutswangwa, E., Chagonda, I., Masere, P., Dimes, J., Murewi, C.: Use of indigenous knowledge systems and scientific methods for climate forecasting in Southern Zambia and North Western Zimbabwe. Zimbabwe J. Technol. Sci. **1**(1), 19–30 (2010)
5. Masinde, M., Bagula, A.: Itiki: bridge between african indigenous knowledge and modern science of drought prediction. Knowl. Manage. Dev. J. **7**(3), 274–290 (2011)
6. Sillitoe, P.: The development of indigenous knowledge: a new applied anthropology 1. Current anthropology **39**(2), 223–252 (1998)
7. Akanbi, A.K., Muthoni, M.: Towards semantic integration of heterogeneous sensor data with indigenous knowledge for drought forecasting. In: Proceedings of the Doctoral Symposium of the 16th International Middleware Conference. ACM (2015)

Green IT Applications and Security

Part II Application and Results

Prospect of Reduction of the GreenHouse Gas Emission by ICT in Africa

Telesphore Tiendrebeogo$^{(\boxtimes)}$

Polytechnic University of Bobo-Dioulasso, Bobo-Dioulasso, Burkina Faso
tetiendreb@gmail.com

Abstract. In recent year, reducing global warming is becoming one of the most challenging research topics in Information and Communication Technologies (ICTs) because of the overwhelming utilization of electronic devices and of Petroleum products.

Current solutions mainly focus on energy efficiency for saving power consumption by virtual machine consolidation on one hand, and on the on the other hand, by minimization of the consumption of petroleum products through Teleservices. The latter that must be used via data center whose we try to reduce energy consumption.

In this paper, we propose a dynamic consolidation method of virtual machines (VMs) using the alive migration and the switching of nodes idle and allowing to the suppliers of Cloud to optimize the use of the resource and to reduce the energy consumption. Furthermore, we show how Teleservices can participate in the reduction of the emissions of greenhouse gases in Africa.

Keywords: Global warming · ICT · Petroleum products · Data center · Consolidation · Teleservices · Carbone dioxide · Virtual machine

1 Introduction

For several decades, the man has been at the origin of a vicious circle, having grave environmental consequences: the atmospheric pollution due to Green House Gas emissions (GHG) favours the degradation of lands, which, in his turn, stresses the phenomenon. Furthermore, nowadays, cloud computing has become a popular computing paradigm for hosting and delivering services over the Internet [1]. Indeed, the Cloud computing model leverages virtualization of computing resources, allowing customers to provision resources on-demand on a pay-as-you-go basis [3]. In a prospect of a reduction of the capital cost of IT infrastructures and computing software, the cloud seems necessary. The proliferation of Cloud computing has resulted in the establishment of large-scale data centers containing thousands of computing nodes and consuming enormous amounts of electrical energy. In this regard, power management in cloud data centers is becoming a crucial issue since it dominates the operational costs. Moreover, the power consumption in large-scale computer systems like clouds based on the trends from

© ICST Institute for Computer Sciences, Social Informatics and Telecommunications Engineering 2016
R. Glitho et al. (Eds.): AFRICOMM 2015, LNICST 171, pp. 113–122, 2016.
DOI: 10.1007/978-3-319-43696-8_13

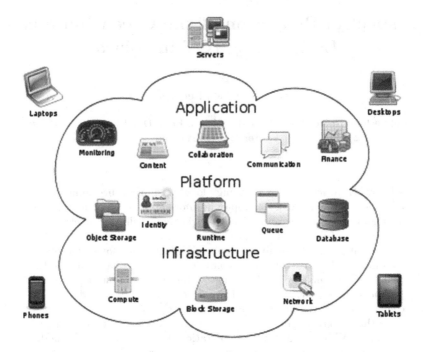

Fig. 1. Cloud computing model [14].

the American Society of Heating, Refrigerating and Air-Conditioning Engineers (ASHRAE) [4], it has been estimated that by 2014 infrastructure and energy costs would contribute about 75 %, whereas ICTs would contribute just 25 % to the overall cost of operating a data center [5] (Fig. 1).

On one hand, the emergence of cloud computing has made a tremendous impact on the ICT's industry over the past few years, where large companies such as Amazon, Google, Salesforce, IBM, Microsoft, and Oracle have begun to establish new data centers for hosting cloud computing applications in various locations around the world in general and in particular in Africa, to provide redundancy and ensure reliability in case of site failures. On the other hand, Teleservices offer a solution in the reduction of the emissions of greenhouse gases, because allowing to limit the motorized movements which have the effect of increasing the atmospheric pollution.

In this paper, we are interested in a raising awareness in a usable of the Teleservices, which allows to reduce enormously CO_2 emissions in an African context or remains a means of not economic transportation in term of consumption of petroleum products. This solution does not cancel these emissions, that is why we suggest mutualizing the servers of the operator of telephony on one data centers. We also propose a solution of consolidation of the latter with the aim of reducing the energy consumption.

The remainder of this paper is organized as follows. Section 2 presents the related work. Section 3 gives an overview onto virtual machines consolidation principle. Section 4 shows our technical of reduction of energy consumption by consolidation algorithm's of data centers. Section 5 presents the impact of the Teleservices on greenhouse gas emissions. Section 6 concluded our study and presents our perspectives.

2   Related Work

Several issues about green ICT and energy reduction in modern cloud computing systems are receiving huge attention in the research community. Several other efforts have been made to build energy consumption models, develop energy-aware cost, manage workload fluctuation and try to achieve an efficient trade-off between system performance and energy cost. Furthermore, most of the research agrees that the main reason of the climate changes is the green house effect caused by Green House Gases where carbon dioxide is a key factor. It is a challenge that not only jeopardizes the sustainability of our planet; it poses significant, long-term threats to the global economy. Among the main power consumption industries, Information and Communication Technology (ICT), with its annual growing rate of 9 % [6], contributes approximately two per cent to the global GHG emissions, and this amount will almost double by 2020 [7]. One of the first works, in which power management has been applied in the context of virtualized data centers, has been done by Nathuji and Schwan [8]. The authors have proposed an architecture of a data center's resource management system where resource management is divided into local and global policies. At the local level the system leverages the guest OS's power management strategies. The global manager gets the information on the current resource allocation from the local managers and applies its policy to decide whether the VM placement needs to be adapted. However, the authors have not proposed a specific policy for automatic resource management at the global level. Kusic et al. [9] have defined the problem of power management in virtualized heterogeneous environments as a sequential optimization and addressed it using the Limited Lookahead Control (LLC). The objective is to maximize the resource provider's profit by minimizing both power consumption and SLA violation. Energy management techniques in cloud environments have also been investigated in the past few years. In [10] described how servers can be turned ON/OFF uses Dynamic Voltage/Frequency Scaling (DVFS) approach to adjust servers's power status. The power modelling techniques have been proposed by several authors. The power consumption model proposed by Buyya et al. [11] observed a correlation between the CPU energy utilization and the workload with time. Bohra et al. [12] also proposed a power consumption model that observed a correlation between the total system's power consumption and component utilization. The authors created a four-dimensional linear weighted power model for the total power consumption. The power modelling techniques for the physical infrastructure (power and cooling systems) in data centers, proposed by Pelley et al. [13]

is most relevant for us. They worked out first models which try to capture a data center at large.

Besides, the digital book represents only 6.4 % [14] of the sales of books in France and yet more weak in Africa today, a figure however in constant increase. Moving forward the argument of the dematerialization of cultural property, as in a time the MP3 was able to go out of fashion our CD, the digital book boasts of reducing the paper needs, and thus of helping in the fight against the deforestation. With the introduction of the Internet and the increasing amount of services are being provided electronically, eBooks and eReaders are gaining momentum and will significantly change the book industry [15]. Chowdhury [19] opines that the production and distribution costs of digital knowledge products are negligible compared to the environmental costs of production and distribution of printed knowledge products. Fat Knowledge [20] agrees with the above statement saying that the eBooks are better for the environment than their paper brethren and presumes that reading the physical version of the New York (NY) Times for a year uses 7,300 MJ of energy and emits 700 kg of CO_2 and reading it on a Kindle (digital version) uses 100 MJ of energy and emits 10 kg of CO_2 thereby reducing about 70 % of CO_2 emission. These figures clearly show that electronic media can be a safe and better alternative but the dark face of technology also needs to be understood as indicated by below mentioned studies.

In summary, we want to show that the frame of we consist in saying that ICT's deployment can have both a positive and negative impacts on GHG emissions. It may enable GHG emission reduction in a variety of sectors and through many different channels by playing a significant role in reducing the remaining 98 % in particular by enabling smart energy efficiency and providing a substitute for the physical transport of goods and people. But we must also face the challenge of using ICTs to help other industries such as paper-maker or cloud promoters's to realize greener objectives, whether self-imposed or externally regulated.

3   Virtual Machines Consolidation Principle

3.1   Consolidation's Aims

Consolidating disparate data centers into large scale shared premises logically reduces the net environmental impacts. But it is worthwhile to review the ways in which these benefits are realized in practice. Its purpose is:

- Reducing total infrastructure allocation,
- Leveraging multi tenancy,
- Maximizing utilization rates,
- Improving the data center efficiency.

3.2   Migration's Cost

Consolidation principle is associated with the virtual machine migration. In this section we apply competitive analysis [21] to analyze a sub-problem of the problem of energy and the performance service efficient dynamic consolidation of

VMs. There is a single physical server, or a host and M VMs assigned to this host. In this problem the time is discreet and can be divided into frames of time N, when frame every time is 1 s. It is calculated as $C_p t_p$, where C_p is the cost of power (i.e., energy per unit of time), and t p is a time period. The resource capacity of the host and resource usage by VMs are characterized by a single parameter, the CPU performance. The VMs experience dynamic workloads, which means that the CPU usage by a VM arbitrarily varies over time. The host is oversubscribed, i.e., if all the VMs request their maximum allowed CPU performance, the total CPU demand will exceed the capacity of the CPU. We define that when the demand of the CPU performance exceeds the available capacity, a violation of the SLAs (Service-Level Agreement) established between the resource provider and customers occurs. An SLA violation results in a penalty incurred by the provider, which is calculated as $C_v t_v$, where C_v is the cost of SLA violation per unit of time, and t_v is the time duration of the SLA violation. Without loss of generality, we can define $C_p = 1$ and $C_v = s$, where $s \in \mathbb{R}+$. This is equivalent to defining $C_p = 1/s$ and $C_v = 1$. At some point in time v, an SLA violation occurs and continues until N. In other words, due to the over-subscription and variability of the workload experienced by VMs, at the time v the overall demand for the CPU performance exceeds the available CPU capacity and does not decrease until N. It is assumed that according to the problem definition, a single VM can be migrated out from the host. This migration leads to a decrease of the demand for the CPU performance and makes it lower than the CPU capacity. We define n to be the stopping time, which is equal to the latest of either the end of the VM migration or the beginning of the SLA violation. A VM migration takes time T. During a migration an extra host is used to accommodate the VM being migrated, and therefore, the total energy consumed during a VM migration is $2C_p T$. The problem is to determine the time m when a VM migration should be initiated to minimize the total cost consisting of the energy cost and the cost caused by an SLA violation if it takes place. Let r be the remaining time since the beginning of the SLA violation, i.e., $r = n - v$.

4   Consolidation's Model of Data Centers

4.1   Approach's Model

In this section, we propose a new approach allowing to make a reliable strategy of consolidation in cluster of data centers. This approach uses a Poincaré disk model that is a unit's ray disk centred to origin, in which, we can consider an hyperbolic tree. We present here, the hyperbolic AntTree algorithm applied to hyperbolic plane that is based on the self assembly behaviour observed in certain species of ants, where the living structures are used as bridges or auxiliary structures to build the nest. In this model, we refer to points by using complex coordinates. We can find in the literature all the necessary information to understand the hyperbolic plane [2]. The structure is built by using an incremental process in which ants joint a fixed support or another ant for assembling. The Hyperbolic

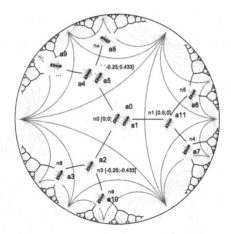

Fig. 2. Hyperbolic AntTree in Poincaré disk model.

AntTree builds a tree structure representing a hierarchical data organization which divides the whole of the data center. Each Ant represents a single datum from the data center and it moves in the structure according to its similarity to the other ants already connected to the tree under construction.

Each node with which we associate a virtual coordinates in the hyperbolic tree structure represents a set of Ants (Ants a4 and a5 is associated to node n2 in Fig. 2) and each ant represents a single datum of data center. The key aspect in AntTree is the decision about where each Ant will be connected to the data center.

Each ant with which we associate an identifier to be connected to the hyperbolic tree represents a datum to be classified. Starting from an artificial support called n0 (containing ants a0 and a1), all the ants will be incrementally connected either to that support or to other already connected ants. This process continues until all ants are connected to the structure, i.e., all data are already clustered. Each ant identifier's is used to compute the location in the hyperbolic tree [22].

4.2   Algorithm of Connection to the Tree

In Algorithm 1, we can consider a system of N data centers, hyperbolic AntTree degree is d and depth is p. Every resource is mapped in key of 256 bits then subdivided into r sub-keys of k bits. One sub-key randomly is chosen and used to determine a point on the edge of the circle of ray 1. Then the resource is stored in the closest data center to the point calculated according to [22].

4.3   Algorithm of Migration on the Tree

Resources migration's in hyperbolic tree uses a Greedy AntTree Colony Forwarding (GATCF) algorithm, the mechanism of which is described in the Algorithm 2.

Algorithm 1. Connection algorithm in hyperbolic AntTree

1: **function** CONNECTPROCESS($PrimeDataCenter\ AntDatum$) **return** 0
2:     $AntID \leftarrow AntDatum.GetID()$
3:     $Key \leftarrow Hash(AntID)$
4:     **for** A doll $r \in R_{Circular}$
5:         $d \leftarrow P_{Max}$
6:         $i \leftarrow 1$
7:         $SubKey[r] \leftarrow Randomly(Resource\_Subkey(Key)[r])$
8:         $TgDataCentAddr[r] \leftarrow DataCenter\_Addr(SubKey[r])$
9:         $TgDataCent \leftarrow GetTg(TgDatCentAd[r])$
10:        **if** $route(AntID, TgDataCent)$ **then**
11:            $i++$
12:            $put(AntID, Datum)$
13:        **end if**
14:        $d--$
15:     **end for**
16:     **return** 0
17: **end function**

Thus, every dated center containing a resource to make migrate question the root data center (coordinates(0;0)) to find the data center of the destination towards where to send the resource. Afterward, every data center containing the resource estimates the smallest hyperbolic distance's [22] which separates his data center neighbour of data center destination and forwards it step by step to the destination as described the Algorithm 2.

Algorithm 2. Migration in hyperbolic AntTree.

1: **function** GETNEXTHOP($DataCenter$, $AntDatum$) **return** DataCenter
2:     $w = AntDatum.destinationDataCentCoords$
3:     $m = DataCent.Coords$
4:     $d_{min} = argcosh\left(1 + 2\frac{|m-w|^2}{(1-|m|^2)(1-|w|^2)}\right)$
5:     $p_{min} = DataCenter$
6:     **for all** $neighbor \in DataCenter.Neighbors$ **do**
7:         $n = neighbor.Coords$
8:         $d = argcosh\left(1 + 2\frac{|n-w|^2}{(1-|n|^2)(1-|w|^2)}\right)$
9:         **if** $d < d_{min}$ **then**
10:            $d_{min} = d$
11:            $p_{min} = neighbor$
12:        **end if**
13:     **end for**
14:     **return** p_{min}
15: **end function**

---

5   Teleservices as Way of Reduction of the Global Warming

To know an enemy is essential to be able to face him. In the search to decrease the carbon footprint of the human activity he is before any necessity to know his importance.

Nowadays, advent of ICTs generally in the world and more particularly in Africa has allowed to reduce in a considerable way the time puts to realize certain activities as well as the average partners. Indeed, the development of Teleservices allows us to realize the payments of electricity bill among others without having to move and consequently without burning with any fuel which participates actively in the greenhouse gas emission. It is, for example important to note that one liter of gasoline, diesel frees respectively 2.28 kg and 2.67 kg of CO_2 [17]. Besides, respectively 57 g and 7.6 g of CO_2 are emitted for 1 min of communication, respectively, for a USSD (Unstructured Supplementary Service Data) transaction's [16]. A study led in 2007 show that 2 % of the emission of CO_2 is attributable in ICTs against 40 % for petrol [18]. CO_2 emissions bound to Teleservices is thought of the main part side server (at the operator of telephony). Indeed, every query of call or USSD requires the execution of an energy-consuming process and consequently source of greenhouse gas emission. The study made in the Sect. 4 shows how we can reduce this consumption by the use of data to center that we could strengthen with the algorithm of hyperbolic AntTree. This study suits well in Africa, which has some more of solution of Teleservices to be developed to participate, so in the fight against the global warming.

6   Conclusion and Future Work

Our study allowed us of shown one of the contributions of ICTs in the reduction of greenhouse gas emissions. So, the use of Teleservices contributes to reduce the atmospheric pollution by petroleum products with one against unimportant part. Of more the use of data centers by the operators of telephony as well as the application of the solution of consolidation of the latter assure a low consumption of energy and participle at the same time to reduce the global warming. The African continent being emergent in general in term of presence of Teleservices, we say that the development of the latter are opportunity which is offered to reduce the vehicle movements which engenders a cost mattering regarding emission of CO_2. In ours future works, we plan to make an in-depth study on the statistics in term of presence of Teleservices in Africa and to proceed to a simulation of our algorithm of consolidation of data centers based on the hyperbolic AntTree.

References

1. Zhang, Q., Cheng, L., Boutaba, R.: Cloud computing: state-of-the-art and research challenges. J. Internet Serv. Appl. **1**(1), 7–18 (2010)
2. Beardon, A.F., Minda, D.: The hyperbolic metric and geometric function theory. In: International Workshop on Quasiconformal Mappings and Their Applications (2006)
3. Buyya, R., Yeo, C.S., Venugopal, S., Broberg, J., Brandic, I.: Cloud computing and emerging IT platforms: vision, hype, and reality for delivering computing as the 5th utility. Future Gener. Comput. Syst. **25**(6), 599–616 (2009)
4. ASHRAE Technical Committee 99.: Datacom equipment power trends and cooling applications (2005)
5. Belady, C.: The data center, power and cooling costs more than the it equipment it supports (2007). http://www.electronics-cooling.com/articles/2007/feb/a3/
6. Kurp, P.: Green computing, are you ready for a personal energy meter? Commun. ACM **51**(10), 11–13 (2008)
7. The Climate Group: SMART2020: enabling the low carbon economy in the information age. In: Report on behalf of the Global eSustainability Initiative (2008)
8. Nathuji, R., Schwan, K.: Virtualpower: coordinated power management in virtualized enterprise systems. ACM SIGOPS Operating Syst. Rev. **41**(6), 265–278 (2007)
9. Kusic, D., Kephart, J.O., Hanson, J.E., Kandasamy, N., Jiang, G.: Power and performance management of virtualized computing environments via lookahead control. Cluster Comput. **12**(1), 1–15 (2009)
10. Shang, L., Peh, L.S., Jha, N.K.: Dynamic voltage scaling with links for power optimization of interconnection networks. In: The 9th International Symposium on High-Performance Computer Architecture (HPCA 2003), Anaheim, California, USA, pp. 91–102 (2003)
11. Rajkumar, B., Anton, B., Jemal, A.: Energy efficient management of data center resources for cloud computing: a vision architectural elements and open challenges. In: Proceedings of International Conference on Parallel and Distributed Processing Techniques and Applications (PDPTA 2010), Las Vegas, USA, pp. 12–15 (2010)
12. Bohra, A., Chaudhary, V.: VMeter: power modelling for virtualized clouds. In: International Symposium on Parallel & Distributed Processing, Workshops and Phd Forum (IPDPSW), 2010 IEEE, pp. 1–8, 19–23 April 2010
13. Pelley, S., Meisner, D., Wenisch, T.F., VanGilder, J.W.: Understanding and abstracting total data center power. In: WEED: Workshop on Energy Effcienct Design (2009)
14. Book vs eBook. http://www.consoglobe.com/livre-papier-vs-livre-numerique-lequel-est-le-plus-ecolo-cg
15. Turning the page: the future of eBooks. PWC. http://www.pwc.com/gx/en/entertainment-media/publications/future-ofebooks.Jhtml
16. Emission de CO_2 pour 1 minute de communication. http://www.ginjfo.com/espace-environnement/green-it/science-et-technologie/
17. Quantité de CO_2 par volume de carburant. http://www.carte-grise.org/explication_calcul_bilan_co2.htm
18. Par des TICs dans l'émission des gaz à effet de serre. http://www.afdel.fr/static/2012/10/08/guide-software-for-green.pdf
19. Carbon footprint of the knowledge sector: what's the future? J. Documentation **66**(6), 934–946. doi:10.1108/00220411011 087878

20. E-Books Vs. Newspapers [Weblog post]. http://fatknowledge.blogspot.com/2008/08/ebooks-vs-newspapers.html
21. Borodin, A., El-Yaniv, R.: Online Computation and Competitive Analysis, vol. 53. Cambridge University Press, New York (1998)
22. Tiendrebeogo, T., Ahmat, D., Magoni, D.: Reliable and scalable distributed hash tables harnessing hyperbolic coordinates. In: NTMS 2012, pp. 1–6 (2012)

Vulnerabilities of Government Websites in a Developing Country – the Case of Burkina Faso

Tegawendé F. Bissyandé[1,2]([⊠]), Jonathan Ouoba[3], Daouda Ahmat[4],
Fréderic Ouédraogo[5], Cedric Béré[2], Moustapha Bikienga[5], Abdoulaye Sere[6],
Mesmin Dandjinou[6], and Oumarou Sié[2]

[1] SnT, University of Luxembourg, Luxembourg, Luxembourg
tegawende.bissyande@uni.lu
[2] Université de Ouagadougou, Ouagadougou, Burkina Faso
{cedric.bere,oumarou.sie}@univ-ouaga.bf
[3] VTT Technical Research Center, Espoo, Finland
jonathan.ouoba@vtt.fi
[4] Université Virtuelle du Tchad, N'Djamena, Chad
daoudique@gmail.com
[5] Université de Koudougou, Koudougou, Burkina Faso
{frederic.ouedraogo,moustapha.bikienga}@univ-ouaga.bf
[6] Université Polytechnique de Bobo Dioulasso, Bobo-Dioulasso, Burkina Faso
{abdoulaye.sere,mesmin.dandjinou}@univ-ouaga.bf

Abstract. Slowly, but consistently, the digital gap between developing and developed countries is being closed. Everyday, there are initiatives towards relying on ICT to simplify the interaction between citizens and their governments in developing countries. E-government is thus becoming a reality: in Burkina Faso, all government bodies are taking part in this movement with web portals dedicated to serving the public. Unfortunately, in this rush to promote government actions within this trend of digitization, little regards is given to the security of such web sites. In many cases, government highly critical web sites are simply produced in a product line fashion using Content Management Systems which the webmasters do not quite master.

We discuss in this study our findings on empirically assessing the security of government websites in Burkina Faso. By systematically scanning these websites for simple and well-known vulnerabilities, we were able to discover issues that deserved urgent attention. As an example, we were able to crawl from temporary backup files in a government web site all information (hostname, login and password in clear) to read and write directly in the database and for impersonating the administrator of the website. We also found that around 50 % of the government websites are built on top of platforms suffering from 14 publicly known vulnerabilities, and thus can be readily attacked by *any* hacker.

Keywords: e-government · Websites · Security · Vulnerabilities · CMS · Developing countries

© ICST Institute for Computer Sciences, Social Informatics and Telecommunications Engineering 2016
R. Glitho et al. (Eds.): AFRICOMM 2015, LNICST 171, pp. 123–135, 2016.
DOI: 10.1007/978-3-319-43696-8_14

1   Introduction

E-government is now a pillar of ICT4D initiatives to improve the life of citizens in developing countries. Generally, it is realized through a web portal (website) where citizens can readily collect information and interact with government officials in an effort for simplifying administrative processes. In their simplest form, government websites are designed to be a reliable data source for all citizens. These websites are thus sensitive sources of information and, as such, they should be resilient to most tampering attempts. Unfortunately, recent high-profile security mishaps across the world, and in particular in developing countries, show that the design and implementation of e-government portals leave security holes that are exploited by attackers.

The primary cause of the precarious situation in which most e-government portals are today, especially in the context of developing countries, is the lack of attention that developers give to the assessment of their installs. A secondary reason is the fact that website design is often outsourced and thus the resulting web site is built in a way that government agents, which are not IT professionals, can easily update text in the web. To that end, Content Management Systems (CMS) are heavily used.

From WordPress to Joomla! and beyond, businesses (such as newspapers or e-commerce companies) and institutions (such as schools or city halls) depend on CMS to maintain online content. Thus, these third-party platforms are everywhere, and like all software, they come with security concerns. Not surprisingly, the popularity of CMS has been an opportunity for malicious hackers, since CMS provide a much larger attack surface. Before the proliferation of CMS, hackers had to focus on finding a vulnerability in a single identified target (e.g., a bank) and then attacking it to compromise its services (e.g., Denial of Service attacks) or to steal data. Today, however, with the vast opportunities presented by CMS, hackers take the path of least resistance (i.e., no time and computing power is wasted on trying to find a vulnerability in a single strong target). Indeed, "use search engines to identify common security vulnerabilities in a CMS platform as a means to accomplish server takeover and data theft" [1]. Unfortunately, as we will show later in this paper, there are literally thousands of security vulnerabilities in CMS platforms. Once such weaknesses are identified, it is again easy to rely on a search engine to fingerprint websites that are built on top of CMS that are affected by the known vulnerability. Doing so, malicious hackers can exploit the vulnerability in multiple CMS in many businesses and institutions, and they can do so very fast.

Nevertheless, businesses and institutions can still defend themselves with some simple tactics. Unfortunately, they are often not aware of the vulnerabilities of such platforms. Our work is part of this effort to sensitize government officials and web developers in developing countries of the perils of overtrusting CMS. The contributions of this paper are as follows:

- We describe and survey the security vulnerabilities that are found in today's popular CMS platforms.

– We investigate government websites in Burkina Faso to study those that are built on top of CMS platforms.
– We develop s2e-gov, a framework for security testing of e-government portals. It exploits a database of known web vulnerabilities and other heuristics to assess the security of web sites.
– We provide guidelines for readily securing e-government websites against common security attacks. In particular we call for the teaching/training of web security basics to the younger generations as we previously did for bootstrapping software engineering teaching in developing countries [2].

The remainder of this paper is organized as follows. Section 2 motivates our work in the context of a developing country, namely Burkina Faso. Section 3 describes web vulnerabilities and presents an overview of their presence within popular CMS. We discuss the implementation of s2e-gov, our e-government security scanning tool, in Sect. 4. Section 5 then details the lessons that we have learned while experimenting with s2e-gov. We discuss related work in Sect. 6 before concluding in Sect. 7.

2   Motivation

During April 2015, a large number of government websites in Burkina Faso were hacked to deliver a single page with a message from a radical group. Major newspapers in the country made headline stories out of these incidents. Observers and readers of online content were led to believe that these attacks were retaliation due to the engagement of the country in the war against terrorism. Online forums have seen discussions on how websites in Burkina Faso were poorly developed with little consideration for security. At that time, our opinion was simply forged by the fact that many other websites in the country, and beyond, had fallen. Given the relatively limited strategic importance of Burkina Faso for hackers, as a researcher we immediately set to understand how such attacks could have been easily, and potentially blindly, performed without specific targets in mind. We then collected the dynamically generated web pages of a number of web sites to study the HTML code. A first review showed that these web pages contained default information on how they were built. In particular, they contained meta-information in HTML headers describing the CMS platform on top of which the web sites are built.

CMS Use in Government Websites in Burkina Faso. To evaluate the penetration of CMS usage in government websites we identify the top government bodies (ministries and departments) as well as institutions (research centers, universities, etc.) and scan their webpages. Our collected dataset includes 42 websites.

Similarly to CMS detectors existing on the web, we compiled a database of fingerprints of CMS versions using hash values of some reference files (e.g., configuration, License and Readme files). While scanning websites from our list, we search for such files and directories in default paths. When they exist, we deduce that the website has been built via a specific CMS. Using the hash values of the reference files we can further identify the CMS version. Table 1 depicts the distribution of CMS usage in government websites. For each CMS version used we refer to the National Vulnerability Database (NVD) hosted by the US Government National Institute of Standards and Technologies (NIST) to determine the number of known vulnerability exposures (CVE) that have been reported for this CMS version.

This first investigation clearly shows that Government websites in Burkina Faso are largely built on top of vulnerable CMS versions. A large proportion of websites have been built with Joomla! 1.5 which was released in January 2008 and which is no longer supported since September 2012: this means that even if vulnerabilities are found today in this version, no Joomla! developer will officially work on releasing a patch for it. Despite the 14 vulnerabilities known for this Joomla! version, relevant government websites have not yet been updated as of June 2015. Yet, the content of the websites are still up to date, implying that they are still important tools of communication for the government.

Table 1. Distribution of CMS usage for government websites in Burkina Faso

CMS	Version	Nb sites	Nb vulnerabilities	CMS release date	End of life
Joomla!	1.5	19	14	22 Jan 2008	Sept 2012
Wordpress	3.5.1	1	13	24 Jan 2013	-
Drupal	-	1	(135)	-	-
Microsoft sharepoint	14.0.0	1	(35)	-	-
SPIP	3.0.17	1	0	August 2014	-
OpenCMS	-	1	(14)	-	-
Static / in-house PHP	-	12	-	-	-
Unreachable hosts	-	6	-	-	-

3   Vulnerabilities in CMS

Software *vulnerabilities* are program defects that provide the opportunity to malicious users to attack a system or application. In the literature, they are often referred to as security bugs [3] or software weaknesses. In this article, we use the terminology of the CVE[1] system to define vulnerabilities: *"An information security "vulnerability" is a mistake in software that can be directly used by a hacker to gain access to a system or network"*[2].

---

[1] Common Vulnerability Exposures.
[2] https://cve.mitre.org/about/terminology.html.

Common security breaches due to software vulnerabilities include sensitive information leakage, modification, and destruction. *Attacks* are successful exploitations of vulnerabilities. We refer to the CVE for our vulnerability counts: it is a system that provides a reference for all publicly known security vulnerabilities. This system is funded by the US government and is managed by the National Institute of Standard and Technology (NIST). To easily share data related to vulnerabilities, each identified and accepted vulnerability receives a unique identifier. Based on this identifier one can retrieve information about the vulnerability, including its description, the product concerned, the version of the product, the date of vulnerability record creation and some comments. In this paper, we use the CVE system as a dictionary for the CMS vulnerabilities that we study. In the same lines, we use the term exposure or exploitable to describe a software vulnerability that was advertised to the public and for which it exists ways to take advantage of it.

There are different types of vulnerabilities that can be found in web applications, including CMS platforms. We describe those vulnerabilities and provide statistics on their appearance in popular CMS platforms.

File Inclusion is a type of vulnerability which allows an attacker to include a file, usually through a script, on the web server. This often occurs due to the use of user-supplied input without proper validation.

Cross Site Request Forgery is a type of vulnerability that makes a malicious Web site, email, blog, instant message, or program cause a users Web browser to perform an unwanted action on a trusted site for which the user is currently authenticated. Attacks based on this vulnerability can result in an unauthorized transfer of funds, changing a password, or purchasing an item in the user's context.

Gain Privileges also known as *Privilege Escalation*, is a vulnerability that allows attackers to gain elevated access to resources that are normally protected from an application or user. This results in them being able to perform unauthorized actions via a vulnerable application.

Bypassing is a vulnerability type where authentication schemes can be bypassed by simply skipping the login page and directly calling an internal page that is supposed to be accessed only after authentication has been performed. Similarly, one can bypass authentication measures by tampering with requests and tricking applications into thinking that we're already authenticated. Bypassing can be accomplished either by modifying a given URL parameter or by manipulating the form or by counterfeiting sessions.

Directory Traversal (also known as *path traversal, directory climbing* and *backtracking*) is a vulnerability where insufficient security validation/sanitisation of user-supplied input file names can be exploited so that characters representing "traverse to parent directory" are passed through to the file APIs.

Code Execution refers to a vulnerability through which an attacker is able to execute any commands of his choice on a target machine or in a target process.

Cross Site Scripting (XSS) attacks where malicious scripts are injected into otherwise benign and trusted web sites. They occur when an attacker uses a web application to send malicious code, generally in the form of a browser side script, to a different end user. XSS vulnerabilities occur anywhere a web application uses input from a user within the output it generates without validating or encoding it.

SQL Injection is a code injection technique in which malicious SQL statements are inserted into an entry field for execution (e.g. to dump the database contents to the attacker). SQL injection attacks exploit vulnerabilities where user input is either incorrectly filtered for string literal escape characters embedded in SQL statements or user input is not strongly typed and unexpectedly executed.

Denial of Service (DoS) attacks are focused on making a resource (e.g., web site or server) unavailable for the purpose it was designed. Denial-of-service attacks significantly degrade the service quality experienced by legitimate users by introducing large response delays, excessive losses, and service interruptions.

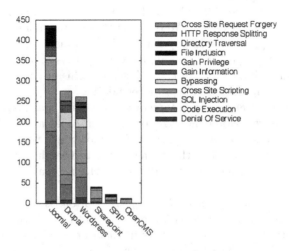

Fig. 1. Distribution of vulnerbaility types in popular CMS – data from NIST as of June 13, 2015

Vulnerability statistics depicted in Fig. 1 show that many CMS suffer from numerous vulnerabilities. Code Execution, SQL Injection and XSS vulnerabilities are the most widespread. Joomla! is the CMS with the most known vulnerabilities.

4   S2e-Gov: Security Scans for E-Government

In this section we propose a framework for security testing of websites. In s2e-gov we automate the process of identifying security concerns, whether known vulnerabilities or misconfigurations, that targeted e-government websites may contain. Figure 2 illustrates the inputs of outputs of s2e-gov. We detail the key aspects of its implementation in this section.

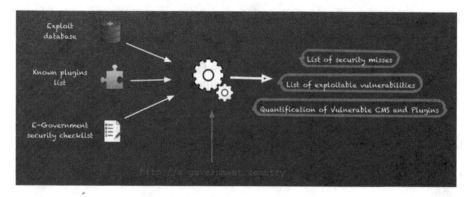

Fig. 2. Schematization of s2e-gov process for security testing of e-government websites

4.1 Default Configuration and Directory Listing

The first feature implemented in s2e-gov is about directory listing: after verification of the HTML code extracted from the index page, we proceed to check
default configuration files and directories in popular CMS. Because a CMS often
includes configuration files where credentials are stored it is important that such
files are not readily accessible for reading. CMS developers hide such information
in PHP files which cannot be read by client browsers. However, when editing
those files with editors such as Vim, Nano, Notepad or Emacs, temporary backup
files are often automatically created. If these are not deleted, all configuration
information are left and become accessible in plain text format.

s2e-gov thus systematically tries to detect unprotected configuration files
which are available on the website. These files usually contain clear text credentials to the login page of the website, or credentials for accessing the backend
databases of CMS platforms.

4.2 Common Security Guards

The second feature implemented in s2e-gov is the verification of common security protocols in websites. For example, transaction data between user web
browsers and government websites must be moved securely across the internet
without any body being able to eavesdrop or tamper with the data. This security is commonly implemented through encryption offered by the Secure Socket
Layer (SSL) to support HTTPS connections. Website administrators must therefore make available a certificate (with their public key) to allow users browsers
to encrypt their requests.

Similarly, the X-Frame-Options HTTP header is commonly known as a good
means to protect websites from Clickjacking attacks which involve fooling users
into clicking on seemingly harmless buttons or links[3]. The vulnerability comes

---

[3] http://jeremiahgrossman.blogspot.de/2008/10/clickjacking-web-pages-can-see-and-
hear.html.

from the possibility to place the targeted web page (e.g., the Adobe Flash settings panel, a Facebook like button or a shopping cart) inside an Iframe and overlay it with a completely different webpage. Such an overlay might then entice users to click on certain buttons or links, leading to Clickjacking, double-click jacking, like-jacking, cursor-jacking attacks. It is possible however to prevent such attacks by simply parameterizing the X-Frame-Options:

* X-Frame-Options: `DENY`: "wont allow the website to be framed by anyone"
* X-Frame-Options: `SAMEORIGIN`: "No one can frame except for sites from same origin"
* X-Frame-Options: `ALLOW-FROM %uri%`: "Only this one URI can frame. No one else"

`s2e-gov` checks for such common security guards in the websites and ensures that they properly set.

4.3   Known Attacks

Although the NVD database shows that the core of all CMS contained at some point some vulnerabilties, security bulletins recurrently point out more security holes in plugins. `s2e-gov` thus implements a plugin detection for popular CMS to collect the list of plugins added to the CMS core. Once this list is known, `s2e-gov` checks whether they contain known vulnerabilities.

Plugin Detection in CMS – Vulnerabilities in CMS are mostly found in extensions code such as plugins, rather than the CMS core code. We first build a list of plugins available on the Internet for the different plugins supported by our tool `s2e-gov`. Then, for each CMS install, `s2e-gov` identifies the included plugins by scanning the web directory: for each plugin, `s2e-gov` attempts to find out whether there exist some known vulnerabilities to report. To this end, we rely on the Exploit database.

Database of Exploits – the Exploit Database[4] is an established archive of attacks that exploited CVE compliant vulnerabilities in various software. We rely on this database to search for vulnerabilities in plugins that have been successfully exploited, either in testing scenario or in harmful hacks.

WordPress TimThumb Exploitation – Website themes in CMS come as add-ons that extend the core layout changes. Often, themes contain variables that refer to dynamic elements such as images. In the popular Wordpress CMS, it has been reported that themes often come with insecure PHP files which are used for caching and or resizing images. The recent "TimThumb" exploitation refers to a project which essentially caches even remote files locally, without doing the necessary proper sanitization: timthumb.php only checked whether the target

---

[4] https://www.exploit-db.com.

file is actually an image or not. This PHP file is used in many themes, with different names.

The Timthumb exploitation is realized simply by tricking TimThumb into believing that a remotely stored file, which may contain malicious PHP for example, is an actual image. Attacks found this trick very simple to perform and many attacks based on the TimThumb exploit were recorded in forums[5].

Joomla Content Editor Bots – JCE is popular component that can be found enabled in most Joomla! sites as a fancy content editor. Unfortunately in its development course, the JCE had once a well known security hole that has since been fixed in Joomla! versions higher than 1.5.x series. This security hole allows anyone to upload arbitrary files to a server. One can easily find a working exploit on the Internet for such a vulnerability. A typical exploitation scenario consists in 3 steps where the attacker scans Joomla! installs looking for vulnerable JCE, then exploits the bug in the JCE image manager to upload a PHP file with an image extension (e.g., .gif) to the images/stories directory. Finally, the hacker can simply rely on a JSON comand to change the file extension to .php. At this point, the attacker has a backdoor to the website and do whatever it wants with the site. Usually, attackers use this strategy to build their botnets.

4.4   E-Government Requirements

More than any other web site, e-Government portals are required to offer reliable services that make the information available to those who need it in a trustable setting. To realize this e-Government portals must setup security policies and enforce security practices during the design, development and production of their services.

Policy – While it is importance to take steps to be secure, it is even better to be sure that one are secure. Security policies are documents that outline the long-term strategy in an organisation to ensure that, when it is respected, information and infrastructure is secured. For example, policy indicates the acceptable use for users and the guidelines for reacting to a web site compromise.

Practice – Security practices, which play a key role for ensure e-Government security, are checklist for actions and advice on how to keep systems secure. Most prominent examples for security practices in e-Government include:

- Authenticate all accounts and make sure that the passwords are difficult to guess. Preferably use One-Time-Password to ensure that no masquerade attack can be performed even if an attacker uses a sniffer to collect passwords.
- Check for resource and sofware integrity regularly by maintaining a list of their MD5 checksums
- Check logs regularly to audit data and early detect anomalies. Possibly, install firewalls to drop unsollicited packets.

---

[5] https://www.exploit-db.com/wordpress-timthumb-exploitation/.

– Always update to the latest software available from the vendor with recent upgrades and patches

Finally, our experience in assessing government websites has shown that their design and implementation require: (1) some degree of obfuscation (e.g., which CMS is used) to complicate the work of attackers; (2) some level of resilience to DoS attacks to ensure availability; (3) a tight control on resource access (e.g., no dynamic loading) to preserve integrity; and (4) a certification/authentication scheme via a Public Key Infrastructure to guarantee confidentiality and integrity in information exchange.

5   Security Issues in Burkina Faso Government Websites

Our experiments with s2e-gov on the government websites have highlighted a substantial number of security holes that make it easy for any hacker, even with limited skills, to take over the administration of the web sites.

5.1   Vulnerability Highlights

– 23 out of 42 (i.e., 54 %) of government websites are built on top of vulnerable CMS platforms
– 4 (i.e., 12 %) websites had accessible temp files with login credentials written in clear
– No government website were SSL compliant leading to insecure connections
– 19 (i.e., 45 %) websites were vulnerable to JCE attacks
– In 5 cases, we found that the database servers were directly accessible (from the internet).

5.2   Lessons Learned

Overall, in developing countries, more than anywhere else, there is a need to strengthen security training for government technicians. We now enumerate the lessons learned from these experiments before providing general advice for e-Government in developing countries.

Harden Websites – The first lesson learned from our study is the need for web maintainers to harden their installs. In particular, trivial steps can be taken to avoid a government web site to be randomnly found attackable. Concretely, a CMS should never be run in its default configuration for a government website. Maintainers should rename directories and tune the settings. For example, by default, Drupal is the only CMS that will lockout user accounts after a certain number of failed attempts. This means that unless a specific security plugin is installed, for other popular CMS such as Joomla! or Wordpress, hackers are free to brute force their login forms.

Always update Core CMS – The second lesson learned is on the need to update to newer versions of CMS, since CMS developers often try to patch vulnerabilities regularly.

Monitor website usage / baseline against abnormal usage – Most attacks, in particularly DoS attacks, can be stopped while they are being performed if their is a monitoring systems that raises alarm when an abnormal behaviour is detected.

Consider adding a firewall to virtually patch vulnerabilities internally – A firewall is a requirement in a government system to filter packets and enforce the accepted usage behaviour.

Separation of concerns: database servers should not be accessible from outside the network domain – Finally, we have found out that in many cases, by obtaining information on the database hosts we were able to directly attack it. It is very easy to address such issues by disallowing requests coming outside the government network domain.

Edition and customization artefacts, typically backup files – By simply scanning web directories for configuration files backed up during edition, a hacker can collect credentials for taking over the administration of a website. It is therefore important to clean web directory regularly during customization.

Taming Security holes This study and others somehow demonstrate that the security threat landscape is large. However, our findings also suggest that will simple tactics e-government portals can defend themselves. The essential of the defense system lies in awareness. In particular, it is important in developing countries that web maintainers understand that by raising the bar on protecting their websites, those will be safe from the attacks of today's industrialsed hacker who is only looking for the weakest web sites.

The second important means to tame security holes is to carefully monitor web services. Indeed, it is important to regularly review server logs to have real-time alert when an abnormal behaviour of the web service is detected so that maintainers can promptly investigate them.

Finally, e-government maintainers should always assume that any third-party code, including the CMS their website is based on, has numerous security vulnerabilities (we have shown it based on NVD data). To address such threats, it is necessary to deploy a security solution like a firewall for virtually patching vulnerabilities and mitigating new attack risks when they arise.

5.3 Discussion and Future Work

In this study all government websites were considered as equally important with regards to security needs. It is possible that some websites appear to be more critical as they allow real interactions through forms and official reports. Others however might have been setup to display information only. In future work we plan to investigate the critical resource in each website to evaluate the potential cost of attack.

Similarly, we plan to investigate in the future the reasons why such vulnerabilities remain unpatched. Typically, we will correlate the number of vulnerabilities with the IT budget of each department.

Finally, in continuity with our previous work [4,5] on identifying safety holes in operating systems, we will invest in the study of popular web programming languages [6] to better understand how vulnerabilities are distributed across them.

6 Related Work

ICT4D research can no longer focus only on getting millions of people out of poverty [7]. Researchers must take into account the security issues that threaten an extended use of ICT. In particular the extended use of open source software comes with the responsibility of understanding that malicious developers have access to the source code, and thus can discover the exploitable vulnerabilities.

Vulnerabilities of E-Government websites across the world have been a concern for years. In 2007, Moen et al. [8] have investigated such websites in 212 countries and found that 81.6 % were vulnerable to XSS and SQL injection. Yet, such simple and well-known web application vulnerabilities can be avoided with well-known techniques. Today, in developed countries, much effort has been put into protecting government web sites. Our study, in particular in the case of Burkina Faso, shows that developing countries are still behind.

Although we have focused on technical aspects, including firewalls and website hardening, to provide the appropriate levels of security, previous work has shown that the human factor is also of high importance. A 2011 study by Bowen et al. have shown how the human factor influences cybersecurity policies and how that work could be used to train government employees to improve the security posture of government departments and agencies.

The literature contains a large body of related work on vulnerabilities. Wang et al. have proposed a mathematical model to calculate the severity and risk of a vulnerability. Their model is time dependent, taking into account exploitability, remediation level, and report confidence attributes [9]. Paleari et al. have focused their investigation on race vulnerabilities for web applications [10]. There have also been a number of research works on the challenges for mitigating program security vulnerabilities [11]. Finally, researchers have focused on proposing practical approaches to detect vulnerabilities in web applications. In this context, Ciampa et al. have focused on SQL injections [12].

7 Conclusion

In this paper we have investigated the security of government websites in a developing country, namely Burkina Faso. We have discussed the development of a E-government security testing framework, s2e-gov, which uncovered numerous vulnerabilities in government websites. In particular, we show how extensive and default configuration of CMS platforms contribute largely to making E-government websites vulnerable.

References

1. Shteiman, B.: How your CMS could be breeding security vulnerabilities (2013). http://www.itproportal.com/2013/10/08/how-your-cms-could-be-breeding-security-vulnerabilities/
2. Bissyandé, T.F., Ouoba, J., Ahmat, D., Sawadogo, A.D., Sawadogo, Z.: Bootstrapping software engineering training in developing countries. In: Nungu, A., Pehrson, B., Sansa-Otim, J. (eds.) AFRICOMM 2014. LNICSSITE, vol. 147, pp. 261–268. Springer, Heidelberg (2015). doi:10.1007/978-3-319-16886-9_27
3. Tan, L., Liu, C., Li, Z., Wang, X., Zhou, Y., Zhai, C.: Bug characteristics in open source software. Emp. Softw. Eng. **19**(6), 1665–1705 (2014)
4. Bissyandé, T.F., Réveillère, L., Lawall, J.L., Muller, G.: Diagnosys: automatic generation of a debugging interface to the linux kernel. In: Proceedings of the 27th IEEE/ACM International Conference on Automated Software Engineerinh, ASE 2012 (2012)
5. Bissyandé, T.F., Réveillère, L., Lawall, J.L., Muller, G.: Ahead of time static analysis for automatic generation of debugging interfaces to the linux kernel. Autom. Softw. Eng. **23**, 1–39 (2014)
6. Bissyandé, T.F., Thung, F., Lo, D., Jiang, L., Réveillere, L.: Popularity, interoperability, and impact of programming languages in 100,000 open source projects. In: Proceedings of the 37th Annual International Computer Software & Applications Conference, COMPSAC 2013, pp. 1–10 (2013)
7. Bissyandé, T.F., Ahmat, D., Ouoba, J., Stam, G., Klein, J., Traon, Y.: Sustainable ICT4D in Africa: where do we go from here? In: Bissyandé, T.F., Stam, G. (eds.) AFRICOMM 2013. LNICSSITE, vol. 135, pp. 95–103. Springer, Heidelberg (2014). doi:10.1007/978-3-319-08368-1_11
8. Moen, V., Klingsheim, A.N., Simonsen, K.I.F., Hole, K.J.: Vulnerabilities in e-governments. Int. J. Electron. Secur. Digit. Forensic **1**(1), 89–100 (2007)
9. Wang, J.A., Zhang, F., Xia, M.: Temporal metrics for software vulnerabilities. In: Proceedings of the 4th Annual Workshop on Cyber Security, Information Intelligence Research: Developing Strategies to Meet the Cyber Security and Information Intelligence Challenges Ahead, CSIIRW 2008, pp. 44:1–44:3. ACM, New York (2008). Observation of strains. Infect Dis Ther. 3(1), 35–43 (2011)
10. Paleari, R., Marrone, D., Bruschi, D., Monga, M.: On race vulnerabilities in web applications. In: Zamboni, D. (ed.) DIMVA 2008. LNCS, vol. 5137, pp. 126–142. Springer, Heidelberg (2008). doi:10.1007/978-3-540-70542-0_7
11. Shahriar, H., Zulkernine, M.: Mitigating program security vulnerabilities: approaches and challenges. ACM Comput. Surv. **44**(3), 11:1–11:46 (2012)
12. Ciampa, A., Visaggio, C.A., Di Penta, M.: A heuristic-based approach for detecting sql-injection vulnerabilities in web applications. In: Proceedings of the 2010 ICSE Workshop on Software Engineering for Secure Systems, SESS 2010, pp. 43–49. ACM, New York (2010)

Paying with a Selfie: A Hybrid Micro-payment Framework Based on Visual Cryptography

Stelvio Cimato[1], Ernesto Damiani[1,2], Fulvio Frati[1(✉)],
Joël T. Hounsou[3], and Judicaël Tandjiékpon[3]

[1] Department of Computer Science, Università degli Studi di Milano, Milan, Italy
{stelvio.cimato,fulvio.frati}@unimi.it
[2] Etisalat British Telecom Innovation Center, Khalifa University, Abu Dhabi, UAE
ernesto.damiani@kustar.ac.ae
[3] Institut de Mathématiques et de Sciences Physiques, Porto Novo, Benin
joelhoun@gmail.com, judicaeltandjiekpon@yahoo.fr

Abstract. In developing countries, the mobile revolution is happening in these days, and technology is now improving life conditions and providing new opportunities for the developing of the economies. In this paper, we provide a micropayment framework that can be used to conclude everyday financial transactions. The novelty of the approach relies on the usage of techniques of easy understanding and application, even for uncultured people. The security of the system is also ensured by exploiting visual cryptography schemes, whose reconstruction phase requires no particular technical skills and relies only on human activities. The description of usage scenarios and the prototypal architecture of the framework are provided together with the initial plan for the experimental deployment.

Keywords: Micro-payment · Visual cryptography · Mobile

1 Introduction

A common feature of nowadays is the ubiquitous usage of information and communication technologies for different activities in everyday life. In developed economies, mobile phones are considered a normal part of the life, and the functions they provide extend the usual way in which customers do business, get educated or informed, and socialize, getting in touch with family and friends through emails, messaging, and social networks [9].

Even in developing countries, where satisfying basic needs often is an issue, the number of people accessing to mobile phones is surprisingly increasing from year to year. According to a report from IAMAI (Internet and Mobile Association of India), in 2012 there were 120 million people connected to the internet each week (doubling the total population of the UK, but getting less than 10 % of Indian population). According to recent reports, there are currently more than four billion mobile phones across the world, of which 64 % are used in a developing country [1].

The possibility to have easily simple voice and text communication has started a revolution in accessing financial, health, agricultural, and educational services for many

© ICST Institute for Computer Sciences, Social Informatics and Telecommunications Engineering 2016
R. Glitho et al. (Eds.): AFRICOMM 2015, LNICST 171, pp. 136–141, 2016.
DOI: 10.1007/978-3-319-43696-8_15

communities, increasing the working opportunities. As an example, many people living in rural areas of Africa and Asia have started using SMS services to find out daily prices of agricultural goods, to improve their bargaining position in local markets, and to select markets that offer the maximum income [2]. Another example of the possibilities offered by the connection to remote services comes from the UNICEF's RapidSMS initiative, which is a SMS-based open-source framework for the collection of dynamic data. Thanks to this initiative across six countries in Sub-Saharan Africa, 200,000 users in some of the most underserved and rural communities can access health services and receive support from the central places, saving money and, sometimes, lives. In Ghana, the same service is used by a local entrepreneur to monitor the sales of cook stoves around the country [2].

The process that in the rest of the world is replacing many paper-based procedures with digital information processing, is of utmost importance in the developing economies, where it can support the creation of new business opportunities and overcome some of the constraints coming from the cultural and social context. A field that is in rapid expansion is the development of mobile digital-money frameworks, giving the possibility to conclude transactions and/or transfer small amounts of money among users. Airtime [3] and MPESA [4] are two examples of mobile cash transfer systems that are being used in different countries to provide citizens with financial services that can significantly improve their lives. Still several challenges remain to be solved, including the need to overcome cultural barriers and support trust in non-traditional financial services. Applications need to be developed taking into account a better analysis of the ways in which people interact with money in developing countries, being flexible enough to be customized to different cultural patterns. In this paper, we present a mobile payment framework that leverages on face-to-face exchanges, where pictures taken with mobile phones are used to support the successful conclusion of a financial transaction. Trust is enhanced by relying on Visual Cryptography (VC) schemes that make possible the creation of shares, whose ownership ensures the correctness of the transaction [5]. The novelty of the proposed approach relies on the usage of simple techniques such as taking pictures and over-stacking images. Such actions are of easy understanding also for uncultured people. Today, people of all cultural backgrounds take pictures or selfies, since even the cheapest smartphones enable photo taking and require virtually no training or technology awareness. The human visual system has always been used by humans to establish the context (purchaser/supplier roles, object of the transaction, price) of commercial transactions. In our system, group selfies are used as context representations, where all the parties participating in a payment protocol can be represented in a self-validating way: the purchaser, the supplier, the purchased goods or service, the amount, time, and place of the transaction. On the other side, visual cryptography is used as a tool to build systems where the degree of trustworthiness that the user needs to have in the system is reduced. VC is a technique where a secret image is split into random-looking images printed on transparencies [6]. The most relevant property of VC schemes is that the reconstruction of the original image can be performed by simply stacking the shares, using the human visual system to perform the decoding operation, releasing any need for trust in the hardware. Furthermore, the computation of the shares requires simple procedures and low computational power. In literature, an example of hybrid systems, where visual cryptography is used as a tool to provide additional trust without leveraging on the digital equipment is Chaum's voting system [7], while a complete survey of applications of VC can be found in Cimato and Yang (2011).

2   Usage Scenarios

The mobile payment system we propose is not intended to replace the existing payment infrastructures, but to extend their reach. The goal is to enable commercial transactions in low or no connectivity areas involving non-IT-savvy or even illiterate parties. All parties must do at the time of purchase is *(i)* take a group selfie, *(ii)* compute and exchange shares. Shares are then sent to a trusted service point who reconstructs the image and (interacting with a traditional payment infrastructure) ensures that the supplier gets the cash, and that the buyer gets the goods. The proposed system supports three transaction styles, of which a simplified description is given in the following.

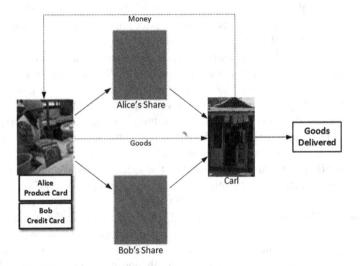

Fig. 1. *Cash and Carry* transaction style.

Cash then Carry. Alice and Bob meet somewhere outside the range of the mobile network. They both carry a simple phone. In order to commit to selling a product/service to Bob, Alice takes out a pre-marked product card (with her name, the product name and an amount, say 10 cents) and gives it to Bob. In turn, Bob takes Alice's product card, puts it and his own micro-credit card side by side and takes a photo with his phone. Bob's phone contains a simple app that computes two visual shares of the picture. One share stays with Bob, the other goes to Alice. Alice gets back her product card and keeps her product. Once Bob and Alice get mobile coverage (without needing to sync and in no particular order), they send their shares to Carl, a trusted operator who runs a point-of-service equipped with a desktop computer and an Internet connection. Carl puts together the two shares, uses the image to debit Bob's micro-credit card, prepares 10 cents cash, and sends a message to Alice. Alice drops by Carl's shop, gets the money and leaves the product, which can be delivered to Bob. If Carl receives only one share, the missing party is blacklisted. The scenario is depicted in Fig. 1.

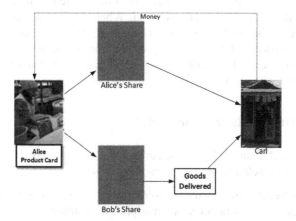

Fig. 2. *Carry then Cash* transaction style.

Carry then Cash. In this style (see Fig. 2), when Alice gets her share, she directly delivers the good to Bob. Alice and Bob later sends their shares to Carl, who notifies Alice to pass by the point of service and redeem the share to obtain the cash. Alice can decide to wait until notified amounts add up to a given value, or leave permanent money transfer instructions to Carl. If Carl receives only one share of the transaction, the missing party is blacklisted and will be excluded from the service.

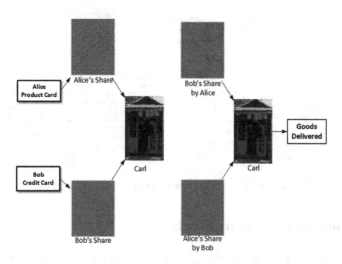

Fig. 3. *Guaranteed Future Contract* transaction style.

Guaranteed Future Contract. This style, depicted in Fig. 3, requires two photos, one of the micro-credit card and the other of the product card. First, Carl collects one share of Bob's micro-credit card and of Alice's product card.

At the time of transaction, Alice collects the other share of Bob's credit card and gives Bob the other share of her product card. When Alice comes to Carl's point of service, she matches the other share of Bob's card held by Carl. Carl debits Bob's micro-credit account, beyond Bob's control to pull out from the transaction. In turn, Bob matches the product card share with the one stored by Carl on Alice's behalf and will collect the product without Alice being able to pull out.

3   Architecture of the Framework

The mobile payment framework presented in this paper will be implemented as a simple software toolkit that includes three components (Fig. 4):

- **The share generator and share stacker utilities.** The share generator utility will create the shares and will target cheap smartphones, including the ones designed with developing countries in mind, in the line of Mozilla's $25 smartphone idea. The share stacker will be available under smartphone, tablet, and desktop platform, and it will reconstruct the image using the available shares.
- **The integrator tool.** This component will be installed at the point of service and act as a glue between share stacker and the current systems handling e-payments and money transfers in developing countries. The integrator prototype will be built according to West Africa specifications (Benin, Ghana, Togo and Nigeria)[1] [8].

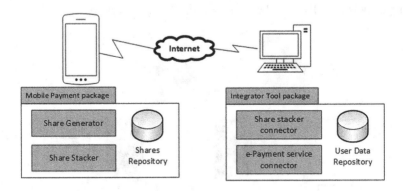

Fig. 4. Mobile payment framework component diagram.

4   Conclusions and Future Work

The continuing growth of mobile devices in developing countries represents a tremendous business opportunity. The features of this new potential market differ completely

---

[1] Source: http://www.itu.int/ITU-D/cyb/publications/archive/wmrcjune00/ntoko.html.

from the ones of the occidental world, where, for example, companies in Silicon Valley are fighting to develop the top app in a certain category. In developing countries, business developers are required to be able to think the design of their applications from a different viewpoint, considering the different contexts, environmental constraints and scenarios, and the motivations, experiences, needs of end users. The mobile payment framework we propose faces some of these challenges, not requiring any specific technological skill for its use, and, at the same time, relying on strong security techniques such as visual cryptography. We plan to perform functional and acceptance tests in collaboration with mobile phone companies operating in the rural area of Porto Novo (Benin), where many of the features above described are present. Although the illiteracy level in Benin reaches 60 % in rural areas, virtually everyone has a mobile phone. The framework will be tested out by a selected group of students of the local University, coordinated by graduate students and professors. Specific acceptance test and survey will be administered in order to evaluate the quality of the service and the user experience, to evaluate how and in which measure such service could be useful in rural areas. In particular, the test will report the number of transactions, the amount of exchanged money, and the number of users that have been blacklisted for misusing the service.

References

1. Business case studies: using technology to improve economies (2015). http://businesscasestudies.co.uk/vodafone/using-technology-to-improve-economies/
2. Kochi, E.: How the future of mobile lies in the developing world (2012). http://techcrunch.com/2012/05/27/mobile-developing-world/
3. The Economist: Airtime is money (2015). http://www.economist.com/news/finance-and-economics/21569744-use-pre-paid-mobile-phone-minutes-currency-airtime-money
4. Safaricom: M-PESA (2015). http://www.safaricom.co.ke/personal/m-pesa
5. Cimato, S., Yang, C.-N.: Visual Cryptography and Secret Image Sharing. CRC Press Inc., Boca Raton (2011)
6. Naor, M., Shamir, A.: Visual cryptography. In: De Santis, A. (ed.) EUROCRYPT 1994. LNCS, vol. 950, pp. 1–12. Springer, Heidelberg (1995)
7. Chaum, D.: Secret-ballot receipts: true voter-verifiable elections. IEEE Secur. Priv. 2(1), 38–47 (2004)
8. Jagun, A., Heeks, R., Whalley, J.: The impact of mobile telephony on developing country micro-enterprise: a nigerian case study. Inf. Technol. Int. Dev. 4(4), 47–65 (2008)
9. Brazier, C.: Computers and cellphones in the developing world (2013). http://newint.org/books/reference/world-development/case-studies/2013/03/14/computers-cellphones-in-developing-world/

Are the Days of Field-to-Laboratory Analysis Gone? Effects of Ubiquitous Environmental River Water Quality Assessment

K.B. Goodman Makojoa and Isaac O. Osunmakinde[✉]

School of Computing, College of Science, Engineering and Technology,
University of South Africa, P. O. Box 392, 0003 Pretoria, South Africa
44170637@mylife.unisa.ac.za, osunmio@unisa.ac.za

Abstract. As the human population growth and industry pressure in most developing countries continue to increase, effective water quality assessment has become critical for river waters. A major challenge, however, faced in water quality assessment is the process of data capturing and chemical laboratory approaches, which could be expensive and time consuming. This work develops ubiquitous particle swarm optimization (PSO) made-easy framework for mobile networks. The framework experimentally assesses water health status of Southern Africa river waters. Simulation results show that the proposed framework is able to obtain good results with economical solution when compared with assessment results obtained by the state of the art.

Keywords: Framework · E-Services · Environment · Ubiquitous network · PSO · Water quality · Fuzzy · Developing country

1 Introduction

The rate of increase in population, urban, and industrial activities has raised researchers concern about water quality. Surface water quality in a suburban depends on the nature and extent of industrial, agricultural, and other activities in the catchment. Therefore, surface water contamination from agricultural and urban runoff and waste water discharges from industrial activities is of major concern [1]. Water quality is determined by assessing biological, chemical, and physical characteristics. Due to their dynamic nature and easy accessibility through tributaries, rivers are affected by contaminants.

Pathogenic microbes spread directly through contaminated water cause waterborne diseases. Most waterborne diseases cause diarrheal illness. Eighty-eight percent of diarrhea cases worldwide are associated to unsafe water, inadequate sanitation, or insufficient hygiene. These cases result in 1.5 million deaths yearly affecting mostly young children in developing countries [2]. Figure 1 shows total water-related deaths in the years 2000–2020 years. Red lines show ranges of death likely to occur without United Nations Millennium Development Goals (UN MDG). Blue lines show range of deaths even if MDGs are achieved.

Recently, surface water quality monitoring and evaluation has attracted attention of scholars. To protect water quality resources, scholars work on pollution degree and the

© ICST Institute for Computer Sciences, Social Informatics and Telecommunications Engineering 2016
R. Glitho et al. (Eds.): AFRICOMM 2015, LNICST 171, pp. 142–164, 2016.
DOI: 10.1007/978-3-319-43696-8_16

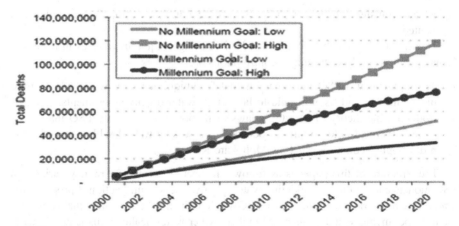

Fig. 1. Total Water-Related Deaths between 2000-2020 [5]. (Color figure online)

development of trends models in surface waters. Various techniques for monitoring and predicting surface water quality were developed [3]. In [4], a multi-variate, principal component analysis (PCA) was applied to evaluate correlation of river water parameters. This work demonstrates that PCA results for physico-chemical parameters are less important in explaining the annual variance of the data set. However, only one-year annual mean values of water quality parameters were used in this study.

Finally, in [6] a comparison of biotic and physicochemical indices approach is presented for monitoring and assessing water heath quality of a river. The approach used biotic and 28 physico-chemical and habitat parameters to calculate six indices to assess water quality and the impact of human activities in the Tajan River, Iran. Results showed a reduction in water quality and ecological from upstream to downstream. The reduced water quality was revealed by biotic indices better than the abiotic indices that were linked to a variety of ecological water scales.

There exist several optimization techniques for assessing the quality of water. However, particle swarm optimization (PSO) presents many advantages over other swarm intelligence techniques. Yet in spite of its simplicity and few parameters involved, PSO still presents a number of drawbacks, such as being stuck in local minima. It is therefore of special relevance to address these drawbacks for the benefit of other researchers.

1.1 Contributions and Outline

Rapid evolution of ubiquitous technologies in developing countries is spreading rapidly and has motivated an explosion of initiatives to explore the use of these technologies in a number of water issues. Smart phones are becoming pervasive computing, communications platform, and the variety and number of mobile applications has increased recently. Since mobile phones are affordable, easy to use and can transmit multiple types of information over long distances, the development of ubiquitous network utilizing these devices is of great significance for e-Services. Ubiquitous devices can collect and transfer data in a variety of formats: voice, text, images and video and augmented reality.

This research study therefore focused on utilizing ubiquitous devices in resources management. Therefore the major contributions are:

- Development of a PSO made-easy model for ubiquitous framework, which minimizes time lag and risks in field-to-laboratory water quality assessments.
- Modelling the theory of Newton's laws of motion equations into PSO made-easy model integrated onto ubiquitous devices for assessing water health status of rivers in developing countries, such as Mohokare River.

The structure of this paper is as follows: In Sect. 2, we briefly review variants of PSO models and laxities of modeling water quality assessment. Section 3 proposes the ubiquitous network integration with PSO made-easy model in water quality assessment. Experimental evaluations on Mohokare River water health status is presented in Sects. 4 and 5 outlines the conclusions.

2 Theoretical Background

2.1 Variants of PSO Models

In this section, we review the available basic variants of PSO models, together with their advantages and disadvantages. The existing basic PSO variants are velocity clamping, inertia weight, constriction coefficient, synchronous versus asynchronous updates.

Basic PSO Model. A more detailed description of PSO algorithm is presented in [7, 8]. In PSO, the potential solutions, called particles, move iteratively within the search area according to the historical experiences of their own and that of their neighbors. The position of particle i at iteration t can be expressed as

$$x_i^t = \{x_1^t, x_2^t, \ldots, x_n^t\},$$

and the velocity of the ith particle at iteration t can be expressed as

$$v = \{v_1^t, v_2^t, \ldots, v_n^t\}.$$

In order to reach the solution, each particle changes its searching direction according to these factors: the particle's best position, called p_{best} and the best particle's position in the entire swarm called g_{best}. In [9] the p_{best} and g_{best} are called cognitive and social parts respectively. During PSO iteration, the particle's velocity is updated according to its local information and particle's global position using Eq. (1). The particle's position is updated using Eq. (2).

$$v_i^{t+1} = v_i^t + c_1 \times r_1 \left(p_{best} - x_i^t \right) + c_2 \times r_2 \left(g_{best} - x_i^t \right). \tag{1}$$

$$x_i^{t+1} = x_i^t + v_i^{t+1} \tag{2}$$

In [10], analysis of PSO is carefully looked at. Since PSO is based on intelligence, it can be applied into both scientific research and engineering. PSO does not have overlapping and mutation calculation. Search can be carried out by the speed of the particle. Only the most optimistic particle can transmit information onto other particles, and the speed of researching is fast. Another advantage of PSO is that it adopts real number codes, and is decided by the solution. Consequently, PSO has its drawbacks as it easily suffers from partial optimisms, which causes less exact at the regulation of its speed and the direction. The PSO method cannot work out problems of scattering and optimization and problems of non-coordinate system.

Modified PSO Exploiting Areas around Known Solutions [11]. The drawbacks of PSO have let to developments of several PSO variants. These variants improve the speed of convergence and quality of solution found by PSO. Quite a number of control parameters influence these PSO variants. In this section, we discuss the modified PSO variants that exploit areas around known solutions.

Synchronous versus asynchronous updates. In synchronous update, particles update their velocities considering the current best position found by their neighborhoods. The fitness of all particles is computed and shared within neighbors. This leads to a slower feedback and better g_{best}. On the other hand, in asynchronous update, particles update their velocity immediately after computing the fitness function and consequently, the update is performed with particles having imperfect information about their neighborhoods.

Velocity clamping. Velocity clamping controls the global exploration of the particle. Suppose velocity v of a particle i exceeds the maximum allowed speed limit, velocity clamping assigns that particle the maximum velocity allowed. Velocity clamping reduces the size of the step velocity and controls the movement of the particle. However, should the velocities equal to the maximum velocity; particles will continue searching within a hypercube and would likely remain in the optima without convergence. Velocity clamping is adjusted using Eq. 2 in [12].

Constriction coefficient. Constriction coefficient is used as a natural, dynamic way to ensure that particles converge to a stable point without clamping. The velocity update Eq. (1) becomes (7) in [12]. The constriction coefficient approach is employed under the constraints that $\beta \geq 4$ and $k \in [0, 1]$, and this constraints guarantees that the swarm converges.

Modified PSO with Inertia Weight Exploring New Areas of the Search Space

Inertia weight. In the original PSO, inertia weight controls particle's exploration and exploitation. It controls the momentum of the particle by weighing the contribution of the previous velocity. Inertia weight also eliminates the idea of velocity clamping. An inertia weight w is introduced into the Eq. (1) and the original equation becomes Eq. (5) in [12]. Inertia weight has been developed by some researchers [11].

Dynamic Environment with PSO. In dynamic environments, the PSO should be fast to allow quick re-optimization. The idea is to find a good solution before the next environment can change. A dynamic environment changes the standard velocity update equation to (9) as in [12]. Several solutions were developed for dynamic environments.

Multi-objective optimization with PSO. The multi-objectives optimization (MOO) problem is defined as:

$$\text{minimize}: f(x),\ x = (x_1, x_2, \ldots, x_n)$$
$$\text{subject to}: g_i \leq 0,\ i = 1, \ldots, m$$
$$h_i = 0,\ i = 1, \ldots, p$$

The objective of the MOO approach is to find a set of solutions that will optimally balance the trade-offs among the objective of a MOP. This approach differs from the basic PSO that return one solution [11].

Niching with PSO. Niching algorithms are algorithms that locate multiple solutions. Speciation is the process of finding a niche [11].

Single solution PSO. Single solution PSO development is to obtain single solutions to continuous-valued, unconstrained, static, and single-objective optimization problems [13].

2.2   Survey on Laxities of Water Quality Assessment Models

River water quality has become a hot research topic for many scholars. Researchers are engaged in finding quick and modern techniques for river water assessment. In [4], a multivariate analysis is used to assess the quality of water in a river. The first step is to collect data on a monthly basis during June 2005 to May 2006 collecting eight physico-chemical parameters from Bennithora River. Water samples were taken to the laboratory for further analysis. Principal component analysis (PCA) was performed to identify the potential reduction of physico-chemical parameters. Results showed that there was a potential for improving the efficiency and economy of the monitoring network by reducing the number of monitoring parameters from 8 to 3.

Chemometrics was used to assess the quality of water in Langat River [3]. Discriminant analysis (DA) was used to confirm the hierarchical agglomerative cluster analysis (HACA) results. The application of these different pattern techniques reduce the complexity of large data sets and proved to give better interpretation and understanding of water quality data. The projects mentioned above contributed significantly to river water quality monitoring. These projects demonstrate potential benefits achieved by laboratory and statistical techniques in environmental management. However, there are challenges faced by these approaches, including:

- Fieldwork for data collection takes a long time.
- There is a need for sophisticated laboratory buildings and laboratory instruments for data analysis.
- Collected water samples require specialized storing facilities.

- Collected water samples need to be transported from the field to laboratory hence specialized care should be maintained in terms of storage and handling not to distort data.
- Field workers need a special training in handling and taking specimen of parameters.
- It is expensive and manually intensive.

3 Proposed Ubiquitous Network Integrated with PSO Made-Easy Model

3.1 Establishing the Framework

In view of the above challenges faced with traditional techniques in water quality assessment, we describe in details our proposed design of ubiquitous network integration with PSO made-easy model for river water assessment. As illustrated in Fig. 2, the proposed framework consists of two layers: hardware and software layers. Hardware architecture is composed of field equipment for data collection (smartphones, personal digital assistant (PDAs, tablet computers)), a server computer with intranet and internet connection, workstations connected to the server allowing access and renewing data at the server. The framework shows mobile devices equipped with water sensors to detect water quality parameters, pH, Temp, Turb, TDS, and DO and these sensors provide general characteristics of water quality. Ubiquitous devices acquire data from sensors using a Bluetooth or Wi-Fi connection and then transmit data to the application server through broadband cellular connections. The transmitted data is in a

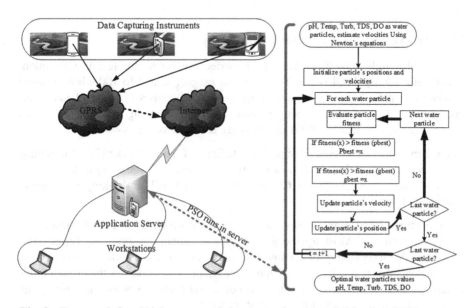

Fig. 2. Framework for ubiquitous network for pso made-easy model for river health status.

form of an SMS, which contains water parameter values. The software architecture is composed of PSO made-easy analysis and visualization tools. Raw data acquisition and transmission is performed at each mobile device using a custom-built integration software. A stream of data is transmitted to an application server running an intelligent PSO made-easy application. The framework allows users to reduce human power for data collection. It is much cheaper in cost and time. The devices consumes less power since and they are not connected with wires and these mobile devices are battery driven and it is easy to replace battery or recharge batteries. Data may be captured on hourly basis or at different times of a day and this helps in conserving the devices battery power. It is in the application server where actual water quality analysis is performed.

When developing the framework, issues taken into account were that:

- Data capturing equipment should better fit practical utility needs and should be easy to operate and maintain.
- Available technology should link to water quality regulations.
- Technologies and practices are developed to manage the large quantities of data transmission.

Additional benefits of the proposed framework are:

- It saves money.
- It speeds up data collection as data is transmitted thorough the network.
- It reduces time-consuming filed work.
- Storage of samples not needed which might require special storing facilities.
- It does not require laboratory analysis experiments.
- It does not need transportation.
- It does not need laboratory buildings.

3.2 Parameters of River Water Particles [14]

Water quality index (WQI) attempts an imperfect answer to non-technical questions about water quality. WQI is a unit less number ranging from 1 to 100 where a higher number indicates a better water quality. Multiple constituents are combined and results are aggregated to produce a single score for each sampling site. Water quality parameters used in defining WQI in this study are described as follows:

pH. pH measures the degree of acidity or alkalinity of the water. A pH of 7 is neutral, values below 7 are acidic, and values above 7 are alkaline. Some organism survives better in waters with pH between 6.5 and 8.5. Acceptable pH for drinking water ranges between 6.5 and 8.5.

Temperature. River water temperature is very important as it directly affects the biochemical process. Most aquatic life survives in certain temperatures. Temperature influences the acceptability of a number of other inorganic constituents and chemical contaminants that may affect taste. High water temperature enhances the growth of the microorganisms and increases taste, odor, color, and corrosion problems. The recommended temperature for drinking water shall not exceed 5°C.

Turbidity. Turbidity measures the transparency/clarity of water. The high measures of turbidity in water reduce light penetration resulting in waters being unable to support a wide variety of aquatic life. High turbidity can protect microorganisms from the effects of disinfection, stimulate growth of bacteria and give rise to a significant chlorine demand. The recommended turbidity level for drinking water is between 0.5 NTU to 1.0 NTU.

Total dissolved Solids. Total dissolved solids (TDS) measure the amount of solids materials dissolved in water. These materials include salts, some organic materials. If TDS is too high or too low, it might affect the aquatic life leading to death. Recommended TDS for drinking water is from 25 to 100 mg/l.

Dissolved Oxygen. Dissolved oxygen (DO), an important indicator of the water quality measures the amount of life-sustaining oxygen in the water. Lower levels of dissolved oxygen in water signify that there is a possibility of pollution. High levels of DO are good for drinking water as the water tastes better. Drinking standard for DO is 1.3 mg/l.

Table 1. PSO made-easy algorithm for assessing river health status

ALGORITHM 1. PSO-made easy model for assessing river water health status
INPUT: Water parameters captured from a river **OUTPUT**: optimal p*best* and *gbest* of the rivers

STEP 1:	Initialization $c_1=0$, $c_2=c_3=2$, $u_1=0.2$, $u_2=0.4$, $u_3=0.3$, $r_1=0.73$, $r_2=0.25$
STEP 2:	Set iteration $t=0$
STEP 3:	particles positions $x_i^0, i=1,...,n$
STEP 4:	particles velocities $v_i^0, i=1,...,n$, for $-v_{max} < v_i^0 < v_{max} i=1,...,n$
STEP 5:	For each particle, assign particle best $p_{best,i}^v = [p_{best,1}^v = x_1^v,...,p_{best,i}^v = x_i^v, i=1,...,n], f_i^{P_{best}}(p_{best,i}^v, i=1,...,n)$
STEP 6:	For all particles, assign global best $g_{best} = \{f_i^{best,i}, i=1,...,n$
STEP 7:	$t=t+1$
STEP 8:	Update particle velocity by $v_i^{t+1} = c_1 u_1 v_i^t + \left(c_2 u_2 r_1 \left(p_{best,i} - x_i^t\right)\right) + \left(c_3 u_3 r_2 (g_{best} - x_i^t)\right)$
STEP 9:	Update particle position by $x_i^{t+1} = x_i^t + v_i^{t+1}$
STEP 10:	Evaluate each particle best if $f_i^t(x_i^t, i=1,...,n) < f_i^{P_{best}}(p_{best,i}^{t-1}, i=1,...,n)$ then
STEP 11:	$f_i^{P_{best}}(p_{best,i}^t, i=1,...,n) = f_i^t(x_i^t, i=1,...,n)$
STEP 12:	else
STEP 13:	$f_i^{P_{best}}(p_{best,i}^t, i=1,...,n) = f_i^{P_{best}}(p_{best,i}^{t-1}, i=1,...,n)$
STEP 14:	Update global best $f^{g_{best}}(g_{best,i}^t, i=1,...,n) = min\{f_i^{P_{best}}(p_{best,i}^t, i=1,...,n)\}$
STEP 15:	if $f^{g_{best}}(g_{best,i}^t, i=1,...,n) < f^{g_{best}}(g_{best,i}^{t-1}, i=1,...,n)$ then
STEP 16:	$f^{g_{best}}(g_{best,i}^t, i=1,...,n) = f^{g_{best}}(g_{best,i}^t, i=1,...,n)$
STEP 17:	else
STEP 18:	$f^{g_{best}}(g_{best,i}^t, i=1,...,n) = f^{g_{best}}(g_{best,i}^{t-1}, i=1,...,n)$
STEP 19:	$t=m$ stopping condition is met, display output or go to step 7

3.3 PSO Made-Easy Algorithmic Analysis

We now describe the specific PSO algorithm used in this work. The implementation is an improvement on the standard PSO introduced in [15].

Our approach uses a fully connected topology where nodes are directly connected among each other. This topology is also known as PSO's g_{best} version where all particles in the swarm direct their movement toward the best particle found in the whole swarm. That is

$$g_{best} = min\left\{f_i^{Pbest}(p_{best,i}^t, i = 1, \ldots, n\right)$$

PSO's g_{best} is known to converge more rapidly but also susceptible to converge to a local optima [16].

PSO Made-easy algorithm steps. Algorithm 1 in Table 1 presents the steps for the PSO made-easy for assessing river health status.

Step 1 initializes the values $c_1, c_2, c_3, u_1, u_2, u_3, r_1, r_2$, t (number of iterations), and n swarm size. The values of $c_1, c_2, c_3, u_1, u_2, u_3, r_1, r_2$ are taken from [17]. Step 3 initializes particle's position, x_i^t, with river water particles values. Step 4 initializes particles velocities using the Newton's laws of motion equations. Step 5 assigns each particle with particle's best position, $p_{best,i}^t = [p_{best,1}^0 = x_1^0, \ldots, p_{best,i}^t = x_i^t$, $i = 1, \ldots, n]$, $f_i^{Pbest}(p_{best,i}^t, i = 1, \ldots, n)$. Step 6 assigns a global best for all particles, $g_{best} = min\left\{f_i^{Pbest}(p_{best,i}^t, i = 1, \ldots, n)\right.$. Step 7 increases the iteration number to $t = t + 1$. The particle position is updated in step 8 using equation. Step 9 updates the particle position. Steps 10-13 evaluate each particle best. In our model, the particle best is evaluated by. Steps 14-18 evaluates swarm global best. The process iterates until convergence step 19 or stopping condition is met, or go to step 7.

For PSO made-easy algorithm, particle's velocities are estimated using Newton's law of motion Eqs. 3, 4, and 5.

$$F = m \times a. \tag{3}$$

$$s = ut + \frac{1}{2}at^2. \tag{4}$$

$$v = \frac{distance}{time}. \tag{5}$$

Where F represents force, S is measured distance in kilometers from first sampling point to the second and so forth. Acceleration factor a is changes in observed parameter from first sampling point to the second and so forth at time t. initial speed u, initialized to zero.

Water quality index using fuzzy logic. One of the research fields in Artificial Intelligence is fuzzy logic. It is based on mathematics of fuzzy sets [18]. A fuzzy set is defined in terms of membership functions. Membership function of a set is 1 within the

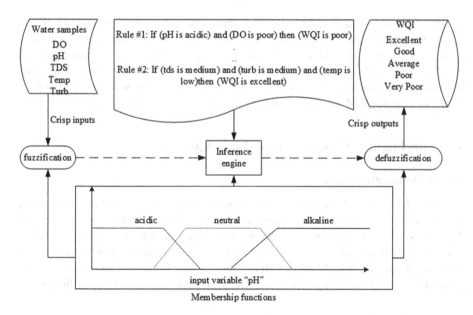

Fig. 3. Different components of the FIS for river water quality index

boundaries of the set and 0 outside. Membership function maps the domain of interest onto the interval (0, 1). The symbol μis used to represent the fuzzy memberships and if x represents the value of sample variable, the μ(x) corresponds to its membership. Fuzzy method utilizes max-min operator to perform fuzzy inference system (FIS) and the standard fuzzy set operations are intersection (AND), complement (NOT), and union (OR).

Fuzzy methodology is developed to propose a new water quality index for Mohokare River. Memberships functions for different water parameters were developed considering boundaries from [14]. Fuzzy inference system was designed to and classifies water quality with membership grade and the components of the FIS are depicted in Fig. 3. To generate membership function, the two pieces of intervals about the same water quality are merged. For example, for pH to be considered as "acidic", pH measurements must fall within [0, 6.5]. For example, for our water quality index assessment using a pH parameter for fuzzy set inputs we have "acidic", "neutral", and "alkaline" and for the output we have "poor", "bad", "average", "good", and "excellent". Trapezoidal membership functions define these fuzzy sets.

In the fuzzy language, it could be:

Rule 1: If (pH is acidic) and (temperature is low) and (turb is bad) and (tds is bad) and (do is bad) then (wqi is very poor).

Rule 2: If (pH is normal) and (temperature is good) and (turb is good) and (tds is good) and (do is good) then (wqi is good).

The last step is defuzzification. The input for defuzzification process is the aggregate output fuzzy set and the output is a single number for each parameter. Parameters included in the fuzzy-based index were selected as key indicators of drinking water quality. These parameters were weighted according to their importance for health implications on human health. Direct weighting factors were assigned to each parameter and the final score was calculated based on these weights.

4 Experimental Evaluations of Mohokare River

4.1 Experimental Setup

Mohokare River (Fig. 4) is an important source of potable water for Maseru City and other industrialized places in Lesotho. It forms an international boundary with the Republic of South Africa in the Free State province. It is about 200 km long. The river faced huge threats from various types of agricultural and industrial activities. In this study, water samples from Mohokare River were collected from four different sampling points as shown in Table 2 in Universal Transverse Mercator (UTM) coordinates.

Fig. 4. Mohokare River, sampling point near Maseru Industrial Site (Yellow flag). (Color figure online)

These sampling points were selected at strategic locations with reference to industries and human activities that are potential sources of pollution to avoid momentary fluctuations in the target parameters because of surface run-off from rain or any other discharges into the river, samples were collected on the same day.

Our implementation platform was carried out on Matlab 2012, a mathematical development environment. The experiment was performed on Windows 8.1 Pro,

Table 2. Font sizes of headings. Table captions should always be positioned *above* the tables.

Sampling Point	UTM Coordinates	
	S	E
1	28.69633	028.23635
2	28.91041	027.89147
3	29.24457	027.54616
4	*29.30662*	027.49146

Intel R Core(TM) i3-2348 M CPU @ 2.30 GHz 2.30 GHz, 4.00 GB Random Access Memory, 64 bit O/S, x64-based processor, 500.00 GB HDD.

4.2   Experiment 1: Assessing the Health Status with Random Initial Distributions

Table 3 presents the water samples parameters captured from four sampling points. Sampling points are represented by $x_i, i = 1,.., 4$.

Table 3. Measured water samples from Mohokare River.

	pH	Temp.	Turb.	TDS	DO
x_1	7.81	21.2	39.2	0.04	1.98
x_2	7.92	23.5	188	0.08	6.21
x_3	7.94	23.9	946	0.07	5.56
x_4	7.81	25.1	386	0.06	7.21
Min	7.81	21.2	39.2	0.04	1.98
Max	7.94	25.1	946	0.08	7.21

The maximum and minimum values for captured water samples parameters are presented in Table 3 last two rows. Data normalization was calculated using Eq. 6 and the resulting table is shown in Table 4.

$$x_i = \text{Rnd}(x_{min}, x_{max}). \tag{6}$$

To estimate particle's velocities, we used Newton's law of motion equations. For example, for pH, from first sampling point to the second, the distance is 40.63 km and the change in pH is 0.11. Using Eq. (4)

$$s = ut + \left(\frac{1}{2}\right)at^2$$

$$= 0 + \left(\frac{1}{2}\right)(0.11)t^2$$

$$= 40.63$$

$$= 0.055t^2$$

Table 4. Normalized data using Eq. (6).

	pH	Temp.	Turb.	TDS	DO
x_1	7.85	24.64	899.09	0.08	3.24
x_2	7.88	21.20	157.32	0.06	4.84
x_3	7.87	24.06	705.75	0.06	5.93
x_4	7.94	23.01	215.04	0.05	5.66

Then

$$t = \sqrt{738.7273}$$
$$t \approx 27.18 \text{hours}$$

Using Eq. (6)

$$v = \frac{\text{distance}}{\text{time}}$$
$$= \frac{40.63}{27.17954}$$
$$= 1.49.$$

pH velocity from sampling point one to sampling point two is 1.49. Estimated velocities are presented in Table 5.

Table 5. Estimated particle velocities.

	pH	Temp.	Turb.	TDS	DO
v_1	1.49	6.84	54.98	0.90	9.27
v_2	0.79	3.53	153.50	0.56	4.50
v_3	0.97	2.95	63.70	0.27	3.46
v_4	1.08	4.44	90.73	0.53	5.74

Table 6 shows the minimum and maximum velocities used in normalizing initial particle velocities. Equation 7 is used to normalize velocities as presented in Table 8. The minimum and maximum velocities ensure that during PSO iterations, when velocities change, they fall within that boundary. That is particles are constricted in the range [-min, max] (Table 6).

Table 6. Minimum and Maximum velocities

min	-1.49	-6.84	-153.50	-0.90	-9.27
max	1.49	6.84	153.50	0.90	9.27

$$v_i = \text{Rnd}\left(\frac{-v_{max}}{3}, \frac{v_{max}}{3}\right). \tag{7}$$

Table 7. Final velocities obtained by Eq. (7)

	pH	Temp	Turb.	TDS	DO
v_1	-0.07	-1.34	37.40	0.23	-1.45
v_2	0.36	-1.85	-26.21	0.11	2.98
v_3	-0.31	0.95	-0.62	-0.07	1.99
v_4	-0.31	2.25	-9.12	-0.15	2.86

According to algorithm 1, the following steps are performed until all particles converge to a certain value, global best or gbest.

Step 1: Initializes other PSO made-*easy* algorithm parameters by $c_1 = 1$, $c_2 = c_3 = 2; u_1 = 0.2, u_2 = 0.4$, and $u_3 = 0.3$; and $r_1 = 0.73, r_2 = 0.25$. Step 2 sets iteration number to 0. Table 8 shows results of step 3 and 4, initialization of particle position and velocities.

Table 8. Initialization of positions and velocities

i	1	2	3	4	5
	pH	Temp	Turb.	TDS	DO
x_{1i}^0	7.85	24.64	899.09	0.08	3.24
v_{1i}^0	−0.07	−1.34	37.40	0.23	−1.45
x_{2i}^0	7.88	21.29	157.32	0.06	4.84
v_{2i}^0	0.36	−1.85	−26.21	0.11	2.98
x_{3i}^0	7.87	24.06	705.75	0.06	5.93
v_{3i}^0	−0.31	0.96	−0.62	−0.07	1.99
x_{4i}^0	7.94	23.01	215.04	0.05	5.66
v_{4i}^0	−0.31	2.25	−9.12	−0.15	2.86

Table 9. Assigning each particle with p_{best}

i	1	2	3	4	5
	pH	Temp	Turb.	TDS	DO
x_{1i}^1	7.85	24.64	899.09	0.08	3.24
x_{2i}^{12}	7.88	21.29	157.32	0.06	4.84
x_{3i}^1	7.87	24.06	705.75	0.06	5.93
x_{4i}^1	7.94	23.01	215.04	0.05	5.66

Step 5 of the algorithm assigns particle best to each particle in the swarm as shown in Table 9. Step 6 assigns global best for all particles as presented in Table 10 below.

$$G_{best} = \min \left\{ p_{best,i}^t \text{ where } i = 1, 2, 3, 4, 5 \right\}$$

At this stage, PSO iterates to $t = t + 1$ and go to step 8 for velocity updating. This is achieved by step 8 and the updated velocities are shown in Table 11.

Table 10. Finding g_{best}

i	1	2	3	4	5
	pH	Temp	Turb.	TDS	DO
$g_{best,i}^1$	7.85	21.29	157.32	0.05	3.24

Table 11. Updated particle velocities v_i^{t+1}

i	1	2	3	4	5
	pH	Temp	Turb.	TDS	DO
v_{1i}^1	−0.01	−2.28	−437.58	0.03	−0.29
v_{2i}^1	0.05	−0.37	−5.24	0.02	−0.37
v_{3i}^1	-0.07	-1.47	-329.18	-0.02	-1.22
v_{4i}^1	−0.11	−0.58	−36.46	−0.03	−0.88

In case some velocities moved outside the range, and Eq. 8 is used to clamp them. The algorithm then moves to step 9 for particle position updates and the result are shown in Table 12. It should be noted that after updating, some position fell outside the original maximum and minimum values hence position adjustment was done using

$$x_i^{t+1} = \begin{cases} x_{min} \text{ if } x_i^{t+1} < x_{min} \\ x_{max} \text{ if } x_i^{t+1} > x_{max} \end{cases}. \tag{8}$$

Table 12. particle position update x_i^{t+1}

i	1	2	3	4	5
	pH	Temp	Turb.	TDS	DO
x_{1i}^1	7.84	22.36	461.50	0.08	2.95
x_{2i}^1	7.88	21.20	152.07	0.04	4.48
x_{3i}^1	7.81	22.59	376.57	0.04	4.71

Table 13. Evaluate current positon with previous position

i	1	2	3	4	5
	pH	Temp	Turb.	TDS	DO
x_{1i}^1	7.84	22.36	461.50	0.08	2.95
x_{2i}^1	7.88	21.20	152.07	0.04	4.48
x_{3i}^1	7.81	22.59	376.57	0.04	4.71
x_{4i}^1	7.82	22.43	178.58	0.04	4.78

Steps 10–13 of the proposed PSO made-easy cater for particle position update and the results are shown in Table 13. Steps 14–18 of the algorithm evaluate the new g_{best} against the previous g_{best} and the updated g_{best} is presented in Table 14 below.

Table 14. Final global bests for each particle

i	1	2	3	4	5
	pH	Temp	Turb.	TDS	DO
$g_{best,i}^1$	7.81	21.20	124.68	0.04	2.69

If the values of x_{1i}^{t+1} do not converge, PSO algorithm increments the iteration number and go to step 8 of the algorithm, otherwise stop the iteration and output the results. The computation continued until convergence. However, it should be noted that not all the particles converged on the same iteration, for example pH and TDS converged at t = 5, temperature at t = 6, O_2 at t = 8 and TDS at t = 14.

Table 15 presents the optimum PSO values for all parameters in Mohokare River. Closely looking at the values, some of them converged to a known value for example pH, temperature, and Total dissolved solids all converged to the same values as measured. However, that is not the case with turbidity and dissolved oxygen since they converged to new values, 124.68 and 2.69 respectively.

4.3 Experiment 2: Deriving the Consensus Health Status

Figures (5, 6, 7, 8 and 9) shows the PSO iteration against the measured water parameters. In all the figures, on the legend, sp 1, sp 2, sp 3, and sp 4 means sampling points 1, 2, 3, and 4 respectively. All the graphs reveal how each particle at each sampling point converges to the optimum value, global best. Figure 5 shows the pH graph for all 4 sampling points and how pH converges at each point. Carefully looking at the graph, we observe that at iteration number 3, all sampling points' values started coming to a single value. Figure 6 shows how temperature for each sampling point performs.

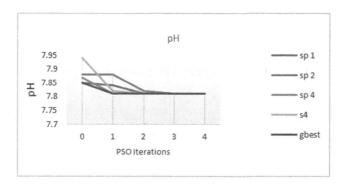

Fig. 5. pH Sampling points convergence vs gbest

Observation on the graph shows temperature coming close to a single value at iteration number 4. Figure 7 presents how turbidity behaves as iterations increase. This particle took much iteration to converge than other parameters. At iteration number 15, we observe turbidity coming to optima. Total dissolved solids (TDS) convergence graph is shown in Fig. 8. TDS converged to 0.04 mg/l at iteration number 4. Figure 9 shows the convergence of dissolved oxygen (DO) parameter for all sampling points.

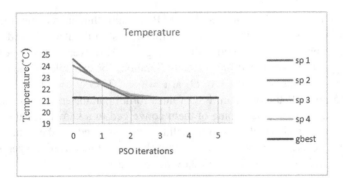

Fig. 6. Temperature sampling points convergence vs gbest

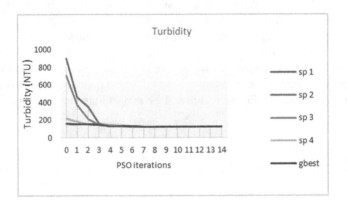

Fig. 7. Turbidity sampling points convergence vs gbest

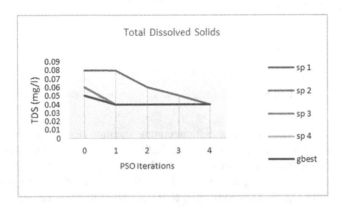

Fig. 8. TDS sampling points convergence vs gbest

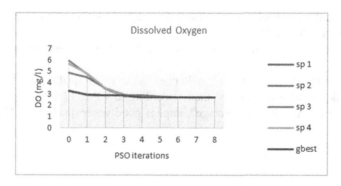

Fig. 9. DO sampling points convergence vs gbest

Looking at the graph, DO converged to 2.69 mg/l at iteration number 6.

Fuzzy inference system was proposed to get the overall health status of Mohokare River. In this study, five quality parameters were included in the index based on their importance including pH, temperature, turbidity, total dissolved solids (TDS), and dissolved oxygen (DO) were used as inputs and WQI as the output. The five water quality parameters were divided into different categories, and trapezoidal membership functions were assigned to each. Ranges for fuzzy sets were based on World Health Organization (WHO) standards. WQI is a 100-point index divided into several ranges

Table 15. Water Quality Index Legend [14].

Quality	Very Poor	Bad	Average	Good	Excellent
Range	7.81	21.20	124.68	0.04	2.69

corresponding to the general terms as shown in Table 15.

Figure 10 below shows a graphical algorithmic flow developed for fuzzy logic process where individual quality variables are processed by inference system producing different groups. As per classification, 3 parameters from optimal PSO made-easy global best values were kept in group 1, 2 parameters were kept in group 2. The two groups were combined by keeping physical parameters together and chemical parameters together. According to Fig. 10, temperature, TDS, and turbidity were combined to output G1, pH and DO were combined to produce G2. Groups G1 and G2 were further combined to form group 3 which was processed through fuzzy rules to

Table 16. Water Quality parameter inputs to FIS.

Parameter	pH	Temp	Turb	TDS	DO
Value taken	7.81	21.20	124.68	0.04	2.69

produce overall river health status. Table 16 presents optimal representative values serving as inputs to the FIS.

Following are two sample rules designed for physico-chemical water quality parameters.

Rule 1: if (pH = 7.81, "basic", it implies good water quality) & (DO = 2.69," good", implies good water quality) then (according to Table 17 WQI is good).

Rule 2: if (temp = 21.20, "average", implies good water quality) & (TDS = 0.04,

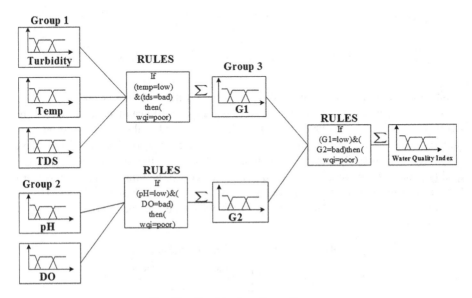

Fig. 10. Graphic flow Fuzzy Process

"good", implies good water quality) & (turb = 124.68, "good", implies good water quality) then according to Table 17, WQI = 50, "average").

According to Table 17, the WQI in Mohokare River was found to be in the 50–70 scale. In order to validate the results of the proposed framework, comparison was made with [19] where most river samples showed increasing trend especially around factories. The WQI also showed to be worsening downstream of agricultural farms and urban settlements downstream of wastewater treatment plant.

4.4   Comparing the Proposed Ubiquitous Network PSO Made-Easy with Other Classical Methods

Table 17 compares our proposed model to other related works in river quality modeling. The major concern in river water quality monitoring is the accuracy, timely, and reliable information in order to avoid disaster.

The method proposed in [20] presented water quality on a single point rather than other places where there are also potential pollution sources. In [4], few parameters

Table 17. Comparison of the proposed model with Field-to-Laboratory Models

Proposed Model/ Related methods	Problem addressed	Method	Result	Limitations
Physico-Chemical Assessment of Pollution in the Caledon River Around Maseru City [20]	Automatic calibration of river water system.	CE-Qual and principal component analysis	Experimental results show that their method produced good results. Details in [20]	The complexity increase in the system could the computational and memory requirements for large number of function evaluation may restrict performance hence computational burden.
Monitoring and assessment of water health quality in the Tajan River, Iran using Physico-chemical, fish, and macroinvertebrates indices [6]	Assessment of river water in the Tajan River, Iran.	Measured data on biotic and abiotic elements were used. GIS, univariate, and Multivariate statistics have been used to assess the correlation between biological and environmental endpoints.	Results showed that ecological condition and water quality were reduced from upstream to downstream. Reduced water quality was better revealed by biotic indices than abiotic indices. Details in [6]	Though the proposed method seem promising, it takes a longer time to do the analysis before the results can be published especially in a country like Iran which is located in a mid-dry area where resource management is particularly urgent and important.
Assessment of Water Quality of Bennithora River in Karnataka through Multivariate Analysis [4]	Karnataka River water quality assessment	Multivariate analysis with laboratory experiments and principal component analysis	Results showed that there is potential in improving the efficiency and economy of the monitoring network. Analysis	One-year mean values of water quality parameters were used and prior to making any critical decision in

(Continued)

Table 17. (*Continued*)

Proposed Model/ Related methods	Problem addressed	Method	Result	Limitations
			further showed there is potential in reducing water quality parameters. Details in [4]	eliminating water quality parameters, the PCA with longer time scale should be performed. Principal factor analysis is also needed to identify important parameters
Proposed model	Assessing river water quality	Real-time ubiquitous network and swarm intelligence	Experimental results show that proposed model obtain satisfactory results as shown in Sect. 4	Experimental results show that proposed model obtain satisfactory results as shown in Sect. 4

were chosen to assess the river quality making it difficult to judge the quality of water in that river since water quality index is based many parameters. The study presented in [6] provides an assessment and comparison of biotic and abiotic indices based approach for river water quality. Furthermore, authors could not claim that their proposed choice of indices will work in other regions. Compared to other classical models in assessing water quality of Mohokare River [19], the proposed model produced better results in a shortest time. In [19], quality of Mohokare River showed to be worsening especially downstream of garments factories and wastewater plants. The proposed model transmitted data on water quality parameters faster and reduced time-consuming fieldwork. The PSO-made easy algorithm converged after a few iterations. Furthermore, the proposed model proved to be economically since it does not require laboratory experiments.

5 Conclusion

Literature survey indicates that several researchers introduced modern techniques in assessing river water quality. This work presents the design, implementation and evaluation of ubiquitous PSO made-easy framework for assessing river health status through e-Services. The aim of the framework is to ensure real-time water data capturing and water quality assessment using PSO made-easy algorithm to address the drawbacks of the traditional methods of water assessment. The proposed framework showed the flow of data from capturing devices in a river to a PSO made-easy analysis system. Furthermore, the experiment showed PSO model calculations from start to finish. The model was experimented to assess water health status of a Suburban river. The results showed that ubiquitous PSO made-easy framework could be used as a tool for finding solutions to real-world optimization problems such as air quality monitoring, earthquake warnings, tracking health indicators and treatments. The proposed model produced good results because it is better, faster, and economically sound hence the model could be extended to distributed river networks.

Acknowledgement. The authors gratefully acknowledge the resources made available by the University of South Africa and Lesotho Department of Waters Affairs for providing surface waters.

References

1. Wechmongkhonkon, S., Poomtong, N., Areerachakul, S.: Application of artificial neural network to classification surface water quality. World Acad. Sci. Eng. Technol. **6**(9), 205–209 (2012)
2. Prüss-Üstün, A., Bos, R., Gore, F., Bartram, J.: Safer water, better health, p. 53 (2008)
3. Juahir, H., Zain, S.M., Aris, A.Z., Yusoff, M.K., Bin Mokhtar, M.: Spatial assessment of Langat River water quality using chemometrics. J. Environ. Monit. **12**(1), 287–295 (2010)
4. Thareja, S., Trivedi, P.: Assessment of water quality of Bennithora River in Karnataka through multivariate analysis. Nat. Sci. **8**(6), 51–56 (2010)
5. Gleick, P.H.: Dirty Water: Estimated deaths from water-related diseases 2000–2020. Pacific Inst. Res. Rep., pp. 1–12, 2002
6. Aazami, J., Esmaili-Sari, A., Abdoli, A., Sohrabi, H., Van den Brink, P.J.: Monitoring and assessment of water health quality in the Tajan River, Iran using physicochemical, fish and macroinvertebrates indices. J. Environ. Heal. Sci. Eng. **13**(1), 29 (2015)
7. Kennedy, J., Eberhart, R.C.: A discrete binary version of the particle swarm algorithm. In: 1997 IEEE International Conference on Systems, Man, Cybernetics Computer Cybernetics Simulation, vol. 5, pp. 4–8, (1997)
8. Eberhart, R., Kennedy, J.: A new optimizer using particle swarm theory. In: MHS 1995 Proceedings of the Sixth International Symposium Micro Machine Human Science, pp. 39–43 (1995)
9. Shi, Y., Eberhart, R.: A modified particle swarm optimizer. In: 1998 IEEE International Conference Evolutionary Computation Proceedings. IEEE World Congress on Computational Intelligence (Cat. No. 98TH8360), pp. 69–73 (1998)
10. Bai, Q.: Analysis of particle swarm optimization algorithm. Comput. Inf. Sci. **3**(1), 180–184 (2010)
11. Zhang, Y., Wang, S., Ji, G.: A comprehensive survey on particle swarm optimization algorithm and its applications (2015)
12. Dian, P.R., Siti, M.S., Siti, S.Y.: Particle swarm optimization: technique, system and challenges. Int. J. Comput. Appl. **14**(1), 19–27 (2011)
13. Peer, E.S., Van Den Bergh, F., Engelbrecht, A.P.: Using neighbourhoods with the guaranteed convergence PSO. In: Proceedings of the 2003 IEEE Swarm Intelligence Symposium. SIS 2003 (Cat. No. 03EX706), no. 2 (2003)

14. Gordon, B., Callan, P., Vickers, C.: WHO guidelines for drinking-water quality. WHO Chron. **38**(3), 564 (2008)
15. Clerc, M.: A method to improve Standard PSO. Technical report, pp. 1–18 (2009)
16. Kennedy, J., Eberhart, R.C., Shi, Y.: Swarm Intell. Scholarpedia **2**(9), 1462 (2001)
17. Clerk, M.: Stagnation analysis in particle swarm optimization or what happens when nothing happens. no. CSM-460 (2006)
18. Zadeh, L.: Fuzzy sets. Inf. Control **8**, 338–353 (1965)
19. Pullanikkatil, D.: Water quality assessment of mohokare river
20. Tanor, E.B., George, M.J.: Physico-Chemical Assessment of Pollution in the Caledon River Around Maseru City, Lesotho, pp. 776–782 (2014)

Health and Communication Infrastructure

Healthcare Systems in Rural Areas: A Cloud-Sensor Based Approach for Epidemic Diseases Management

Sarra Berrahal[2(✉)], Noureddine Boudriga[2], and Antoine Bagula[1]

[1] University of the Western Cape, Cape Town, South Africa
bbagula@uwc.ac.za
[2] Communication Networks and Security Research Lab, University of Carthage, Tunis, Tunisia
berrahal.sarra@gmail.com, noure.boudriga2@gmail.com

Abstract. The recent advances in wearable and integrated sensing devices, such as Wireless Body Area Networks (WBANs), have enabled a wide range of advanced and real-time sensing and monitoring issues. However, as stand-alone systems, WBANs are likely to face many challenges in terms of communication range, data security and privacy, storage and processing of the huge amount of data collected. In this context, we propose in this paper a novel healthcare system that relies on a cloud-sensor based approach for epidemic disease management in rural areas. The proposal tries to optimize epidemic diseases detection and tracking through the management of alerts generated by WBANs carried by individuals and belonging to public and private clouds. It also tries to report on the evolution of particular diseases and implement a query management system allowing cooperative answers from the aggregated clouds.

Keywords: WBAN · Sensor-cloud · Rural areas · Diseases · Continuous querying

1 Introduction

In recent years, the world has witnessed an exponential escalation in the occurrence of many epidemic diseases such as the Ebola virus. Such epidemic diseases are among the major threats that affect public safety in its large-scale and cause untold suffering to mankind [15]. In this context, governments and international organizations such as the Pan African Union and the World Health Organization (WHO) have set up healthcare surveillance systems to monitor diseases and to predict epidemic's occurrence [11]. Consequently, designing efficient healthcare systems can assist caregivers to diagnose, monitor, and manage critical health indicators, as well as to provide appropriate medical treatments once epidemic's occurrence is confirmed.

The recent advances in mobile communication systems as well as wearable and integrated sensing devices, such as Wireless Body Area Networks (WBANs), have given tremendous opportunities to enable advanced sensing purposes including monitoring, tracking and controlling systems and health states [4]. Accordingly, networks of WBANs can be utilized as ad-hoc mobile sensor infrastructures to actively monitor patient's health status, to provide early diagnosis of disease-related symptoms, and ultimately to prevent the occurrence and the spreading of epidemiological diseases.

© ICST Institute for Computer Sciences, Social Informatics and Telecommunications Engineering 2016
R. Glitho et al. (Eds.): AFRICOMM 2015, LNICST 171, pp. 167–177, 2016.
DOI: 10.1007/978-3-319-43696-8_17

Managing epidemic diseases in rural areas is, however, a challenging task that may impede the undertaken of a well-coordinated decision. In addition, when the WBANs are implemented as stand-alone systems, they are likely to face many limitations and challenges in terms of communication, reliability, security and privacy, the mobility of the monitored users, and the scarcity of wireless network resources. Besides, communication infrastructure in the monitored area may be overloaded in case of emergency, destroyed and even non-existent as is the case of many rural areas. Consequently, there is a growing need for implementing an infrastructure to enable ubiquitous, convenient, on-demand access to a shared pool of configurable computing resources (e.g., networks, storages, servers, applications, and services) that can be rapidly provisioned and released with minimal management effort or service provider interaction [5].

Cloud computing provides a configurable platform to support collaborative services and presents a huge transformation in the information and communication technology [2, 6]. According to [10], the major benefits of cloud computing in healthcare applications are: (a) Enabling on-demand access to a shared pool of computing and large storage services; (b) Supporting huge amount of health-related records as well as burdensome medical tasks including radiology images and genomic data offloading from many hospital departments; (c) Providing an easy sharing of information among authorized physicians and hospitals in various geographic areas; and (d) Enabling more real-time access to health-related information and minimizing the need for duplicate testing. Accordingly, the management of WBANs, despite their aforementioned limitations, can be tackled by exploiting Cloud computing to provide an integrated cloud-sensor based platform that provides a scalable and distributed storage system in rural areas. The presence of backup copies in the cloud reinforces data reliability and guarantees that the applications can continue running in the cloud without interruption [16].

Several solutions for the integrating WBANs with cloud computing have recently been reported in the literature [3, 7, 12, 14]. In these works a typical healthcare application is described. It aims at providing ubiquitous collection, access, process, and sharing of patient data from different hospitals in dedicated health services networks. The mobility of patients is restricted to the hospital environment or to the area within the communication ranges of the WBAN system, his house for example. In addition, the proposed querying mechanisms in these works only take into consideration data already stored in the cloud servers. The stored data should satisfy temporal and freshness requirements to reflect the current status of the monitored phenomenon. Nevertheless, epidemic diseases management is a mission-critical application where WBAN users, typically, deliver data in streams continuously at defined time intervals. These streams have to be processed in real-time manner as data arrives and need active real-time querying that implements cooperation among the cloud platform and the distributed WBAN nodes.

Motivated by all these observations, we propose in this work a novel healthcare system that relies on a cloud-sensor based approach for epidemic disease management in rural areas. The major contributions are summarized in the following.

- We propose a system model that, specifically, considers different networks of wearable sensors in the form of WBANs carried by individuals moving in a rural area and belonging to public and private clouds. This system allows continuous collection and transmission of health-related and environmental information and tries to optimize epidemic diseases detection and tracking through the management of alerts generated by distributed WBANs.

- We implement an epidemic diseases management system that tries to report on the evolution and intensity of particular diseases and adapts an active querying management approach that allows cooperative answers from the aggregated clouds, which facilitates the decision making process in health related issues.

The remainder of this paper is organized as follows. In Sect. 2, we propose a cloud-sensor based architecture for epidemic diseases management in rural areas. A continuous querying approach is proposed in Sect. 3 to allow cooperative answers from the aggregated clouds and to facilitate the decision making process in healthcare issues. Section 4 proposes the tracking of a specific disease as a case study to evaluate the proposed approach. And the last section concludes the work.

2   A Cloud-Sensor Based Architecture for Epidemic Diseases Management

The core idea behind this section is to propose a healthcare system that relies on the interaction between cloud platforms and WBANs as an infrastructure for continuously tracking epidemic diseases' occurrence in rural areas.

2.1   Epidemic Disease Propagation

An epidemic may be defined as the occurrence of disease or health related condition in excess of the common frequency in a given area or among a specified group of people over a particular period of time. It spreads through human populations by direct contact between individuals carrying the disease's virus and susceptible members of the population to which they belong. The spread intensity of epidemics varies depending on the related disease and the geographic locations of infections. In addition, high human density would increase the spread of epidemic diseases. Some epidemics such as Ebola are introduced into the human population through close contact with infected animals such as chimpanzees, bats, monkeys, mosquitoes, parasitic worms, and so forth. The major signs and symptoms for deciding whether an individual has critical health condition include fever, fatigues, diarrhea, and muscle aches. An investigation of a given epidemic should take into consideration the detection time and place of the person under test.

2.2   A Cloud-Sensor Based Architecture in Rural Areas

We describe in this section the general architecture of a cloud-sensor based approach for epidemic diseases management in rural areas. The whole architecture is illustrated in Fig. 1. As we can see, it integrates three main layers, namely a central public cloud, a private cloud as well as a cloudlets of WBANs.

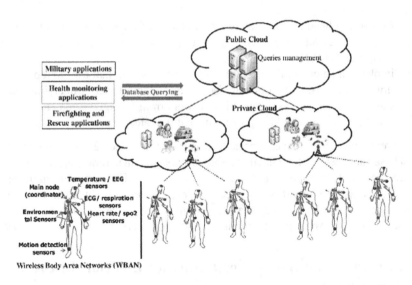

Fig. 1. A cloud-sensor based architecture for epidemic diseases management

The first level defines networks of wearable sensors embedded on mobile individuals in the form of WBAN systems to measure health parameters, motion parameters, and environmental parameters. Every WBAN node should be able to continuously collect vital signs parameters such as body temperature, electrocardiogram (ECG), electromyogram (EMG), oxygen saturation, blood pressure, breathing rate, among other parameters. The environmental sensors aim to measure parameters that may be favorable to epidemic disease propagation such as the ambient temperature and humidity, the water pollution, and the presence of particular types of flora and fauna. Indeed, by monitoring environmental conditions as well as by providing localization information, the wearable healthcare system is able to record the location and the time of disease detection and the related geographical expansion. The WBANs act together in a given monitored area in order to establish a common target of epidemic disease diagnosis. In this context, we consider that the different WBAN nodes in close vicinity of each other are able to form mobile cloudlets. The latter is a new architectural element that emerges from the improvement in mobile communication systems and cloud computing. It represents a fully cloud system capabilities but in small scale in order to bring the cloud capabilities closer to the users [13]. Any WBAN node in the cloudlet domain is in charge of collecting disease-related data.

The second level defines a private storage system of a given healthcare institution that is in charge of monitoring and tracking patients' health statuses as well as epidemics evolution. The private cloud includes the set of WBANs' cloudlets. The geographical proximity of private cloud and WBANs using the set of cloudlets enables a reduced access and communication delays. The private cloud provides a centralized management along with storage points where data collected by different mobile WBANs are stored in order to be processed and queried in real-time manner. In addition, the private cloud stores sensitive and private information, including the patient's profile, the patient's health-related information, the history of medical treatments, the history of special diseases' occurrence and the medical staff information. All this information is useful in order to monitor patients' health status and track epidemic diseases. Real-time measurements must be sent to the destination within a specified deadline; otherwise, the collected information expires and is no longer useful.

Disease management may require the intervention of more than one healthcare organization and in critical cases such as in epidemic detection the intervention of other organizations and safety providers would be needed. To this end, the third layer in the proposed architecture defines a global, centralized and public storage infrastructure where abnormalities and irregular measurements reported by the private clouds are logged to be available for other organizations that are interested in a certain type of data and for further investigation.

2.3   WBANs for Epidemic Diseases Management

To efficiently manage epidemic diseases the following properties should be considered: (a) Every WBAN node acts as a temporary storage system that enables instantaneous monitoring and tracking of patient-related information; (b) The WBAN encompasses heterogeneous sensors in charge of generating priority-based traffic including critical information in form of alerts, real-time information, and normal information; and (c) Every WBAN node is in charge of collecting both, health-related and environmental information. The major objectives of using WBAN systems for epidemic diseases management in rural areas are:

Providing a Communication Platform: the WBAN nodes provide a mobile platform for data collection and processing according to traffic priority. At any given instant, a mobile WBAN user in the rural area can be in one of following scenarios: (i) it is in the communication coverage of a private cloud, then the user can transmit data packets directly to the associated private databases; (ii) it is only in the communication range of another WBAN node, which is directly connected to a private cloud. Then a cloudlet domain may be formed and the WBAN user can transmit data packets to the private databases using multi-hop communication; (iii) it is out-of-coverage where no communication infrastructure is available. In this case, a priority-based communication approach is implemented. If the WBAN node tries to transmit a high priority traffic, the WBANs in its vicinity are solicited to form a mobile cloudlet domain that will be in charge of relaying the generated traffic; otherwise, the WBAN node should delay transmission until one of the previous scenarios becomes available.

Building Epidemic Disease Databases: the proposed architecture will provide a useful support for medical professionals (such as doctors, therapists, and caregivers) as well as governments to manage large-scale epidemics through the fast identification of epidemic's sources, the prediction of its geographical expansion and the number of affected individuals, and the provision of appropriate medical interventions and treatments to moderate future aggravation. The system must provide building multi-databases as a service by invoking autonomous and private clouds to contribute to the collection and monitoring of health parameters.

3   Querying Databases

In contrast to traditional real-time cloud databases querying model, rather than collecting, storing and then analyzing large amount of real-time data, we describe here a novel querying mechanism that allows immediate evaluation of the incoming data before being stored. Managing continuous data streams imposes new requirements on querying approaches to handle the unbounded nature of data streams. Based on the proposed architecture two levels of queries are considered: the Ascendant Queries (AscQ) and the Descendant Queries (DesQ).

3.1   Continuous Query Language

We use the Synchronized SQL (SyncSQL) language as a reference to manage continuous data streams generated by the WBAN nodes. SyncSQL is among the continuous query languages that support stored data and continuous data streams. A continuous query over n tagged streams, $S_1 \ldots S_n$, is semantically equivalent to a materialized view that is defined by an SQL expression over the time-varying relations, $R(S_1) \ldots R(S_n)$. The output of a query can be provided either as a COMPLETE output, where, at any time point, the query issuer has access to a table that represents the complete answer of the query (the output in this case is non-incremental), or as a STREAMED output, where the query issuer receives a tagged stream that represents the deltas (the output in this case supports incremental changes) to the answer. Then, considering SynchSQL semantics, a simple query may be expressed as follows:

$SELECT\text{-}[STREAMED\text{—}COMPLETE]\text{-}<select\text{-}item>\psi$
$FROM\text{-}R(Si)\text{-}$
$[WHERE\text{-}<condition>]\text{-}$

Typically, in healthcare application the arriving streams may comprise private tuples (e.g., personal information of patients). Restricted access to such information can be achieved in SyncSQL by means of views that projects out the private attributes [8]. Based on privileges attributed to user groups multiple views can be defined. SyncSQL implements views as a means for enhancing data privacy.

$CREATE\text{-}[STREAMED]\text{-}view\text{-}<view\text{-}name>\psi as\text{-}$
$SELECT\text{-}<select\text{-}item>\psi$
$FROM\text{-}R(Si)\text{-}$

$[WHERE\text{-}<condition>]\text{-}$

The view is refreshed when either the streaming S_i is updated or Now is changed. This query encompasses a window that is defined by the clause WHERE and that allows to output a relation containing all the items collected by a WBAN node and referenced in the clause SELECT up-to current time Now.

3.2   Descending Queries (DesQ)

Descendant Queries (DesQ) are reading queries that can be completed by the content of a query on a database, but can be also inserted using additional lecture from the cloud or the WBAN nodes. DesQs are, typically, generated after a query sent by a user. When the answer to the received query is not available in the database, the database management system decomposes the global query into a one or several sub-queries, which are sent to appropriate private cloud databases.

The implementation of a query (we specify, precisely, the implementation of queries on real-time video streams) is coordinated by a broker that, after receiving a query, checks the validity of the stored video streams and accordingly generates a query execution plan.

(i) If the required video data is available in the private database and is recent enough to reply the query within its response delay, Timestamp + maxvalid > timequery, then the query may be implemented locally in the public databases and the requested information is sent back to the user. The maximum validity (maxvalid) of a real-time video streaming should be short enough to guarantee the freshness and validity of its content. Such a query can be answered in SyncSQL by maintaining a COMPLETE (not STREAMED) query that contains the videos that are currently available in the database as follows.

$SELECT\text{-}[COMPLETE]\!<\!video\clubsuit segment\!-\!value\!>\!\psi$

$FROM\text{-}R(S_i)\text{-}$
$[WHERE\!<\!condition\!>]\text{-}$

We consider that a query on a stored video may specifies videos, segments of videos, or values of variables related to the environment where the video was filmed. A video is retrieved from a WBAN node, a segment from a video, and a value may be deduced from a segment. The clause WHERE may specify temporal, spatial, spatio-temporal, and application query conditions.

(ii) If the requested video content is not available or it does not satisfy the temporal and validity requirements, then the broker should send the query to the nearest cloudlets (which normally provides fresher data than those stored in the private database) that execute similar processes. If the video is not available, each cloudlet targeted by the user query solicits its affiliated WBAN nodes to collect live video streams for more detailed views of the monitored phenomenon, if any.

3.3   Ascending Queries (AscQ)

The Ascendant queries (AscQ) are generated by the WBAN nodes to implement write and read transactions on the private cloud databases. In addition, they are useful to provide cooperative answer among aggregated actors of the cloud-sensor based system. Ascending data stream collection is, generally, triggered by an event occurrence and alerts generated by a WBAN user. TinyDB is a distributed query processor for smart sensor devices that supports events as a mechanism for initiating real-time data collection using ON EVENT clause. Every time an event occurs, the query is issued from the detecting node and the required parameters are collected from nearby WBAN nodes [13]. In this context we propose a new language that integrates, both TinyDB and SyncSQL languages to provide a uniform ascendant query. The latter may be expressed by:

ON-EVENT-event-detection-():-
SELECT-[STREAMED|COMPLETE]<select-item>ψ

FROM-R(Si)-

[WHERE-<condition>]-

The AscQ queries can be also executed to read from the private cloud databases and to request on-demand services. For example, if the WBAN user is unable to move to a hospital in case of emergency, it can request the cloud to look for a doctor in its entourage. In this case, we consider that medical staff, in rural areas, including doctors, nurses, and other health providers should be equipped with a WBAN system to enable additional medical measurements and enhanced communication supports.

4   Case Study

In this section, we propose a cloud-sensor based network to continuously manage the evolution of a specific epidemic. In particular, to validate the effectiveness of the proposed approach, a detection scenario of Ebola virus disease (EVD) is investigated. The diagnosis of suspected patients begins by monitoring the early symptoms of Ebola, following an incubation period of 2/21 days, including fever, severe headache, shivers, muscle aches, and weakness. With the progression of the disease, suspected patients may develop other additional symptoms such as vomiting, abdominal pain and diarrhea, nausea, difficult breathing, hypovolemic shock, pharyngitis, conjunctivitis, to dysfunction organs, and bleeding. The terminal phase of this disease is the death. Accordingly, we propose a scenario where patients and medical personnel equipped with WBANs are moving in a large scale area. This area is divided into adjacent sub-areas. Each is supervised by at least one cloud or one WBAN. Two types of WBAN systems are considered. The Patient-WBAN system is embedded on the monitored patients and the Medical-WBAN system is embedded on medical staff. Under these assumptions we describe an active querying approach using successively descending queries and ascending queries. We consider that the Patient-WBANs-Collection and Medical-WBAN-Collection streams are referring to the set of continuous streaming generated by the Patient-WBAN system and Medical-WBANs system, respectively. The corresponding tagged stream and time-varying relation are denoted $WBAN_{MCOL}$ and $R(WBAN_{MCOL})$, respectively.

Case 1. The medical department executes a descending query on the private database that consists to continuously keep tracking of the temperature measurement of all patients in the monitored area that have temperature greater than 38°C. Such a query may be expressed by:

Query-1:-SELECT-*STREAMED*-id<ψtemperatureψ
FROM-$\mathcal{R}$(WBANCOL)Rvψ

WHERE-Rv▷temperatureψ>ψ38-
GROUP-BY-idψ

In this query, the keyword STREAMED indicates that the output includes either insert or update operations for patients that qualify the predicate "R.temperature > 38" and/or delete operations for previously quali_ed patients that disqualify the predicate.

Case 2. As we are dealing with Ebola virus, the medical institution is interested at a given point of time T by monitoring additional vital signs of all patients in the monitored that have temperature greater than 38°C for the last two days. The inputs of such a query are the WBAN id, the temperature level, the sweat level, and the blood saturation.

Query-2:-CREATE-*STREAMED*-view-TwoDaysWindow-as-
SELECT-id,ψtemperature,ψsweat,ψbloodψ
FROM-$\mathcal{R}$(WBANCOL)Rvψ

WHERE-Nowψ↖←-2-<ψRv▷Timestampψ≤←Nowψ
GROUP-BY-idψ
Query-2-1:-SELECT-STREAMED-id<ψtemperature<ψsweat<ψbloo
dψ
FROM-R(*TwoDaysWindow*)Rvψ
WHERE-Rv▷temperatureψ>ψ38-

In this query a sliding window over WBANCOL of size 2 time units (i.e., two days in our case) is created. This sliding window defines a view that, at any point of time, contains all the required information reported between times Now-2 and Now. To report information belonging to patients that qualify the predicate "Rv.temperature > 38", a query 2-1 can be expressed in terms of TwoDaysWindow view.

Case 3. In this case, we generate a cooperative querying approach between the WBAN nodes and the private clouds. To this end, we consider that at a given instant of time, an alert generated by the WBANs generates an ascending query that reports all the information concerning the patient. The generated alert that we call HealthDegradation(temperature, blood) defines the rapid degradation of vital signs (e.g., the temperature and the blood saturation) of the patient in a short period of time.

Query-3-ON-EVENT-Health-Degradation-(temperature,-blood):-
CREATE-*STREAMED*-view-ALERT-as-
SELECT-*-
FROM-$\mathcal{R}$(WBANCOL)Rvψ

Upon receiving this query the healthcare institution, precisely the medical staff, generates a descending query that aims to keep tracking the location of the concerned patient.

Query-3-1:-SELECT-*STREAMED-id‹ψlocation*ψ
FROM-R(*ALERT*)-

ALERT is a view that contains all the information concerning the WBAN node that
detected the event Health-Degradation (temperature, blood). Upon receiving the output
of this query the healthcare institution generates a second descending query that aims
to check the availability of healthcare providers (e.g., doctors or nurse) in the close
vicinity of the patient.

Query-3-2:-SELECT-STREAMED-id,-location,-video-
FROM-R(WBANMCOL)Rv-
WHERE-distance(R.location,-p(id))-¡-dmin-and-R.status-=-0-

Where p(id) returns the location of the WBAN node contained in Query 3-1 and
status is a Boolean parameter that refers to the availability of medical staff (available:
0, not available: 1). This query outputs the id, the location and video from all available
medical staff (status = 0) located at a maximum distance dmin from the patient.

5   Conclusion

In this paper, we investigated the benefits of integrating WBANs and Cloud Computing
to build a Cloud-sensor platform to support medical diagnosis of epidemic diseases
monitoring in rural areas. First, we proposed an architecture that integrates three main
layers, namely distributed WBAN nodes for data collection, private clouds that manage
WBAN collections (e.g., real-time analysis, continuous querying and secure storage)
and a central public cloud that attributes privileges to other groups of users in order to
retrieve disease-related information. The proposed solution tries to optimize epidemic
diseases detection and tracking through the management of alerts generated by WBANs
carried by individuals and belonging to public and private clouds. It also tries to report
on the evolution of particular diseases and implement a query management system
allowing cooperative answers from the aggregated clouds. In our future work we will
evaluate, through simulations, the performance of the proposed approach to ensure
effective and real-time monitoring of epidemic diseases. For this purpose, the following
metrics will be assessed: (i) The effectiveness of the proposed model to generate real-
time alerts and forward them timely in case of epidemics detection; (ii) The effect of
user mobility on responses to queries containing real-time constraints; and (iii) The
impact of the number of the deployed clouds and users per cloud on the quality of service.

References

1. Al-Mulla, M.R., Sepulveda, F., Colley, M.: An autonomous wearable system for predicting
   and detecting localized muscle fatigue. Sensors 11, 1542–1557 (2011)
2. Alamri, A., Ansari, W.S., Hassan, M.M., Hossain, M.S., Alelaiwi, A., Hossain, M.A.: A
   survey on sensor-cloud: architecture, applications, and approaches. Int. J. Distrib. Sens. Netw.
   9, 1–18 (2013)

3. Almashaqbeh, G., Hayajneh, T., Vasilakos, A.V., Mohd, B.J.: Qos-aware health monitoring system using cloud-based wbans. J. Med. Syst. **38**, 121 (2014)

4. Chammem, M., Berrahal, S., Boudriga, N.: Smart navigation for firefighters in hazardous environments: a ban-based approach. In: Proceedings of the 7th International Conference on Pervasive Computing and Application (ICPCA) and the 4th International Symposium of Web Society (SWS), Turkey (2012)

5. Dash, S.K., Sahoo, J.P., Mohapatra, S., Pati, S.P.: Sensorcloud: assimilation of wireless sensor network and the cloud. In: Meghanathan, N., Chaki, N., Nagamalai, D. (eds.) Advances in Computer Science and Information Technology. Networks and Communications, pp. 455–464. Springer, Heidelberg (2012)

6. Fortino, G., Fatta, G.D., Pathan, M., Vasilakos, A.V.: Cloud-assisted body area networks: state-of-the-art and future challenges. Wirel. Netw. **20**(7), 1925–1938 (2014)

7. Fortino, G., Parisi, D., Pirrone, V., Fatta, G.D.: Bodycloud: a SAAS approach for community body sensor networks. Future Gener. Comput. Syst. **35**, 62–79 (2014)

8. Ghanem, T.M., Elmagarmid, A.K., Larson, P.-A., Aref, W.G.: Supporting views in data stream management systems. ACM Trans. Database Syst. (TODS) **35**(1), 1–47 (2010)

9. Hossain, S.M., Muhammad, G.: Cloud-based collaborative media service framework for healthcare. Int. J. Distrib. Sens. Netw. **10**, 11 (2014)

10. Naikodi, C., Philip, B.A., Puneeth, P., Shenoy, P.D., Venugopal, K.R., Patnaik, L.M.: Wsn integrated cloud computing for n-care system (ncs) using middleware services. Int. J. Innov. Technol. Exploring Eng. (IJITEE) **3**(1), 194–208 (2013)

11. Oldstone, M.B.A.: Viruses, Plagues, and History Past, Present and Future. Oxford University Press Inc., Oxford (2009)

12. Dialloa, O., Rodrigues, J.J.P.C., Seneb, M., Niuc, J.: Real-time query processing optimization for cloud-based wireless body area networks. Inf. Sci. **284**, 84–94 (2014)

13. Quwaider, M., Jararweh, Y.: Cloudlet-based effcient data collection in wireless body area networks. Simul. Model. Pract. Theor. **50**, 57–71 (2015)

14. Rolim, C., Koch, F., Westphall, C., Werner, J., Fracalossi, A., Salvador, G.: A cloud computing solution for patient s data collection in health care institutions. In: Proceedings of the Second International Conference one Health, Telemedicine, and Social Medicine. ETELEMED 2010, pp. 95–99, St. Maarten (2010)

15. Schlipkoter, U., Flahault, A.: Communicable diseases: achievements and challenges for public health. Public Health Rev. **32**(1), 90–119 (2010)

16. Wan, J., Ullah, S., Lai, C., Zhou, M., Zou, X.W.C.: Cloud-enabled wireless body area networks for pervasive healthcare. IEEE Netw. **27**, 5 (2013)

Managing Personal Health Records in an Infrastructure-Weak Environment

Nicolas Anciaux[1(✉)], Sébastien Guillotton[2], Luc Bouganim[1],
Sergio Ilarri[3], Alain Kamgang[4], Abraham Ngami[5],
Christophe Nouedoui[4], Philippe Pucheral[6], and Maurice Tchuente[5]

[1] Inria, Rocquencourt, France
nicolas.anciaux@inria.fr
[2] Ensta, Palaiseau, France
[3] University of Zaragoza, Saragossa, Spain
[4] Hospital Central, Yaoundé, Cameroon
[5] University of Yaoundé, Yaoundé, Cameroon
[6] University Versailles Saint-Quentin-en-Yvelines, Versailles, France

Abstract. There are currently more than half a million diabetes cases in Cameroon and the deaths caused by diabetes complications will double before 2030. Diabetes complications mostly occur due to a bad follow-up of patients. In this paper, we propose a new IT architecture for diabetes follow-up and introduce the bases of a new distributed computation protocol for this architecture. Our approach does not require any preexisting support communication infrastructure, can be deployed at low cost, and provides strong privacy and security guarantees. This work envisions an experiment in the field we plan to conduct under the authority of the Cameroonian National Center for Diabetes and Hypertension, with a potential for generalization to other diseases.

1 Introduction

According to the World Health Organization, 347 million people worldwide have diabetes [1]. This is a chronic and incurable disease, for which good treatments do exist. Diabetes is however currently the direct cause of 1.5 million deaths [2] with more than 80 % of deaths in low and middle income countries [5] and deaths caused by diabetes are expected to double before 2030 [4].

Diabetes follow-up plays an important role to orchestrate the treatments, which are indeed a combination of insulin drugs, appropriate and healthy diet, regular physical activities, and patient monitoring. An incorrect follow-up of patients may cause hyperglycemia, which over time would provoke an alteration of the nerves and blood vessels with many bad effects on the body. These diabetes complications might cause severe problems like hypertension, blindness, feet problems leading to amputations, kidneys failure, and myocardial or heart stroke with significant morbidity. Fortunately, they can be avoided if there is a good follow-up of diabetes patients. Our discussions with doctors from the *Cameroonian National Center for Diabetes and Hypertension* (NCDH) have led to three main requirements to improve patients follow-up: (1) Patients should own a Personal Health Record (PHR) and make it available to the

© ICST Institute for Computer Sciences, Social Informatics and Telecommunications Engineering 2016
R. Glitho et al. (Eds.): AFRICOMM 2015, LNICST 171, pp. 178–191, 2016.
DOI: 10.1007/978-3-319-43696-8_18

practitioners at the time of the consultation; (2) global statistics on populations of patients should be computed easily for a better understanding of diabetes evolution, its complications and co-morbidities, in order to adapt prevention actions and treatments to local populations; and (3) a synthetic view of the PHR of each patient could be maintained on a server in the different services or hospitals. We concentrate in this paper on the first two points and let the third one for future work. It should be noted that the benefit of a PHR even goes beyond the case of diabetes [9].

The use of e-services is unavoidable to reach such objectives, as exposed by Pr. Walinjom Muna from NCDH [8]. However, providing any IT solution for developing countries has to face a specific set of requirements, mainly linked to the inherent lack of a reliable infrastructure, weakness in the commercial and industrial environment, and the limited financial resources of governments.

Two main approaches have been envisioned to provide data services (such as health related data services) in developing countries. The first one is to provide a global and reliable electronic health record infrastructure. It usually requires huge financial investments, transversal agreements between the legislator, government, commercial partners and health practitioners. Besides, it faces problems related to network connectivity and coverage, central system architecture, administration and maintenance costs, unified data models and norms, security procedure and trusted authorities, legal and ethical frameworks, authentication and unique identification numbers for patients, etc. Representative initiatives of this approach include Google "Loon for All" and Facebook "Internet.org" projects. The focus of these initiatives is on improving network connectivity, by means of high altitude balloons or drones that act as gateways to the Internet. These projects are amazing and aim at bridging inherent lacks of developing countries, but they face difficult technological issues (e.g., Google solar helium balloons can only fly for a few days) and merely address a single dimension of the problem (network connectivity), ignoring other issues that need to be overcome to support reliable data-oriented services. Building a complete EHR following this approach can thus be considered as long-term initiative, with uncertain outcomes. The second approach for providing data services in developing countries consists in using existing infrastructure, whatever weak, with the target to quickly and practically offer working solutions to specific problems. Representative of this approach are solutions based on the use of phones and text messages to address specific issues, like keeping track of vaccine cold chains [12] or reminding medical appointments to patients. Many mHealth applications are envisioned on such basis [7]. As another example, we can indicate the existence of applications that connect patients and health counselors to help improve habits that may reduce the impact of a given disease [13]. However, while the advantages may be achievable in the short term, such proposals usually focus on specific scenarios and cannot be generalized to a broader scope of data-driven applications.

Motivated by the aforementioned shortcomings, we try here to bridge the gap between the two approaches (at least partially). We have recently proposed the vision of Folk-IS (Folk-enabled Information System) [14, 15], a new generic information system suited to provide generic data-oriented services. This proposal matches three requirements identified with NGOs (non-governmental organizations), which must be met by any practical ICT solution: (1) **Self-sufficiency**: the solution must not rely on any quick improvement of the existing software and hardware infrastructure but should benefit from it; (2) **Low cost**: very low initial investment, deployment and maintenance costs are assumed, the usual scale being a few dollars per user; and (3) **Privacy-by-design**: security and privacy are major prerequisites due to the lack of a global IT security infrastructure, secured servers, trusted authorities, and legal frameworks, leading to a self-enforcement in IT of citizens' privacy principles. The system would thus be based on some hypotheses made in the second approach mentioned above (exploiting the existing infrastructure), but with a wider potential in terms of application scope.

Folk-IS builds upon the emergence of very low-cost and highly-secure devices, and uses people moves to transparently and opportunistically perform data management tasks, so that IT services are truly delivered by all the folks (thus the acronym Folk-IS). The system raises new research challenges exposed in [14, 15] linked to the support of various architectural settings and personal devices, diverse data models, and heterogeneous, open and distributed infrastructures. In this paper, we instantiate the Folk-IS vision to provide PHRs, and turn Folk-IS into reality in the context of diabetes follow-up programs. Our contributions concentrate on (i) the design of an architecture which satisfies the use case without assuming any preexisting communication infrastructure, with strong privacy guarantees for the patients and at very low and incremental deployment costs; and (ii) new algorithms to enable the computation of global statistics on populations of patients with strong privacy and security guarantees.

The rest of this paper is organized as follows. Section 2 presents the diabetes follow-up use case. Section 3 proposes an architecture for diabetes follow-up based on PHRs, using the principles proposed in the Folk-IS vision. Section 4 investigates global computations with strong privacy and security guarantees. Section 5 concludes the paper.

2 Diabetes Follow-up Use Case

In Cameroon, more than 30.000 diabetic patients are followed by the *Cameroonian National Center for Diabetes and Hypertension* (NCDH). The current follow-up is based on paper folders. A first folder (*hospital folder*) is kept by the hospital and contains a summary of the most important information about the patient: personal attributes, treatments, and the results of the main medical examinations. A second folder (*patient folder*) is kept by the patient and contains his/her complete medical history. The patient provides it to the practitioner at the time of a consultation.

In practice, practitioners fill in the patient folder, which is the most complete one, and summarize some information in the hospital folder. Doctors also conduct epidemiological studies, by reporting data from the patient folder into the hospital folder during the consultation, such that after a given time period (e.g., one month), these data can be aggregated. These statistical studies are crucial for a good diabetes follow-up, because many important variables for the treatments depend on the location and the population's habits.

Some problems reduce the efficiency of the follow-up. First, the hospital folder may not be available during the consultation. Indeed, the hospital folder is sometimes kept by another service of the hospital, or remains at the archives department when the consultation has not been anticipated. Second, patients may lose their folders, and no backup is available. Third, statistics are difficult to compute since only a small subset of practitioners are involved in the collection of the data to perform a given statistics. To improve the follow-up at a low cost, we propose to replace the second folder by an electronic PHR held on a personal and secure portable IT device. In this way, the practitioners would have an easy access to the synthesis (equivalent to the hospital folder) from the patient folder even when the hospital folder is not available, and this synthesis may be synchronized on a server available in the hospital services (e.g., cardiology, ophthalmology, etc.) or other hospitals the patient visits. Moreover, the medical history would be searchable and more easily browsed. To avoid potential loss of data, the medical folders would be (securely) backed up and recovered if needed. And finally, a protocol would enable a convenient automatic computation of global statistics on many more patients (typically, all the patients visiting one or several hospitals in a given time frame) without hurting the privacy and security level of the system.

3 A Secure and Low Cost Architecture for Diabetes Follow-up

Our target is to reach the above objectives without relying on an existing infrastructure. Therefore, we use here the Folk-IS paradigm [14], which builds upon personal and secure devices currently emerging under different names and shapes (e.g., smart USB keys, secure SD cards, smart tokens, etc.). We term these devices *Folk-nodes*. From a hardware point of view, a folk-node is assumed to provide: (1) enough stable storage to host the complete medical history of its holder, (2) enough computing resources to securely run a server managing the data and enforce access control rules locally, (3) a tamper-resistant smart card to hold secrets (e.g., cryptographic material, certificates, passwords), (4) a biometric sensor (e.g., fingerprint reader) to ease the authentication of users, and (5) input/output capabilities (e.g., USB connector, and/or a wireless communication module) to interact with external devices (e.g., computers, smart phones, tablets, etc.).

The token pictured in Fig. 1 (left) is called *PlugDB* (see https://project.inria.fr/plugdb/en/) and is representative of what a folk-node can be. Inria provides it in open hardware, such that any electronic manufacturer can build it. When ordered in small quantities, its cost is around 60€. This is of the order of the average cost of one month of treatment for diabetes patients in Cameroun [6]. To further reduce this cost without jeopardizing the functionalities and privacy level, we propose to share the most expensive hardware components by integrating them on *Docking stations*. Docking stations would thus be required wherever the patient's PHR must be used. Typically, they could be placed in the consulting rooms, in the hospital hall, and at the registration desk of the hospital or service. Technically, building docking stations is easy since they simply integrate a subset of the hardware components of a folk-node, a USB slot, and a power outlet.

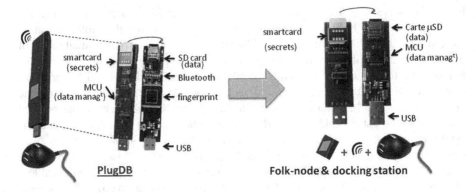

Fig. 1. Folk-nodes.

The wireless communication module and the fingerprint sensor are the two most expensive components of PlugDB. They can be integrated on shared docking stations as shown in Fig. 1 (right), thus reducing the price of the folk-node by an important factor (we estimate it at around 2 according to recent interactions with different manufacturers). Whenever a communication module is integrated on the docking station, the patients can plug their folk-node into the USB slot of the docking station to interact wirelessly with any practitioner device.

The fingerprint sensor is more difficult to share in the general case without reducing the security guarantees. Nevertheless, in a medical scenario, the system must only prevent folk-nodes from being used by somebody else than the patient owning it. To support these functionalities, the "fingerprint minutiae" of the patient and the code confronting the sensed fingerprint with these minutiae can be embedded in the patient's folk-node. The fingerprint sensor can thus be shared without lowering security, since it does neither store patients' minutiae nor the comparison algorithm resulting in unlocking the folder. Remark that we have also placed Flash memory sticks on the docking stations to be able to store (encrypted) data, e.g., intermediate results used while computing statistics, backup information, etc.

The overall architecture that we propose is pictured in Fig. 2. Each patient is equipped with a folk-node which contains his/her personal health record. Docking stations may be situated in the consultation rooms, at the registration desk and in the hospital hall. For simplicity, a local WiFi hotspot, which does not need to be connected to the Internet, is used to synchronize the data stored among the docking stations, to provide backup and global computations services (and potentially other distributed data services). Note that alternatively, opportunistic data exchanges could also be exploited (see [15] for details), but these techniques are not further considered here. Professionals can interact with the folk-nodes using a computer or their own personal device (smart phone or tablet), as advocated by BYOD (Bring Your Own Device) initiatives [10].

From the functional point of view, the patient first personalizes the folk-node at the first connection: a cryptographic public/private key pair is derived by the folk-node from a passphrase provided by the patient and his/her fingerprint is enrolled. At the time of the consultation, the patient unlocks her folk-node by using her finger, and the practitioner accesses the health record and may append new information. Any data inserted into the folk-node is also stored encrypted on the docking stations to generate an archive, and a synthesis view of this information can be synchronized on a hospital server if available. This will ensure the persistence of the data even if the folk-node experiences any problem. Thus, any lost folk-node could be restored from a blank (i.e., empty) folk-node, using the personal passphrase of the patient to regenerate the keys and access the backup information from any docking station. Similarly, patients who forgot their folk-node when coming to the hospital may borrow a blank folk-node at the registration desk, recover their folder from any docking station, and consult the practitioner using the borrowed folk-node. Any new data appended to the folder during the consultation will be integrated in the backup. The borrowed folk-node could then be reset after the consultation, since the new data will be integrated within the (forgotten) patient's folk-node at the next visit.

The backup and recovery mechanisms are not further described in this paper, but the reader can see [15] for information. Similarly, the embedded data management engine in charge of storing, indexing, querying and authenticating users on folk-nodes is out of the scope of this work; for more details, we refer the reader to two recent studies presenting an embedded relational database system [16] and a search engine designed for smart objects [17]. These proposals have been validated by a demonstration [18] and by an experiment in the field involving 40 patients and 80 medical-social professionals (see https://project.inria.fr/plugdb/category/medical/). The kernel of an embedded data management engine integrating these different proposals and a data recovery protocol based on the use of (encrypted) external storage will be provided as open source by Inria.

4   Distributed Computations

In this section, we investigate the problem of computing global statistics with strong privacy and security guarantees. We only concentrate on the computation of simple statistics (like average, sum, count, min, and max), and leave more complex computations for future work. We first introduce a basic algorithm without taking security into account. We then discuss techniques to enforce the security and privacy and propose an algorithm matching these requirements.

We describe the problem as follows. Some people are able to issue queries and are called *queriers* (e.g., practitioners, PhD students, researchers conducting an epidemiological study, etc.). They are equipped with personal devices (e.g., a smartphone or tablet). In several medical centers or hospital services, we deploy a set of docking stations. The set of docking stations deployed in the same hospital service can communicate synchronously using a WiFi spot. Each set of docking stations is called a *query spot*. Several *query spots* can be settled. We do not assume that all the queriers' personal devices and all the *query spots* can be accessible from the Internet, but we benefit from such Internet links when they exist. We propose to compute each query in three steps as follows:

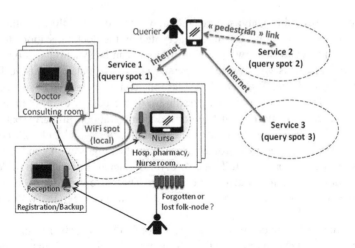

Fig. 2. Diabetes follow-up architecture.

1. First, the query is defined by a *querier*, and is transmitted to a single docking station of each *query spot*. The query can be either transmitted through the Internet if available, or by physically entering in the wireless communication scope of a given docking station of each of the *query spots* with the querier device using WiFi (or Bluetooth). The query is then automatically propagated to the other docking stations of the *query spot*.

2. Then, the folk-nodes connecting to a docking station in a given query spot will successively contribute to the running queries by enriching the intermediate results stored on the docking station. Docking stations act as transit points for intermediate results, processed and enriched successively by the participating folk-nodes. A given intermediate result on a docking station, when it aggregates enough contributions, is transmitted to all the docking stations of the query spot, and will not be modified anymore. By transmitting the results to all the docking stations instead of choosing only one, the querier does not need to connect to a specific docking station to retrieve the results.

3. Finally, the querier collects all the intermediate results available on each query spot by physically accessing a given docking station in each query spot, and merges together all the intermediate results to obtain the query result. If a sufficient number of contributions have been integrated into that result, the query can terminate, and all data related to that query are removed from the docking stations in the query spots.

The implementation of the first and third steps is simple and are thus not described in more detail. The second step deserves more explanation and a first (unsecure) implementation is given in Algorithm 1, considering the example of an average computation (other computations like sum, min and max can be deduced easily in a similar way). We assume in the algorithm that each query posted by a querier during step 1 generated an initial intermediate result that is set at 0 propagated to all the docking stations of the query spot. Then step 2 can be implemented as follows. When a folk-node connects to the docking station, the algorithm identifies the intermediate results the folk-node is eligible to contribute to, and updates the corresponding intermediate results by integrating its own contribution. Being "eligible" means that (the data of) the patient data does match the *scope of the query* (i.e., the specific query constraints that restrict which values will be considered to compute the required aggregation) and that the folk-node has not contributed to that query yet. When the folk-node contributes to an intermediate result, the number of contributions for that result is incremented by one. When the number of contributors reaches a given threshold, the folk-node transmits the intermediate result to all the other docking stations of the query spot.

Algorithm 1.   Average query computation (launched when the folk-node connects to a docking station)

Input:

Q a set of tuples $\{ < id, id_q, s_q, v_q, n_q > \}$ describing the intermediate results of the queries, with id the identifier of the intermediate result, id_q a query identifier, s_q the scope of the query, v_q an intermediate result and n_q the number of contributors to this intermediate result;

D a set of personal values $\{d\}$ belonging to a certain patient;

P a set of query identifiers for which the folk-node has already contributed;

/* Note: Q is stored on the docking station, D and P are stored in the folk-node */

Output: $\emptyset$.

1. **while** $\exists\, q \in Q,\ id_q \notin P$ **do** /* *while the folk-node is eligible to a query q* */
2. $Q_r = \{\, r \in Q, r.id_q = q.id_q,\ r.n_q < threshold\,\}$;
3.   /* *Qr the set of tuples below the threshold for this query* */
4. $v = 0$; /* *initialize the intermediate result value at 0* */
5. $n = 0$; /* *initialize the number of contrib. to the intermediate result at 0* */
6.   **for each** $r \in Q_r$ **do** /* *for each interm. res. to be processed* */
7. $v = (\, r.v_q * r.n_q + v * n\,)\, /\, (r.n_q + n\,)$; /* *aggr. the interm. res. values* */
8. $n = r.n_q + n$; /* *increment the number of contributions* */
9.   Delete the tuple with $id{=}r.id$ from the docking stations in the query spot;
10.   **endfor**;
11.   **if** $q.id_q \notin P,\ \exists\, d{\in}D,\ s_q(d) = true$ **then** /* *if the folk-node must contribute* */
12. $v = v * n + d$; /* *add the adequate contribution d to the intermediate result* */
13. $n {+\!+}$; /* *increment the number of contribution by 1* */
14.   **endif**;
15. $id = $ generate_id( ); /* *generate an id for the interm. result with the help of the docking station* */
16.   Delete the tuples in Q_r from the docking stations of the query spot;
17.   Insert $< id, q.id_q, q.s_q, v, n >$ on the docking station;
18. $P = P \cup \{q.id_q\}$; /* *add the query to the set of queries the folk-node has already contributed* */
19. **endwhile**;

4.1   Ensuring Privacy and Security

The privacy and security of the patients' data must be guaranteed. First, to prevent from snooping intermediate results on the docking stations, which may lead to reveal individual contributions, we must encrypt the intermediate results. The tamper resistance smartcard embedded in each folk-node can be used to store the encryption key. A simple solution would be to distribute a shared secret key in each folk-node (stored in the tamper resistant smartcard and never exposed outside) and add an encryption/decryption operation in Algorithm 1 when the folk-nodes write/read intermediate results on/from the docking stations. However, although the smartcards exhibit a high level of tamper resistance [11], it is not possible in practice to totally prevent from any tampering against opponents that would be sufficiently motivated and equipped. In practice, if all the folk-nodes hold the same secret key, an attack targeting a single folk-node would potentially compromise all the successive intermediate results and all the individual contributions. To maximize privacy and security, two main conditions must be met: (condition 1) each folk-node must hold a unique private key, and (condition 2) the algorithm must lead each folk-node to be able to decrypt very few intermediate results. These two conditions are required to prevent from data snooping and ensure that attacking a single patient folk-node would only compromise a very small portion of the data, leading to a very low ratio between the cost of the attack (tampering into a smartcard is highly difficult and expensive) and its benefit (few intermediate results are revealed).

To satisfy the first condition, we consider that each folk-node holds a unique private/public key pair. To adapt our algorithms to the second condition, (i) we make the assumption that it is possible to know with a good probability the next folk-nodes which will connect to the docking stations in a query spot, and (ii) we design the algorithm in such a way that the querier cannot obtain intermediate results before a sufficient number of contributions (above a threshold) are aggregated, and (iii) we involve each contributing folk-nodes in the computations evenly, each one processing only a few intermediate results when connected to a docking station. Of course, the challenge is to adapt the algorithm without reducing the efficiency, i.e., the number of patients' folk-nodes which effectively contribute to a query within a given time frame. We show below that Algorithms 1 and 2 are comparable in terms efficiency (in number terms of the number of integrated contributions during a given time frame). A privacy-by-design and secure implementation of three steps of the computation algorithm presented above can be obtained as follows:

1. The querier generates a unique public/private key pair for each query, and posts the public part of the key on the docking stations along with the query.
2. Each folk-node is endowed with a unique public/private key pair, and provides its public key at the reception desk (one per query spot) which is inserted in an agenda and published on all the docking stations of the query spot. When a folk-node f_i connects to a docking station, among the intermediate results generated by previous folk-nodes f_j (different from f_i), a very small subset can be decrypted by f_i. If f_i can process intermediate results of a same query, it merges them into a single intermediate result, and if it is eligible to the query it integrates its own contribution into the intermediate result. If f_i is eligible to queries for which there is no intermediate result it can decrypt, it generates a new intermediate result containing only its own value. All the intermediate results decrypted by f_i are deleted from the docking stations of the query spot. All the intermediate results produced by f_i are encrypted with the public key of another waiting folk-node chosen in the agenda or with the encryption key of the querier if the number of contributions is above a threshold, and are send to all the docking stations in the query spot.
3. The querier collects the intermediate results produced in query spot by accessing a single docking station of the query spot (through the Internet, if available), decrypts them with its private key (only those results reaching a sufficient number of

contributions are accessible to the querier) and merges these intermediate results to obtain the query result. If a sufficient number of contributions have been integrated into the result, the query can be terminated, and all information related to this query is removed from the docking stations.

We show in Algorithms 2 an implementation of the step 2, respecting the security conditions listed above. Step 1 and 3 are not further detailed, due to space constraints. Notice that only the value v_q of each tuple needs to be encrypted, as the rest of elements in the tuple are not considered to be sensitive.

We discuss here some details of Algorithm 2. First, note that if the agenda can be assumed as exactly reflecting the order in which the folk-nodes will connect to the docking stations, the intermediate result produced by a folk-node connected to a docking station could be encrypted with the public key of the longest waiting folk-node in the waiting room, which is the first one in the agenda (i.e., in line 16 of Algorithm 2, we could set $dest = 0$, leading to choose $A[0]$ to encrypt the intermediate results). But in practice, this hypothesis does not hold since the patients do not all wait the same time before their consultation, depending on the type of care they need (e.g., a patient waiting for an injection performed by a nurse may be treated before another patient waiting for its consultation with a doctor, although he/she was registered after by the reception desk, and thus appears after in the agenda). In that case, choosing $dest = 0$ would lead the patients waiting the more to process more intermediate results, leading to hurt the condition 2 expressed above. To solve the problem, and evenly distribute the processing of intermediate results by the folk-nodes, we introduce in line 16 of the algorithm some randomness in the choice of the public key in the agenda used to encrypt the produced results. A second remark is that there is no need to lock the tuples accessed by the folk-node (Q_r accessed in line 3 of Algorithm 2) because these tuples can only be updated by the unique folk-node owning the appropriate private key to decrypt them. Third, at the end of the day, some intermediate results integrating a number of contributions below the threshold may be lost since the agenda is empty (the patients coming the next day may not be known yet). This is however not considered as a big issue, since simple solutions can be proposed. For example, some time before the end of the day, we may stop releasing intermediate results to the querier when the threshold is reached, but instead continue to integrate new values in these results. As a consequence, the values produced at the end of the day would not be lost but integrated into existing intermediate results above the threshold, leading to lose fewer contributions.

Algorithm 2.   Secure average query computation (lauched on the folk-nodes)

Input:

Q a set of tuples $\{<id, id_q, s_q, v_q, K, K_{querier}, n_q>\}$ describing intermediate results of queries, with id the identifier of the intermediate result, id_q the query identifier, s_q the scope of the query, v_q an encrypted intermediate result, K the public key of a folk-node used to encrypt the intermediate result v_q, $K_{querier}$ the public key of the querier and n_q the number of contributions integrated to this intermediate result;

D a set of personal values $\{d\}$ where d belongs to the scope of the query q if $s_q(d) = true$;

P a set of query identifiers for which the folk-node has already contributed;

K_{pub} and K_{priv} are the public and private keys of the folk-node;

nb_active_ds the number of active docking stations in the query spot;

A an agenda with the public keys $[K_{next}]^+$ of the folk-nodes waiting for a consultation, ordered by registration date (a[0] has the oldest date, attributed to the folk node waiting for the longest);

/* Note: Q and A are stored on the docking station; $D, P, K_{pub}, K_{priv}, A$ are stored in the folk-node */

Output: $\varnothing$.

1.	*Remove the entry containing K_{pub} from the agenda A;*
2.	**while** $\exists\, q \in Q, q.K = K_{pub}$ or $q.id_q \notin P$ **do** /* *while the folk-node has to process intermediate results* */
3.	$Q_r = \{\, r \in Q, r.id_q = q.id_q, r.K = K_{pub}\,\}$; /* *$Q_r$ the tuples to be processed* */
4.	$v = 0$; /* *initialize the intermediate result value at 0* */
5.	$n = 0$; /* *initialize the nb of contributions to the intermediate result at 0* */
6.	**for each** $r \in Q_r$ **do** /* *for each interm. res. to be processed* */
7.	$v = (\,\text{Decrypt}_{Kpriv}(r.v_q) * r.n_q + v * n\,) / (\,r.n_q + n\,)$; /* *aggr. the intermediate result values* */
8.	$n = r.n_q + n$; /* *increment the number of contributions* */
9.	Delete the tuple with $id=r.id$ from the docking stations in the query spot;
10.	**endfor;**
11.	**if** $q.id_q \notin P$, $\exists\, d \in D$, $s_q(d) = true$ **then** /* *if the folk-node must contribute* */
12.	$v = v * n + d$; /* *add its contribution d to the intermediate result* */
13.	n ++; /* *increment the number of contribution by 1* */
14.	**endif;**
15.	**if** $n < threshold$ **then** /* *if the nb of contributions is below the threshold* */
16.	$dest = \text{rand\_int}(nb\_active\_ds)$; /* *choose at random an entry between 0 and nb_active_ds* */
17.	$K_{dest} = A[dest]$; /* *read in A the corresponding public key* */
18.	**else** /* *the number of contribution has reached the threshold* */
19.	$K_{dest} = K_{querier}$; /* *choose the public key of the querier* */
20.	**endif;**
21.	$v = \text{Encrypt}_{Kdest}(v)$; /* *encrypt the interm. result with the public key K_{dest}* */
22.	$id = \text{generate\_id}()$; /* *generate an id for the interm. res. with the help of the docking station* */
23.	Insert $< id, q.id_q, q.s_q, K_{dest}, q.K_{querier}, n >$ into the DS of the query spot;
24.	$P = P \cup \{q.id_q\}$; /* *add the query to the set P of query the folk-nodes has contributed to* */
25.	**endwhile;**

4.2   Sample Scenario

To give a rough estimate of the validity of the algorithm, we have implemented a simple simulation set up with representative parameters form the Cameroonian National Center for Diabetes and Hypertension in Yaoundé. We consider a single query spot, with an average of *10* practitioners, nurses and medical assistants available to treat the patients, using *10* docking stations, an additional docking station used at the reception desk to generate the agenda, and around 500 patient's visits per day.

Figure 3 shows the number of contributions being aggregated into the intermediate results for a query and made accessible to the querier along the day. In the X-axis, we plot the number of patients connecting successively along the day (from 1 to 500), and in the Y-axis we give the number of contributions to the query. The reference curve (called *contributions*) gives the total number of contributions made by the patients (one

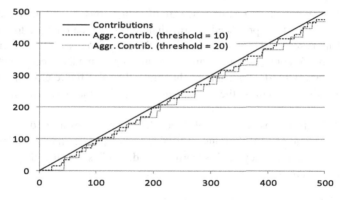

Fig. 3. Number of contributions available to the querier along time.

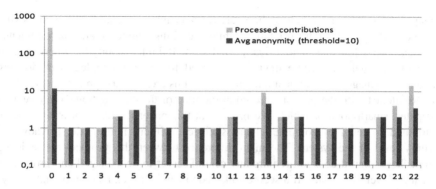

Fig. 4. Number of contributions processed by each participant and anonymity.

contribution per patient). The two dashed curves show the number of contributions integrated in the intermediate results released to the querier with a threshold at 10 and at 20. We conclude that a very small number of contributions escape from the intermediate results (limited to the contributions collected at the end of the day). Note that the third optimization proposed above could solve this problem.

Figure 4 shows the number of contributions that are exposed to the different actors taking part into the computation. In the X-axis, we plot the identifier of the querier (number *0*) and the folk-nodes of the patients successively connecting to the docking stations (for the sake of clarity, only the first 25 interactions are represented, numbered from *1* to *25*, but the data is representative for the next interactions). In the Y-axis, we plot the number of processed contributions (clear grey bar) and their level of anonymity (dark grey bar). A certain number of contributions has been integrated in the intermediate results each folk-node process, and we use the average number of contributions already aggregated in the intermediate result as an anonymity value (the higher the number of aggregated values, the more anonymous the value of each contributor). For example, folk-node *13* aggregates the value of two intermediate results which was obtained by aggregating 8 values, leading to an average anonymity of *4*. Folk-node *22* aggregates four intermediate results made of *14* values thus having an average anonymity of *3.5* (note that the produced intermediate result can be released to the querier, as the threshold is set at *10* in this scenario). At the end of the day, the querier (number *0*) has access to *476* contributions, aggregated into *42* intermediate results with at least a level of anonymity of *10* (the value of the threshold). The figure also shows that the algorithm evenly distributes the processing over all the participating patients' folk-nodes.

We conclude from this section that Algorithm 2 prefigures a good practical solution, with a high rate of contributions accessible to the querier and an implementation which exhibits good privacy and security "by-design" since the three conditions introduced above are well respected.

5   Conclusion and Future Work

This paper proposes a concrete architecture for managing personal health records with a potentially weak infrastructure, while fulfilling three main requirements: self-sufficiency, low cost and privacy-by-design. It builds upon the emergence of low-cost personal and secure devices, so called folk-nodes, coupled with docking stations, to manage personal health records. With this architecture, practitioners will be able to interact with the patient's record at the time of the consultation from a regular computer, smartphone or tablet. We provide in this paper the bases of a new secure distributed protocol to compute global statistics, without hurting the privacy and security level of the system. The main difference between this protocol and existing approaches is that it does not require any central server to be managed and provides a very high level of security. If a secure folk-node is broken (i.e., its cryptographic keys are released), very few amounts of data and intermediate results are compromised. As future work, we plan to precisely evaluate the accuracy and level of privacy of the protocol, and adapt it to support more complex statistics.

Acknowledgement. This work was partially done in the CICYT Project TIN2013-46238-C4-4-R and DGA-FSE.

References

1. Global status report on noncommunicable diseases 2014. Geneva, World Health Organization (2012)
2. International Diabetes Federation. IDF Diabetes Atlas update poster, 6th ed. Brussels (2014)
3. Global Health Estimates: Deaths by Cause, Age, Sex and Country, 2000-2012. Geneva, World Health Organization (2014)
4. Mathers, C.D., Loncar, D.: Projections of global mortality and burden of disease from 2002 to 2030. PLoS Med 3(11), e442 (2006)
5. Liu, L., Yin, X., Morrissey, S.: Global variability in diabetes mellitus and its association with body weight and primary healthcare support in 49 low and middle-income countries. Diabet. Med. 29(8), 995–1002 (2012)

6. Ngassam, E., Nguewa, J.-L., Ongnessek, S., Foutko, A., Mendane, F., Balla, V., Limen, S., Orr-Walker, B., Sobogwi, E., Mbanya, J.-C.: P318. Coût de la prise en charge du diabète de type 2 a l'Hopital central de yaounde. Diabet. Metab. **38**, A105 (2012)
7. Aranda-Jan, C.B., Mohutsiwa-Dibe, N., Loukanova, S.: Systematic review on what works, what does not work and why of implementation of mobile health projects in Africa. BMC Public Health **14**(1), 188 (2014)
8. Muna, W.F.: Comprehensive strategies for the prevention and control of diabetes and cardiovascular diseases in Africa: future directions. Prog. Cardiovasc. Dis. **56**(3), 363–366 (2013)
9. Kyazze, M., Wesson, J., Naude, K.: The design and implementation of a ubiquitous personal health record system for South Africa. Stud. Health Technol. Inform. **206**, 29 (2014)
10. Morrow, B.: BYOD security challenges: control and protect your most sensitive data. Netw. Secur. **2012**(12), 5–8 (2012)
11. Ravi, S., Raghunathan, A., Chakradhar, S.: Tamper resistance mechanisms for secure embedded systems. In: VLSI Design (2004)
12. Chaudhri, R., Borriello, G., Anderson, R.J.: Monitoring vaccine cold chains in developing countries. IEEE PerCom **11**(3), 26–33 (2012)
13. Mamykina, L., Mynatt, E., Davidson, P., Greenblatt, D.: MAHI: investigation of social scaffolding for reflective thinking in diabetes management. In: ACM SIGCHI (CHI 2008), pp. 477–486 (2008)
14. Anciaux, N., Bouganim, L., Delot, T., Ilarri, S., Kloul, L., Mitton, N., Pucheral, P.: Folk-IS: opportunistic data services in least developed countries. PVLDB **7**(5), 425–428 (2014)
15. Anciaux, N., Bouganim, L., Delot, T., Ilarri, S., Kloul, L., Mitton, N., Pucheral, P.: Opportunistic data services in least developed countries: benefits, challenges and feasibility issues. SIGMOD Rec. **43**(1), 52–63 (2014)
16. Anciaux, N., Bouganim, L., Pucheral, P., Guo, Y., Le Folgoc, L., Yin, S.: MILo-DB: a personal, secure and portable database machine. Distrib. Parallel Databases **32**(1), 37–63 (2014)
17. Anciaux, N., Lallali, S., Popa, I.S., Pucheral, P.: A scalable search engine for mass storage smart objects. PVLDB **8**(9), 1–13 (2015)
18. Lallali, S., Anciaux, N., Popa, I.S., Pucheral, P.: A secure search engine for the personal cloud. In: ACM SIGMOD, pp. 1445–1450 (2015)

Simulated Annealing Approach for Mesh Router Placement in Rural Wireless Mesh Networks

Jean Louis Fendji Kedieng Ebongue[1(✉)], Christopher Thron[2],
and Jean Michel Nlong[1]

[1] Computer Science, University of Ngaoundéré, Ngaoundéré, Cameroon
{jlfendji, jmnlong}@univ-ndere.cm
[2] Texas A&M University Central Texas, Killeen, USA
thron@tamuct.edu

Abstract. A critical issue in the planning of Wireless Mesh Networks is the determination of the optimal number and location of mesh router nodes. In this paper, we consider a network model in which the area to cover is decomposed into a set of elementary areas which may be covered; where a node may be placed; and which may be an obstacle for the connectivity. The aim is therefore to determine an optimal number and the positions of mesh router nodes which maximize the coverage of areas of interest, minimize the number of routers while ensuring the connectivity of the network. To achieve this, an approach based on Simulated Annealing algorithm is proposed. It is evaluated on different region instances. It provides area of interest coverage around 98 % with an optimal number of routers 1.3 times the minimum number of router corresponding to the ratio between the area to cover and the area covered by a router.

Keywords: Simulated annealing · Mesh router placement · Rural Wireless Mesh Networks

1 Introduction

Since a decade, there is an emphasis on deploying wireless networks in a mesh topology to form a Wireless Mesh Network (WMN) [1]. This has been shown as a cost-effective approach to extend the coverage of the wireless technology. Despite their cost-effectiveness and their capacity to bridge the digital divide observed between rural and urban regions, WMNs are still lowly deployed in rural regions. In the few deployments, WMNs in rural regions consist usually of one gateway which connects the network to Internet, and a set of mesh routers (MRs). The number and the location of these routers have a direct incidence on the cost and the performance of the network.

As said in [2] the network planning in rural region is coverage-driven rather than capacity-driven. That means we are more concerned by the space to cover than the capacity to provide. In other terms, in the case of WMN planning, the number of routers is determined by their coverage. In rural regions, the main concern when planning a WMN is the cost of the architecture. This cost depends on the number of

© ICST Institute for Computer Sciences, Social Informatics and Telecommunications Engineering 2016
R. Glitho et al. (Eds.): AFRICOMM 2015, LNICST 171, pp. 192–202, 2016.
DOI: 10.1007/978-3-319-43696-8_19

mesh routers and it should be minimized while providing some coverage percentage of a given area.

In this paper, we consider the network model found in [3], wherein a given area to cover is decomposed into elementary areas which can be required or optional in terms of coverage and where a node can be placed or not. This model is extended to consider the presence of obstacles which can hinder the connectivity. The aim is therefore to determine the location of mesh routers which: minimizes the number of MRs; maximizes the coverage of area of interest; and ensures the connectivity of the network.

To achieve this goal, a network model is defined and the placement problem is formulated. Then, a placement approach based on simulated annealing algorithm is proposed. It is evaluated on different regions instances using Scilab 5.4.0.

The rest of the paper is organized as follows: Sect. 2 briefly presents previous work in WMN planning. Section 3 provides the network model and formulates the placement problem. Section 4 explains the simulated annealing approach. Section 5 presents the experimental setup and discusses the results. Conclusion and future work end this paper.

2 Related Work

A good survey on the planning of WMN is found in [4]. This work classifies the planning problem according to the flexibility of the network topology: unfixed (not-predefined) and fixed (predefined). In unfixed topology, we should set the location of at least some nodes in the network: the gateway(s) or the routers. This problem is usually assimilated to the one of facilities and locations with mesh routers representing facilities and the users to serve representing locations.

Different formulations of the placement approach have been proposed in the literature. They depend on the type of node considered in the planning problem: gateway(s) [5], mesh routers [6], or both [7].

To solve this problem, different approaches have been proposed among which: Graph-theoretic-based approaches [8]; Meta-heuristic based approaches [9], and linear programming based approaches [10].

An approach also based on simulated annealing to solve the mesh nodes placement problem is provided in [9]. It aims to find optimal locations of routers that maximize the network connectivity and client coverage, given a two-dimensional area with a number of fixed client nodes.

The placement problem of mesh routers in rural a region has been introduced in [11] and later extended in [3]. They considered the region as decomposed into a set of elementary areas which may require the coverage or where a node may be placed. A placement approach based on metropolis algorithm has been therefore used. We extend this model by considering the existence of obstacles that can prevent the connectivity of the network.

3 Placement Problem Formulation

In the present placement problem, a given region is composed of areas of interest that should be covered as it is in [3]. When an area is not of interest, the coverage of this region is considered as optional. A given region comprised also prohibited areas where a node cannot be placed (lake, river, road...), and a set of obstacles that could hinder the connectivity.

The area to cover is modelled as a two-dimensional irregular form in a two-dimension coordinate plane. We consider the smallest rectangle that can contain the irregular form. Therefore, we assume that this rectangle is decomposed into small square forms. Each discrete point is called elementary area (EA). Each EA can be of one or more types: Elementary Area of Interest (EAI); Non-line-of-sight Elementary Area (NEA); or Prohibitive Elementary Area (PEA).

When an EA is not an EAI, it is automatically an optional EA (OEA). A set of two-dimensional matrices is defined to characterise each EA: *Cover* indicating whether an EA requires coverage; *Place* indicating whether we can place a node in an EA; *CoverDepth* indicating the number of routers covering an EA; and *Pathloss* indicating whether an EA contains an obstacle. Therefore, an EA at position (x,y) can be characterised by (1–4).

$$Cover(x, y) = \begin{cases} 0 \rightarrow coverage\ not\ required \\ 1 \rightarrow coverage\ required \end{cases} \tag{1}$$

$$Place(x, y) = \begin{cases} 0 \rightarrow cannot\ place\ a\ node \\ 1 \rightarrow can\ place\ a\ node \end{cases} \tag{2}$$

$$CoverDepth(x, y) = \begin{cases} 0 \rightarrow no\ coverage \\ n \rightarrow covered\ by\ n\ routers \end{cases} \tag{3}$$

$$Pathloss(x, y) = \begin{cases} 0 \rightarrow no\ obstruction \\ p \rightarrow attenuation\ factor\ =\ p \end{cases} \tag{4}$$

We assume, to alleviate the complexity of the problem, that the attenuation factor of any obstacle in the line of sight between two routers is high enough to prevent any wireless link between those routers. We also assume that all routers are equipped with an omnidirectional antenna all having the same coverage radius (r). The radius is expressed as the number of EAs (r = 6 means that the radius stretches over 6 EAs).

Let l be an EA at position (x,y). If a mesh router is located in l, then the set of EAs covered by this mesh router is given by (5).

$$\forall (a, b), (x - a)^2 + (y - b)^2 < r^2 \tag{5}$$

We assume the number of routers to be placed to be unknown at the beginning.

The mesh router placement problem in rural regions can be described as the determination of a minimum set of positions, which maximizes the coverage of areas of interest, minimizes the coverage of optional areas while maximizing the use of cost effective locations and ensuring the connectivity.

4   Simulated Annealing Approach

4.1   Basic Algorithm

The SA algorithm proceeds as follow: First, an initial solution is generated; several iterations are performed from this solution. A new random solution is generated at each iteration. If the solution improves the value of the objective function, it is directly accepted. Otherwise, this non-improving solution is accepted with a probability depending on the current temperature and the difference E between the value of its objective function and the one of the previous solution. Since the temperature decreases progressively, the probability of accepting non-improving solutions also decreases. Usually, the probability in the SA algorithm follows the Boltzmann distribution $e^{-\frac{\Delta E}{T}}$ [12].

Algorithm 1. Simulated annealing

Input: f **: the objective function to be minimised**

Output: s **: the best solution found**

Begin

   $T := T_{initial}$**;** $s := $ **InitialSolution();** $v := f(s)$

   while (stopping condition not met) do

      while (equilibrium condition not met) do

         $s' := $ **GenerateSolution()**

         $v' := f(s')$

         $\Delta E := v' - v$

         if $\Delta E \leq 0$ **then** $s := s'$

         else accept s` with probability $e^{-\frac{\Delta E}{T}}$

      Update(T)

   return s

End

4.2   Particularization

We use a multi-start SA algorithm in the proposed scheme. It consists of running the SA algorithm many times to keep the best result at the end. The basic SA is adapted according to the flowchart given in Fig. 1.

Initialization. The initial number of routers for a given region is calculated by dividing the total required area by the area covered by a router. Let r be the radius of a router, the minimum number of routers is given by (6).

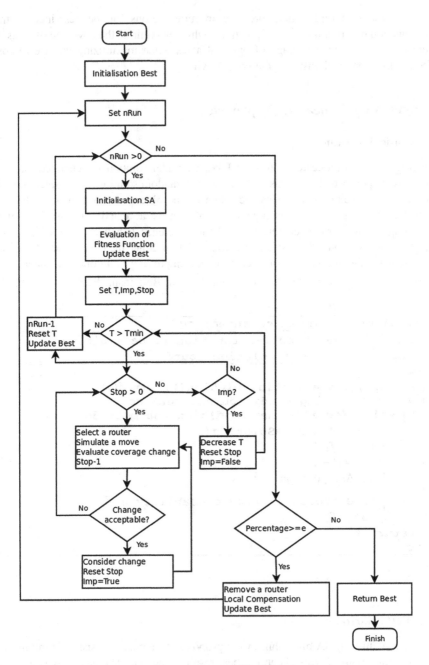

Fig. 1. Flowchart of the modified SA algorithm

$$nr_{min} = \sum Cover(x, y)/(r^2 * 3.14) \tag{6}$$

Since routers should overlap to ensure the connectivity, and because the form of the region is irregular, we use a greater number so that the coverage and the connectivity can be ensured. This number is reduced later while trying to keep the same coverage. However, a too great number at the beginning is not efficient. We choose an initial number of routers between $1.4*nr_{min}$ and $2*nr_{min}$.

Best keep the best solution for each number of routers. *nRun* is the number of times the SA algorithm will be executed. Routers are placed randomly in the region during the initialization phase of the SA algorithm, but only in areas of interest. We randomly select an EA for each router. We check if *Cover*(EA) = 1, and *Place*(EA) = 1, and, if a router is not already set at this location then the current router can be placed there. Otherwise, we continue by selecting another EA. The initialization ends when all routers are placed.

Cooling Schedule. The initial temperature $T = 10$ has been determined empirically. We select a geometric update scheme with $\alpha = 0.5$. When the temperature is less than $T_{min} = 0.001$, the cooling process stops.

Move. We define a set of movements with moving only one router at the same time. We select randomly a distance and a direction; the movement from the current EA_a to the new EA_b is simulated if and only if $Cover(EA_b) = 1$ and $Place(EA_b) = 1$. Initially great moves are selected to allow a rapid convergence. The size of moves decreases with the temperature; when the temperature is close to T_{min}, the size of moves is one EA.

Fitness Function. We count the number of EAIs that are covered to evaluate the fitness function. This is done by (7) after the initialisation.

$$f = \sum sign(CoverDepth \cdot * Cover) \tag{7}$$

Since we move only one router at the same time, we consider also only the EAs which are concerned by the movement.

Acceptance Criterion. When $C_b \geq C_a$, the coverage change is directly accepted. But when the coverage change is negative, the change is accepted with a certain probability following the Boltzmann distribution and influenced by the temperature T to avoid local optimum.

Equilibrium State and Stopping Condition. The equilibrium state is supposed to be reached if after a number (stop) of moves no solution has been accepted. The stopping condition depends on *Imp* and on T_{min}. At each temperature T_i, *Imp* indicates whether the solution has improved. When the equilibrium state at a temperature T_i is reached, before decreasing the temperature we check whether the solution has improved. In case of an improvement, we decrease the temperature and move to the next iteration. But if there is no improvement or the temperature is less than T_{min}, we stop the search process and suppose having reached an optimum.

At the beginning nr_{min} routers are used. The SA algorithm is running *nRun* times at each stage. If the required coverage is satisfied, we remove one router and restart until the coverage can no longer be satisfied.

Nodes Connectivity. The network is connected if for two pair of routers there exists a non-empty set of links that allows a communication between those two routers. At this step we check if each router is connected to at least one router while verifying that there exists no sub-network. This task is more complicated with the presence of obstructions in the model. We must not only check that the router radiuses are overlapping, but also the existence of the line of sight between the routers.

Reducing the Number of Routers. After *nRun* for a given number of routers *nr*, we select the run, which provides the best coverage of the area of interest and we remove one router. To remove a router, three strategies can be used: Remove the router with the minimum single-coverage; Remove the router with the minimum coverage of EAI; Remove the router with the maximum over-coverage. The first appears to be the best among these three strategies.

Local Compensation. When removing one router - if its single coverage is not null - we try to compensate it locally. The idea is to check if by moving its neighbours the compensation can be achieved. So, when removing the router, we keep its coordinates. Then we determine its neighbours and we simulate small moves. We accept a move only if it improves the coverage.

5   Experimental Results

To evaluate our proposed algorithm, we consider a grid of 100×100 with the radius of a router r = 6. The unit is the size of an EA. If size (EA) = 20 m, the grid will be $2 \text{ km} \times 2 \text{ km} = 4 \text{ km}^2$ and the radius r = 120 m. This is realistic since 802.11a routers have a theoretical outdoor transmission range of 120 m, 802.11b 150 m and 802.11n routers 250 m. The other global parameters for the experimentation phase are: nRun = 3, Stop = 500, NumberOfObstruction = 50, $nr_{init} = 1.5nr_{min}$, r = 6, $T_{init} = 10$, and $T_{min} = 0.001$.

We generate two regions with different areas of interest, obstructions and prohibited areas as in Fig. 2. Blue regions represent the area of interest that should be covered and black regions represent optional areas in this figure. Prohibited areas are not directly seen, because some areas of interest and optional areas can also be prohibited areas. Obstructions are placed randomly on regions.

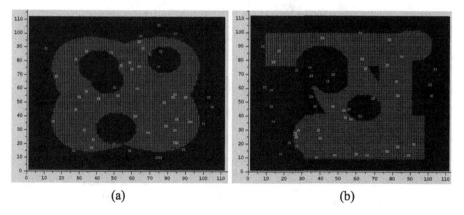

Fig. 2. Region instances: (a) instance 1; (b) instances 2.

6 Results

In instance 1, all the three runs provide a coverage percentage of the area of interest close to 100 % with nr_{init} = 65. All routers are connected and the coverage of the optional area is around 20 %. We observe that with nr = 63 or nr = 62, no run provided a connected network. But with nr between 61 and 58, we get at least one connected network from each run. This is due to the presence of obstructions between routers. That means, in presence of obstructions, augmenting the number of routers is not an efficient strategy to ensure the connectivity of the network. We also observe that with nr = 59 ($1.34*nr_{min}$), we obtain a coverage percentage of the area of interest greater than 99 %, with all the routers connected. This number could be considered as the optimal number to achieve a coverage percentage of the area of interest close to 100 %. This number of routers starts a horizontal asymptote. Augmenting the number of routers will not improve the coverage, since it is close to 100 %.

In instance 2, the initial number of routers nr_{init} = 68 provides a coverage percentage of the area of interest close to 100 %; with all routers connected. As in the first instance, the locations of obstructions in the region influence the connectivity of the network. With nr = 63 or 64, no run provided a connected network. A good trade-off between the number of routers and the coverage percentage of the area of interest is found with nr = 61 ($1.32*nr_{min}$) with a coverage of 98 %.

Figure 3 compares the best and the worst coverage percentage of the area of interest for instance 1, 2 respectively. The almost monotonically increasing curve of the best coverage percentage (maximal) is obtained by keeping the best previous configuration after removing one router and making the local compensation. Apart from some low peaks with a decrease of 5 % from the best, other numbers of routers provide a variation less than 4 % between the best and the worse percentage coverage of the area of interest in Fig. 3. That means, even though the approach is probabilistic, the results are similar.

Figures 4 and 5 show router locations (a), links and obstructions (b), respectively in instance 1, and 2. In Figure (a), blue, red, and white colours represent areas covered

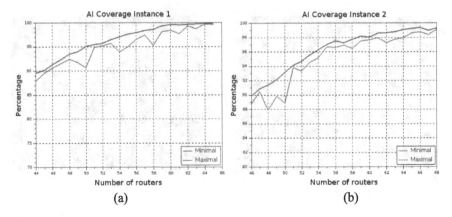

Fig. 3. Coverage percentage of area of interest

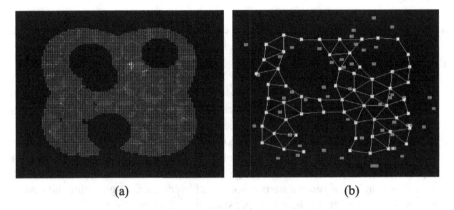

Fig. 4. Router locations and links

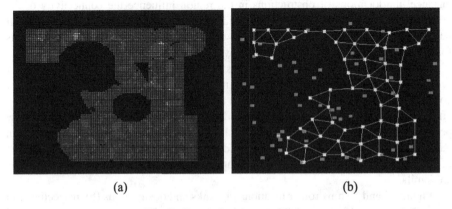

Fig. 5. Router locations and links

respectively by one, two, and three routers. In Figure (b), lines represent links between routers that are represented as white squares. Obstructions are represented as green squares.

59 routers are used in Fig. 4; that corresponds to $1.34*nr_{min}$. 61 routers are used in Fig. 5 ($1.32*nr_{min}$). In Figs. 4a and 5a, we can observe some very small dead spots represented by black space between routers. The fact that they are insignificant also witnesses the suitability of the placement approach.

7   Conclusion

From the two dissimilar instances and different runs of the algorithm, we can generalise some results. The first result is the efficiency of the approach to solve this problem of mesh router nodes placement in regions with different forms. In fact, in the two instances the average coverage is close to 100 % with $nr_{init} = 1.5*nr_{min}$. Secondly, we observe that an optimal number is around $1.3* nr_{min}$, with a coverage percentage of the areas of interest of at least 98 %. This approach improves the coverage percentage provided by using the simple metropolis approach provided in [3], with the same number of routers. However, it always considers the case where the area of interest is continuous. A new approach should therefore be provided to deal with the case of disjoint areas of interest.

References

1. Akyildiz, I.F., Wang, X., Wang, W.: Wireless mesh networks: a survey. Comput. Netw. **47** (4), 445–487 (2005)
2. Bernardi, G., Marina, M.K., Talamona, F., Rykovanov, D.: IncrEase: a tool for incremental planning of rural fixed broadband wireless access networks. In: IEEE Global Telecommunications Conference (GLOBECOM 2011), pp. 1013–1018 (2011)
3. Fendji, J.L.E.K., Thron, C., Nlong, J.M.: A metropolis approach for mesh router nodes placement in rural wireless mesh networks. J. Comput. **10**(2), 101–114 (2015)
4. Benyamina, D., Hafid, A., Gendreau, M.: Wireless mesh networks design—a survey. IEEE Commun. Surv. Tutor. **14**(2), 299–310 (2012)
5. Li, F., Wang, Y., Li, X.Y., Nusairat, A., Wu, Y.: Gateway placement for throughput optimization in wireless mesh networks. Mobile Netw. Appl. **13**(1–2), 198–211 (2008)
6. Xhafa, F., Sánchez, C., Barolli, L.: Genetic algorithms for efficient placement of router nodes in wireless mesh networks. In: 24th IEEE International Conference on Advanced Information Networking and Applications (AINA), pp. 465–472 (2010)
7. De Marco, G.: MOGAMESH: a multi-objective algorithm for node placement in wireless mesh networks based on genetic algorithms. In: 6th IEEE International Symposium on Wireless Communication Systems (ISWCS 2009), pp. 388–392, September 2009 (2009)
8. Wang, J., Xie, B., Cai, K., Agrawal, D. P.: Efficient mesh router placement in wireless mesh networks. In: IEEE International Conference on Mobile Adhoc and Sensor Systems (MASS 2007), pp. 1–9 (2007)

9. Xhafa, F., Barolli, A., Sánchez, C., Barolli, L.: A simulated annealing algorithm for router nodes placement problem in Wireless Mesh Networks. Simul. Model. Pract. Theor. **19**(10), 2276–2284 (2011)

10. Amaldi, E., Capone, A., Cesana, M., Filippini, I., Malucelli, F.: Optimization models and methods for planning wireless mesh networks. Comput. Netw. **52**(11), 2159–2171 (2008)

11. Fendji, J.L. E. K., Thron, C., Nlong, J.M.: Mesh router nodes placement in rural wireless mesh networks. In: Sellami, M., Badouel, E., Lo, M., (eds.) Actes du CARI 2014 (Colloque africain sur la recherche en informatique et mathématiques appliquées). Inria, Colloques CARI, pp. 265–272 (2014)

12. Talbi, E.G.: Metaheuristics: From Design to Implementation. Wiley, Hoboken (2009)

A Public Safety Wireless Sensor Network: A Visible Light Communication Based Approach

Dhouha Krichen[1], Walid Abdallah[1(✉)], Noureddine Boudriga[1], and Antoine Bagula[2]

[1] Communication Networks and Security Research Lab, University of Carthage, Tunis, Tunisia
dhouha.krichen@gmail.com, ab.walid@gmail.com,
noure.boudriga2@gmail.com
[2] Department of Computer Science, University of the Western Cape, Cape Town, South Africa
bagula@gmail.com

Abstract. This paper investigates the design of a wireless sensor network that employs visible light communication technology to ensure an indoor public safety application intended for toxic gas detection within critical locations such as airports. To this end, a specific architecture for the VLC-based WSN was proposed which supports mobility of sensors inside the building. Moreover, an optical encoding scheme that can provide multiple access and quality of service differentiation was developed by combining both OCDMA and WDM techniques to reduce intra and inter cell interference. The quality of service provision is based on a dynamic allocation of optical code-words with variable lengths that depend on the transmission rate requirements of different classes of sensors. To reduce interferences the allocated code-words must be orthogonal. To this end, an appropriate orthogonal code-words generation approach was presented. Finally, a simulation work was conducted to evaluate the proposed network architecture.

Keywords: Public safety network · Wsns · VLC · OCDMA · Qos provision

1 Introduction

Professional Mobile Radio (PMR) public safety networks commonly known as Terrestrial Trunked Radio (TETRA) are evolving from application-specific networks to multi-applications and multi-agencies wide area networks [1]. Moreover, the PMR are scalable and can support different volume of applications from daily control operations to main public occasions such as sport and political events. Many of public safety networks are using LTE/4G thanks to its high capability to support critical voice and data services [1]. However, those LTE-based public safety networks are facing several challenges that are mainly the high cost of the fixed infrastructure and the limited communication which is based on narrow and proprietary bands.

Besides, wireless sensor networks (WSNs) are widely investigated in monitoring applications such as target tracking in border surveillance, controlling the natural environment, and forecasting natural disasters. The ability of WSNs to control physical locations without a prior infrastructure has motivated researchers to use those networks in the context of public safety. However, the radio spectrum which is allocated to sensor

© ICST Institute for Computer Sciences, Social Informatics and Telecommunications Engineering 2016
R. Glitho et al. (Eds.): AFRICOMM 2015, LNICST 171, pp. 203–214, 2016.
DOI: 10.1007/978-3-319-43696-8_20

nodes is becoming very limited creating interference with other radio systems and mainly Wi-Fi devices that are submerging indoor areas like cafes and airports. A potential solution for this problem is the integration of light-based communication technology in the indoor environment.

Indeed, visible light (VLC) is increasingly investigated as a solution instead of radio frequency (RF) communication for many indoor wireless applications. This technique can ensure ubiquitous lighting and communication simultaneously. For this reason it is considered as a potential candidate to enable wireless access in 5G mobile communication networks. Moreover, VLC offers several advantages over RF. First it has license free spectrum which provides huge communication bandwidth to deliver high data rate services. Secondly, it avoids interference with RF systems. It is also nature-friendly, safe for eyes, inexpensive, and provides high secrecy and protection against eavesdropping thanks to its narrow beam width and line of sight (LOS) transmission mode.

In this paper, we investigate the use of visible light communication technology to implement optical wireless sensor networks as a major component of a public safety network implemented in the indoor environment. The envisioned application of this network is to ensure smart surveillance within airports. The surveillance includes the detection of toxic gas within a controlled area and the report of the detected incident to a central coordinator. It is noteworthy that the central coordinator can be an entity of a cloud service that delivers ubiquitous and real time communication to public safety agencies. The designed light-based WSN architecture enables mobile and real time monitoring of critical locations in airports by optimizing LEDs and sensors deployment in specific locations such as passenger's registration points, departure and waiting rooms, hallways intersections, to provide indoor coverage and communication features. Moreover, a multiple access and quality of service provision scheme based on WDM and OCDMA using appropriate optical code generation function was presented to reduce interference among sensor nodes. The code generation approach ensures the building of a set of orthogonal code-words with variable lengths that will be allocated to communicating nodes according to their bandwidth requirements. We show that this allocation approach can provide differentiated QoS for the different classes of sensor nodes. Finally, we propose a mobility management scheme to enable the motion of sensors inside the airports while not affecting the required quality of communication inside the building. The mobility management addresses the possibility of handing over sensor nodes from a VLC cell to another while not affecting the reliability of the surveillance application.

The reminder of this paper is organized as follows. Section 2 details the related work. Section 3 describes the global architecture of the proposed VLC-based public safety network. It also presents the mobility management scheme for the VLC public safety network. Section 4 describes the proposed quality of service provision scheme which is based on a dynamic allocation of optical code-words with variable length. In Sect. 5, the system performance is analyzed using a simulation work. Finally, a conclusion is drawn in Sect. 6.

2 Related Work

The Federal Communication Commission (FCC) has recently allocated a 10 MHz paired spectrum in the 700 MHz band for public safety applications [2, 3]. A unified architecture for a public safety broadband network was proposed and is based on Long Term Evolution (LTE) technology. However, the planned public safety network and existing commercial LTE networks have different characteristics. For example, the commercial networks have a more user equipment (UE) density and targets at providing different services. However, the major purpose of public safety networks is to provide immediate access to the network and a reliable communication with guaranteed quality of service. There have been many studies on public safety networks. In [4], authors developed a model for a public safety traffic under both normal and emergency scenarios. In [5], an analysis of public safety traffic on trunked land mobile radio systems was made. Indeed, it is shown that the average number of occupied channels in most cells of a commercial network is smaller compared to their capacities. In a public safety network, however, the average amount of routine traffic is much lower than that in a commercial network. In [3], a novel architecture of a cost effective broadband public safety network was developed. This architecture consists in fixed and sparsely deployed base transceiver stations (BTSs) as well as mobile BTSs. The fixed BTSs support light routine traffic, while the mobile access points are used to timely report any incident scene. This requires a deep study to determine the adequate density, placement as well as the link technologies to connect all BTSs to the fixed backhaul.

Furthermore, several research works investigated the use of WSNs for public safety purpose. In [6], authors present a general structure of an Intelligent Transport Systems (ITS) where the traffic data collection is mainly based on WSN-monitoring. A set of sensor nodes deployed throughout the roads collects and forwards measurements to a remote server which processes the data traffic and distributes this data to traffic management centers such as road control units. This collected data can be used for road safety applications. In [7], authors implemented a prototype for stadium surveillance based on wireless sensor networks. This prototype provides real time information to notify the occurrence of incidents within the stadium. Moreover, they considered security requirements that are mainly an encryption based access control and the confidentiality of the generated alert. In [8], authors address the main challenges related to resource management and context-awareness in public safety networks (PSNs) that are based on Long Term Evolution (LTE) access technology. Indeed, broadband PSNs deliver more than voice communications to first responders (police, emergency medical services, etc.). For example, PSNs ensure an integrated information database and several tools to improve the efficiency of safety applications. These tools can be either video surveillance cameras, dynamic maps or sensors. The video surveillance cameras can be used by police men to obtain more details about the scene of an incident, while the automated sensors can be used to communicate reports to firefighters or to send traffic and weather information to transportation agencies to improve road safety [9].

On the other hand, the VLC is used for several novel applications such as smart lighting, underwater communications and in-flight entertainment [10]. Furthermore, the VLC is starting to be used to ensure intelligent public safety applications. For example, in [11], authors designed a light-based architecture to enable intelligent transportation in smart cities. Moreover, they introduce issues related to the integration of the VLC technology into the networking infrastructure of the smart city. In the same context, authors in [12] introduce a VLC broadcast system which addresses LED-based traffic lights to build an intelligent transportation system. The use of VLC presents several advantages since it considers existing infrastructures and explores existing traffic lights as VLC-based road side units to build an inexpensive communication system. In addition, using VLC communication to report or prevent from road accidents enhances the road safety application because the visible light technology ensures a reliable real time communication. In this paper, we propose a communication architecture that combines VLC and WSNs capabilities to build a new communication solution for future public safety networks, especially for real time surveillance in airports.

3   A VLC-Based Wireless Sensor Network for Public Safety Control

The main objective of this work is the development of a public safety application to ensure security control in critical environments such as airports against terrorist attacks. We selected the case of the detection of toxic gas that may be spread by attackers. In this section, we describe light based toxic gas detection method by controlling reflection propriety of visible light. In addition, we describe the architecture of the VLC-based wireless sensor network intended for security control in airports and the mobility management scheme to guarantee a reliable communication to optical sensors while moving inside the building to detect security incident events related to the propagation of toxic gas.

3.1   VLC-Based Toxic Gas Detection Approach

Optical gas detection sensors typically exploits the change in intensity in an absorbent medium or the phase change of a light beam. In the first case the sensor is called "intensity detector". However, in the second case the sensors are called "interferometric detectors". Actually, there exists several techniques for gas detection among them we note mainly the technique of "remote sensing" known also as "LIDAR" (Light Detection and Ranging) technique [13]. This technique measures distance by illuminating a target with a laser and analyzing the reflected light. The LIDAR measurements can be used to determine the concentration of a particular gas in the atmosphere and is typically based on Infrared (IR) light.

In this paper, we investigate the VLC technology instead of LIDAR to enable an accurate detection of some gas in the indoor atmosphere of an airport. As shown by Fig. 1, the sensors that are deployed on the floor detect the light beam of the serving VLC cells and measures the illuminance intensity of the received light. If the received luminance is far less from the value obtained in the LOS case, then the sensor triggers the second phase of the detection. During the second phase, the optical sensor captures the deviation of visible light of the serving LED. Based on the direction of a deviated light ray, the sensor uses the Descartes formula to compute the optical index of the potential new environment.

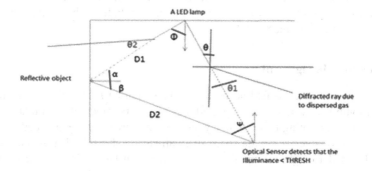

Fig. 1. VLC-based gas detection approach.

The proposed network will notify the appropriate public safety agencies about this new index indicating the emission of certain gas in the atmosphere.

3.2 Public Safety Network Architecture

The architecture of the proposed public safety network is illustrated by Fig. 2. It includes 3 main subsystems:

- The gateway which connects the VLC network to the cloud network. It is responsible for ubiquitous communication of the reported information.
- The VLC network which is composed of a set of light cells covering optical sensor nodes. The light cells are made of LEDs that are deployed in the ceiling of the airport halls and rooms to ensure visible light illuminance and communication with the optical sensor network. Moreover, each cell is allocated a single wavelength according to graph coloring technique to ensure communication with its related

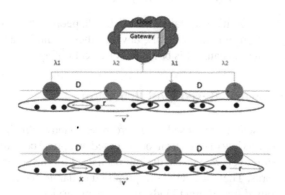

Fig. 2. Global VLC-based public safety network architecture.

nodes. It is noteworthy that graph coloring concept reduces the interference between adjacent VLC cells.
– The optical sensor nodes which are either mobile and generate heterogeneous traffic types with different quality of service requirements. Indeed, they can communicate either multimedia or data traffics.

3.3 Mobility Management

VLC systems can be classified according to their lighting modes that are mainly the "uniform lighting coverage" and "spotlighting". The first mode offers a total coverage by uniformly distributing LEDs with a wide field of view (FOV) on the ceiling. In this case, the area to cover is a wide space like hallways and aisles. The second mode is commonly used to light-up small areas like work surfaces, desktops and airplane passenger seats. Therefore, the range of VLC cells in the spotlighting mode is smaller than the range of cells in the uniform lighting mode. Moreover, the spotlighting is more appropriate for fixed users because the mobility of users is almost absent in this case. Owing to the specific properties of our network, it is more appropriate to consider mobility management only in the first lighting mode of a VLC system.

In mobility scenarios, the users can maintain their connectivity with the serving cell only if the received signal is good enough. Otherwise, the connection will be disrupted. To overcome this problem of session disconnection, we propose that the light cells are overlapped such that sensors are able to continue transmitting their traffic even if they become under the coverage of the target cell. Moreover, because sensors are always covered, they are able to communicate quickly to the new cell. Thus we avoid a long disruption of communication when switching to the target cell. To enable a reliable mobility management for sensor nodes, the following assumptions are taken into consideration:

– The distance separating the VLC cells is D (m)
– The cell range is r, where $D <= 2r$
– The cells are overlapped and the overlapping distance is $x = D - 2r$
– The sensor nodes cross a lighting cell at a constant speed v (m/s)
– Each LED has a constant data rate B (kb/s)

Even though the airport hallway can be crowded with people who could be equipped with smartphones, laptops and other mobile devices, these radio-based devices cannot interfere with our system because it is based on VLC technology.

4 Optical Codeword-Based QoS Provision

In this section, we present the proposed codeword-based bandwidth allocation scheme. First, we present an overview of optical encoding based on optical code division multiple access technique. Moreover, we present the approach used for the generation of orthogonal optical codewords. Then, we detail our proposed dynamic codeword-based bandwidth allocation method for different kinds of classes of service.

4.1 Optical Coding and OCDMA Systems

A communication channel in OCDMA system is uniquely identified by a specific code rather than a wavelength as in WDM systems or a time slot in TDMA systems. One of the main advantages of using OCDMA technique is that it simplifies the network management by almost avoiding the need for channel access control to reduce collision or allocate resources. Moreover, with OCDMA there is no need for synchronization or scheduling operations as in the case of TDMA-based networks. In addition, OCDMA provides larger capacity, and the operation of admission control are less complex than in TDMA or WDM systems. Indeed, in OCDMA each bit is optically encoded by a specific pulse sequence before transmission. The optical encoding represents the data bit by a code sequence which can be in the time domain, in wavelength domain or in both domains. On the other hand, the decoding operation is implemented by an optical receiver to recover the original sequence. The optical coding is defined as the process by which a code is injected into and extracted from an optical signal.

In the time domain, the period of the data bit is splitted into very small time units called chips. However, in the wavelength domain encoding, the bits are physically presented by a unique sequence of wavelengths used during the bit period. Therefore, a two dimensional (2D) coding is the combination of wavelengths used during particular time chips. Moreover, most of the OCDMA systems use the on-off keying technique where only data bits "1" are physically presented by an optical pulse sequence. The bits "0", however, are not presented by any signal. Even if this technique reduces the transmission power, it represents one of the most important vulnerabilities that could be exploited by eavesdroppers.

In our network we use wavelength division multiple access (WDM) to control the optical communication within each VLC cell. We note that we use white LEDs combining several wavelengths that are mainly the red, green and blue. Indeed, all the wavelengths are used for illuminating the airport hallways and rooms. However, a single wavelength is selected to be used for communication in each light cell. To mitigate the inter-cell interference, we affect monochromatic wavelengths to the different VLC cells using graph coloring technique as depicted by Fig. 2. In addition to this wavelength division, we use optical code division multiple access (OCDMA) within each cell. The OCDMA affects for each sensor a different optical code to discriminate between sensors data traffics. However, to overcome the interference problem, the codes should be orthogonal. Furthermore, the sensor nodes may have heterogeneous traffic types (multimedia and data). Thus they have different quality of service (QoS) requirements. Therefore, it is more appropriate that the code allocation process will be dynamic and takes into consideration the quality of service constraints for each sensor node.

4.2 Dynamic QoS-Based Bandwidth Provision

In this subsection we define the properties of orthogonal optical codes (OOC) and we describe our proposed orthogonal optical code generation procedure.

4.2.1   Definition of Optical Orthogonal Codes

We mean by optical orthogonal code a set of (0, 1) sequences of length L and weight w. The weight represents the number of ones "1" in each codeword. In addition, these orthogonal codes have auto and cross correlation properties. Let's take the example of two code words $X = (x_1, x_2, \ldots, x_L)$ and $Y = (y_1, y_2, \ldots, y_L)$ [14]. The autocorrelation of X and the cross-correlation between X and Y should satisfy the constraints given by inequalities 1 and 2:

$$\sum_{i=1}^{L} x_i x_{i+\tau} \leq \lambda_a \tag{1}$$

$$\sum_{i=1}^{L} x_i y_{i+\tau} \leq \lambda_c \tag{2}$$

Where λ_a and λ_c are the auto and cross correlation constraints respectively.

4.2.2   Dynamic Codeword-Based Bandwidth Provision

In this paper, we consider sensor nodes to two types of service class, the multimedia service and the data service. To discriminate between sensors traffics in our VLC system, each node should be allocated an orthogonal optical code. For this purpose, we generated two spaces of codes of different lengths, where each space is reserved for a given type of traffic class. However, the two spaces should be orthogonal to reduce interference between nodes. Moreover, we note that the first code space has codes of length L, whereas the second code space has a length of 2L. Tables 1 and 2 give an example of codes that were used for the two spaces.

Table 1. Example of codes used in the first space.

10001000	00100001

Table 2. Example of codes used in the second space.

1000000010001000	1000000000100010

Recall that in OCDMA a bit is optically encoded by a specific pulse sequence which represents the codeword. Assume that an optical codeword has a length of L chips. Therefore, the bit duration depends on the length of this code. Consequently, the bandwidth required to send a set of bits will depend on the code length. Consequently, the shorter the code is the greater is the allocated bandwidth. Because each sensor data is encoded with a given codeword, the length of the code affects the bandwidth consumption by each sensor. We assume that B is the total bandwidth available in the system and N is the total number of sensor nodes. Consequently, each sensor node will be uniformly assigned a minimum bandwidth of B/N.

However, in our application the sensors are heterogeneous and belong to different classes of service. Therefore, they have different QoS constraints. For this purpose, it is better to allocate bandwidth to the different sensors according to their requirements. This can be done by allowing a dynamic code-word assignment during which the length of optical code-words is dynamic and depends on each senor node requirements in terms of bandwidth. For example, the codes with shorter length will be allocated to multimedia sensors and the code-words with longer length will be affected to sensors that transmit data traffic.

5 Performance Evaluation

In this section, we evaluate the performance of the proposed dynamic codeword-based bandwidth provision. A simulation model is developed by considering a case study of an airport which we aim to secure against malware behaviors. For this purpose, we consider a hallway of length 16 m and width 3 m. In the ceiling of the hallway, we deployed 8 LEDs that are separated by a uniform distance to enable a VLC communication network. In fact, each LED forms a VLC cell of a certain coverage radius. Moreover, the lamps are not used only for illuminating the hallway, but also to communicate security information to the public safety network via a cloud gateway. To save the use of wavelengths, we considered only two colors (the red and the blue) to perform the communication feature. We assume also that each LED has a data rate of 256 kbps.

On the other hand, we consider a set of sensor nodes that are deployed on the floor of the considered hallway. It is worthy to note that the sensors can be either camera nodes, smart phones equipped with cameras, or ordinary sensor nodes that are responsible for detecting suspicious events or behavior and communicate the collected information to the LEDs via VLC links. Moreover, we note that the sensors are heterogeneous and have different traffic types. For example, in our simulations we considered multimedia and data nodes. In addition, the sensors are mobile and have a constant speed. Moreover, we considered the case where the VLC cells have the same coverage radius and are overlapped. Recall that the overlapping distance is the difference between the distance separating the LEDs and the double of the radius.

To discriminate between the sensors channels in the uplink direction, each node is allocated a codeword which should be orthogonal with the other code-words of the other nodes. Because the sensors belong to heterogeneous service classes, the bandwidth allocation should be scalable. For this purpose we consider codes of dynamic code length. Because the multimedia sensor nodes are more demanding in terms of bandwidth than data nodes, we allocated codes of smaller length to the multimedia sensors. In our simulations, we used codes of length 8 for multimedia traffic transmission, whereas data traffic is encoded using codes of length 16. The simulation parameters are given by Table 3.

Figure 4 shows the variation of the average transmission delay in function of the number of sensors that are deployed on the hallway for the two types of traffic. We note by average transmission delay the average time between the first sending of the message and the reception of the proper acknowledgment. As it is shown by the curve, the average transmission delay is an increasing function of the number of sensors due to the interference problem. For data traffic, the transmission delay varies from 7 to 19 ms.

Table 3. Simulation parameters.

Parameter	Value
Code length of multimedia service	8
Code length of data service	16
Data rate (kb/s)	256
Number of Leds	8
Number of wavelengths	2
Distance separating the LEDs (m)	4
Cell range (m)	2
Height of the hallway (m)	3
Number of sensors in the hallway	5,10,15,20,25
Speed of sensors (m/s)	2

However, for multimedia traffic it remains under 10 ms. In fact, with a short code length, multimedia traffic is able to transmit more bits than data traffic. This is because the encoded data for both traffics has the same chip duration but not the same bit duration. We notice that the delay of data traffic is almost two times the delay of multimedia traffic. This can be explained by two reasons. Firstly, multimedia codes have half the length of data codes. Therefore, multimedia sensors transmit with more important data rate. Secondly, multimedia nodes have the priority to transmit in case of interference.

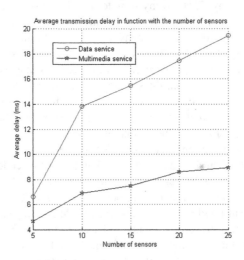

Fig. 4. Average transmission delay in function of number of sensors.

Figure 5 shows the variation of the success rate in function of the number of sensors that are deployed on the hallway for two types of traffic. We note by success rate the rate of packets that were successfully transmitted and acknowledged. As it is shown by the curve, the success rate is a decreasing function of the number of sensors. This is because the interference becomes more important with additional nodes. For data traffic, the success rate decreases from 100 % to 77 %. However, for multimedia traffic it decreases from 100 to 75 %. Indeed, as the multimedia sensors are more demanding in terms of QoS, they are allocated codes with shorter length to allow more bit rate. Because the length of codes of multimedia sensors is half the one of data codes, then the allocated bit rate to multimedia nodes will be the double. This is the reason why the success rate of multimedia service is higher than the one obtained with data service. In addition, we note that the delivery ratio is kept under 75 % which is an acceptable rate. This is ensured thanks to code orthogonality allowing the discrimination between traffics of sensors, which in turn will mitigate the interference problem.

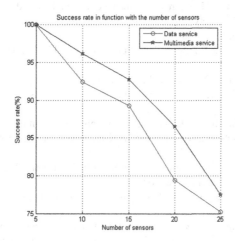

Fig. 5. Success rate in function pf number of sensors

6 Conclusion

In this paper we investigated the use optical WSNs with VLC technology to ensure an indoor public safety application within airports. In addition, we designed an appropriate architecture of the VLC-based WSN. Moreover, we choose a QoS-aware multiple access scheme combining both OCDMA and WDM techniques where codes are dynamically allocated to different sensors according to their requirements in terms of QoS. Finally, simulation results show that the proposed scheme can satisfy QoS constraints by reducing transmission delays and ensuring acceptable success rates. We intend to focus on the nodes energy consumption issue in future works.

References

1. Ceragon Solution Brief: Wireless Backhaul for Public Safety Networks (2012)
2. Manner, J.A., NewMan, S., Peha, J.M.: The FCC plan for a public safety broadband wireless network. In: Telecommunications Policy Research Conference (2010)
3. Xu, C., Dongning, G., Grosspietsch, J.: The public safety broadband network: A novel architecture with mobile base stations. In: IEEE International Conference on Communications (2013)

4. Chen, C., Pomalaza-Raez, C., Colone, M., Martin, R., Isaacs, J.: Modeling of a public safety communication system for emergency response. In: IEEE International Conference on Communications (2009)
5. Sharp, D.S., Cackov, N., Laskovic, N., Shao, Q.: Analysis of public safety traffic on trunked land mobile radio systems. IEEE J. Sel. Areas Commun. **22**, 1197–1205 (2004)
6. Pascale, A., Nicoli, M., Deflorio, F., Chiara, B.D., Spagnolini, U.: Wireless sensor networks for traffic management and road safety. Intel. Transport Syst. **6**, 67–77 (2012)
7. Gomez, L., Laube, A., Ulmer, C.: Secure sensor networks for public safety command and control system. In: IEEE Conference on Technologies for Homeland Security, Boston (2009)
8. El-Mougy, A., Mouftah, H.: On resource management and context-awareness in LTE-based networks for public safety. In: 38th IEEE Conference on Local Computer Networks Workshops, Sydney, NSW (2013)
9. Motorola Solutions: The Future is Now: Public Safety LTE Communications. White Paper (2012)
10. Quintana, C., Guerra, V., Rufo, J., Rabadan, J.: Reading lamp-based visible light communication system for in-flight entertainment. IEEE Trans. Consum. Electron. **59**, 31–37 (2013)
11. Boubakri, W., Abdallah, W., Boudriga, N.: A light-based communication architecture for smart city applications. In: 17th International Conference on Transparent Optical Networks, Budapest (2015)
12. Kumar, N.: Visible light communication based traffic information broadcasting systems. Int. J. Future Comput. Commun. **3**, 26–30 (2014)
13. Rall, J.: LIDAR for atmospheric trace gas detection. In: IEEE Geoscience and Remote Sensing Society
14. Rashidi, C.B.M., Aljunid, S.A., Ghani, F.: Design of a new class of codes with zero in phase cross correlation for spectral amplitude coding. IJCSNS Int. J. Comput. Sci. Netw. Secur. **11**, 237–242 (2011)

Short Papers

Deployment of a WiMAX Solution in a Rural Remote Region of Burkina Faso

Tiguiane Yélémou[1(✉)], Ferdinand Guinko[2], and Aminata Sabané[3]

[1] School of Computer Science, Université Polytechnique de Bobo-Dioulasso,
Bobo-dioulasso, Burkina Faso
`tyelemou@univ-bobo.bf`

[2] Institut Burkinabè des Arts et des Métiers, Université de Ouagadougou,
Ouagadougou, Burkina Faso
`tonguim@univ-ouaga.bf`

[3] Ptidej Team and Soccer Lab, DGIGL, Ecole Polytechnique de Montréal,
Montréal, Canada
`aminata.sabane@gmail.com`

Abstract. WiMAX maybe the solution to open up remote landlocked areas in Africa and particularly in Burkina Faso. In this study, we examine an implementation plan for this technology to open up the Mouhoun administrative region of Burkina Faso, a high agricultural potential area. The opening up of such an area may contribute to the development of the economic sector and consequently to the entire economy of Burkina Faso, that is mainly based on agriculture. A financial estimate and a technical feasibility of the project are done.

Keywords: WiMAX · Wireless networks · Community network

1 Introduction

Wireless communication technologies are a major opportunity to open up rural areas. For a country such as Burkina Faso where the road network is ephemeral and where the landline (wired) telephone and GSM networks are limited to large-sized and medium-sized cities, these technologies should be a springboard to the poverty alleviation. The deployment of communication equipments in these rural areas is considered unprofitable by the telephone operators. WiMAX technology [EL11] is an attractive solution because it is not leading to additional costs regarding civil engineering works nor to high administrative and maintenance costs. In this paper, we present the preliminary results of this Wimax solution.

2 Related Work

WiMAX is a technology suited for remote or very geographically distant metropolitan areas and that do not have an access to the wired Internet circuit nor to a cellular network infrastructure or do not have the means to set

© ICST Institute for Computer Sciences, Social Informatics and Telecommunications Engineering 2016
R. Glitho et al. (Eds.): AFRICOMM 2015, LNICST 171, pp. 217–219, 2016.
DOI: 10.1007/978-3-319-43696-8

one. It belongs to the family of wireless technologies developed as alternatives to the wire based technologies. Many works have been done regarding the use of WiMAX technology to open up and empower rural areas. [ODS11, AES$^+$12] suggest a binding solution of buildings of the Ministry of Food and Agriculture of Ghana; some of those buildings are located in areas that do not have wired circuit to access Internet. [ST10] proposed a WiMAX-based ICT infrastructure for the remote rural area of Mbashe municipality in South Africa.

3 Wimax Deployment Solution

Boucle du Mouhoun is one of Burkina Faso's 13 administrative regions. It is a landlocked area. The quality of the roads is very bad and much of the area is not covered by mobile GSM networks. Our project aims to provide a community network to open up these agricultural and pastoral areas and to facilitate the development of agriculture based business. Several parameters must be taken into account in the deployment of a WiMAX link. These are mainly the performance of interconnection equipment and power attenuation factors of radio waves. The main characteristics of switching equipment to consider in establishing a reliable radio link are the transmission power, the gain, the directivity of the antenna, the reception threshold, the frequency band. To more successfully plan this project, the following are to be considered: a fairly accurate map of the area, an overground database, the coordinates of the sites to link, the height of the antennas. For first simulation tests of this project, we use Google Earth to obtain the geographical coordinates of the locations of the various stations. For this first phase of this project, we use simulation. The network simulation software we use is radio mobile [radio-mobile].

Our equipment choice falls on Alvarion products series: BreezeACCESS VL. The total solution cost is estimated to USD $170 000.

4 Conclusion

This paper presents a technological solution based on the IEEE 802.16 standard to open up the Mouhoun region in Burkina Faso. The solution we propose should enable the development of agricultural and pastoral business and improve the living conditions of aboriginal people in that locality. A detailed study of this project will be presented shortly.

References

[AES$^+$12] Asabere, N.Y., Enguah, S.E., Salakpi, S., Mensah, J.K.A., Ahegbebu, M.K.: Analysis of wi-fi, wimax deployment: a case study of the mofa in the republic of ghana. Cont. J. Inf. Technol. 5(2) (2012)

[EL11] Etemad, K., Lai, M.Y.: Wimax standardization overview. In: WiMAX Technology and Network Evolution, pp. 1–15 (2011)

[ODS11] Ofori-Dwumfuo, G.O., Salakpi, S.V.: Wifi and wimax deployment at the ghana ministry of food and agriculture. Res. J. Appl. Sci. **3** (2011)

[ST10] Siebörger, I., Terzoli, A.: Wimax for rural sa: the experience of the siyakhula living lab. In: Southern African Telecommunication Networks & Applications, South Africa (2010)

Internet of Things Based Framework for Public Transportation Fleet Management in Free State, South Africa

Ahmed Shoman[✉], Muthoni Masinde,
and Mohammed Mostafa Hassan

Unit for Research on Informatics for Droughts in Africa (AfriCRID),
Central University of Technology, Free State - Private Bag,
X20539 Bloemfontein, South Africa
admsho@gmail.com, {emasinde,mmostafa}@cut.ac.za

1 Introduction

The paper is studying the best designed frame work of public transportation using internet of things (IoT). IoT refers to an established communication between identified things through the internet; these could be phones, sensors, tags, Wireless Sensor Network (WSN), Radio-Frequency Identification (RFID), Global Positioning System (GPS), [2], and applications [1].

2 Research Objectives

The overall objective of this research is developing a framework that allows integration of a number of technologies within the IoT paradigm in order to provide an efficient and effective way of managing public transportation in a resource challenged environment such as in Free State. The objective will be achieved through developing IoT integration by identifying applicable IoT technologies to cover existing limitation.

3 Methodology

The study focus on the public transportation system in Free State; which makes it a case study in this area. The study is qualitative by nature. The methodology for this study is a survey that split to several types; first, observation that obtained from the visited places i.e. mini bus. Second, interviews for some of the vehicle's owners. Third, questionnaires that is divided to three (Passengers, Drivers, Owners).

4 Challenges

Part of the challenges are type of passengers who have difficulties with knowledge which is either language or technology uses. No transparency on most vehicles because they are driven by non-owners.

© ICST Institute for Computer Sciences, Social Informatics and Telecommunications Engineering 2016
R. Glitho et al. (Eds.): AFRICOMM 2015, LNICST 171, pp. 220–222, 2016.
DOI: 10.1007/978-3-319-43696-8

5   Recommendations

Make use of Unstructured Supplementary Service Data (USSD) command and SMS for a non-smart phone holder, and install the application on smartphones; using accessible Wi-Fi. Assign an employee to help non-computer literate passengers; a screen to display all taxis/buses position using GPS, WSN, and RFID. Use two Infra-Red (IR) sensors to determine the movement direction of the passengers if it is in or out to count passengers. See Fig. 1 [3].

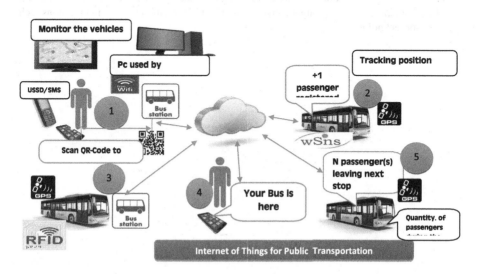

Fig. 1. Example of a designed framework method.

6   Analysis and Result

The study analyses three types of questionnaire; passenger questionnaire; driver questionnaire; vehicles' owners questionnaire. The questionnaire come out with result that the majority of passengers wait for the transportation vehicle. 40 % of the passenger do shopping while they are waiting. Passengers are usually inconvenienced because get disembark further than their stop. Most of the passengers are using smartphones. The passengers are interested in tools like display to monitor their waited vehicle, notify them when it arrives, and notify them and the driver on their detonation stop to stop in the exact place. Almost all the drivers are hired and that because the owners either have more than vehicles or because of their old age. Vehicles' owners believe that most of the hired drivers don't show the full amount of the gained money; which make it a necessary to come with a solution to manage that with IoT and Information and Communications Technology (ICT) [4, 5].

References

1. Atzori et al.: The internet of things: a survey. Comput. Netw., 2787–2805 (2010)
2. Kopetz: Design principles for distributed embedded applications. In: Real-Time Systems, pp. 307–323. Springer US: Springer Science + Business Media, LLC (2011)
3. Kurakova, T.: Overview of the Internet of Things. International Telecommunication Union, Geneva (2014)
4. Mumtaz, S.: Factors affecting teachers' use of information and communications technology: a review of the literature. In: Taylor & Francis Group Content, pp. 319–342 (2006)
5. Target, T.: ICT (Information And Communications Technology - Or Technologies) Definition (2015). http://searchcio.techtarget.com/definition/ICT-information-and-communications-technology-or-technologies

Cloud Computing for a Sustainable Development in Africa

Telesphore Tiendrebeogo[✉]

Polytechnic University of Bobo-Dioulasso, Bobo-Dioulasso, Burkina Faso
tetiendreb@gmail.com

Abstract. Africa is faced with several challenges which negatively affect their growth and sustainability, such as marketing factors, financial issues, management skills and lack of investment in Information and Communication Technology (ICT) on one hand. On the other hand, cloud computing enables users to share resources and carry out tasks remotely. The evolution of ICT solutions such as cloud computing, have the potential to counter some of the challenges that African economies and environments are facing.

Keywords: Cloud Computing · Sustainable development · Information Technology · Global warning · Economy

1 Introduction

Recently, the emerging Cloud Computing offers new computing models where resources such as online applications, computing power, storage and network infrastructure can be shared as services through the Internet [1]. Furthermore, the greatest environmental challenge today is global warming, which is caused by carbon emissions. Besides, African's economy is embryonic and rest dependent on the foreign aid where from the necessity of making an economy of scale regarding acquisition of software for the public administration. In this paper, we propose solutions based on the cloud computing, allowing to realize an economy of scale and to reduce the global warming.

2 Main Objectives

1. Present the financial impact of the cloud on the savings of small, average and big-sized enterprises in Africa on one hand and on the other hand the requirements of the smooth running of the cloud.
2. Give an overview onto the factors of the global warming bound to the use of ICTS and the role that the cloud in the energy saving could play.
3. Show some techniques of reduction of energy consumption by the consolidation of data centers.

© ICST Institute for Computer Sciences, Social Informatics and Telecommunications Engineering 2016
R. Glitho et al. (Eds.): AFRICOMM 2015, LNICST 171, pp. 223–224, 2016.
DOI: 10.1007/978-3-319-43696-8

3 Materials and Methods

Usage of the cloud computing becomes widespread. The data centers associated need in energy, increasing for their supply and their cooling. In 2012, for: $1 spent in material, there was $1 spent on feeding it and cooling it. That is why the reduction of the consumption has a strong economic impact. The challenge of the green Cloud Computing thus, is to minimize the resources usage while continuing to satisfy the quality requirements of services and robustness.

4 Results

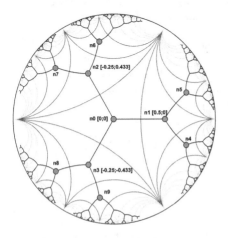

Fig. 1. Virtual machine location in Poincaré disk model.

The solution would be to make a migration of its resources on a low concentration of virtual machine in the aim to reduce the consumption of energy. For that purpose, we propose a model in which, a system of distributed virtual machines on the various nodes of a hyperbolic tree associated with the Poincaré disk model. In reminder, the Poincaré disk model is a unit disk centred at the origin. In this model, each node associated to the data centers is referenced by a name which we use to compute the address and the coordinates of its position in the Poincaré disk model and consequently on the hyperbolic tree (see Fig. 1).

5 Conclusions

In this paper, we show, how the Cloud Computing participates in the reduction of gas emissions and to the creation an economy of scale.

Reference

1. Michael, A., Armando, F., Rean, G., Anthony, J., Randy, H.K., Andrew, K., Gunho, L., David, A.P., Ariel, R., Ion, S., Matei, Z.: Above the Clouds: A Berkeley View of Cloud Computing (2009). http://www.eecs.berkeley.edu/Pubs/TechRpts/2009/EECS-2009-28.html

Adaptive Environmental Management System for Lejweleputswa District: A Participatory Approach Through Fuzzy Cognitive Maps

Mpho Mbele[✉], Muthoni Masinde, and Itumeleng Kgololo-Ngowi

Unit for Research on Informatics for Droughts in Africa (AfriCRID),
Central University of Technology,
Private Bag, Bloemfontein X20539, Free State, South Africa
{mmbele,emasinde,ikgololongowi}@cut.ac.za

Abstract. South Africa is home to some of the deepest mines in the world. Waste from gold mines constitutes the largest single source of waste and pollution in South Africa [2] Though mining industries develop environmental management systems/plans to identify and mitigate the impacts their operations has on the society, their outcome still poses a threat in terms of environmental pollution to communities around them. There are many ICT-based pollution monitoring solutions, but they do not address the needs of the affected mining communities. Some of the reasons for this include lack of relevant tools to access the systems (smartphones, computers) as well as lack of understanding and appreciation of the disseminated information. The mining communities around Lejweleputswa (South Africa) have learnt to depend on their own local knowledge to prevent or mitigate the impacts that mining operations has on them.

Keywords: Fuzzy cognitive maps · Wireless sensor networks · Adaptive · Local communities

1 Introduction

South Africa is home to some of the deepest mines in the world and accounts for almost 50 % of the world's found gold reserves [1]. Waste from gold mines constitutes the largest single source of waste and pollution in South Africa [2]. Though mining industries develop environmental management systems/plans to identify and mitigate the impacts their operations has on the society, their outcome still poses a threat in terms of environmental pollution to communities around them. There are many ICT-based pollution monitoring solutions, but they do not address the needs of the affected mining communities. Some of the reasons for this include lack of relevant tools to access the systems (smartphones, computers) as well as lack of understanding and appreciation of the disseminated information. The mining communities around Lejweleputswa (South Africa) have learnt to depend on their own local knowledge to prevent or mitigate the impacts that mining operations has on them.

Our objectives were: (1) to examine community's local knowledge on environmental pollution caused by mining activities. (2) To explore the usage of fuzzy cognitive

© ICST Institute for Computer Sciences, Social Informatics and Telecommunications Engineering 2016
R. Glitho et al. (Eds.): AFRICOMM 2015, LNICST 171, pp. 225–226, 2016.
DOI: 10.1007/978-3-319-43696-8

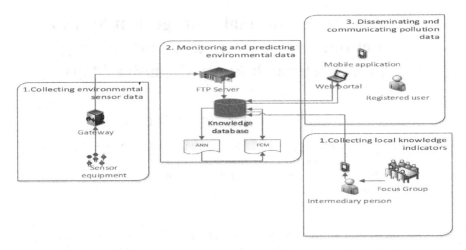

Fig. 1. Conceptual framework, the logic of the system.

maps. (3) To collect pollutants data on the area of interest using sensor nodes. (4) To develop an adaptive and acceptable mobile based environmental management system that integrates local knowledge with wireless sensor data.

Developing an adaptive environmental pollution monitoring system could minimize the impacts that mining operations has on the environment if acceptable and understood by mining communities. An adaptive system involves combining, in a dynamic ongoing process, local and scientific environmental knowledge in the co-management of resources and ecosystems publicizing that knowledge in a well understood manner by our communities [3]. To achieve this dynamism, this research makes use of a local based system capable of tracking, monitoring and reporting on air, soil and water pollution as well as receiving local knowledge from the community members around Lejweleputswa by making use of wireless sensor networks (WSN) to gather scientific knowledge and Fuzzy Cognitive Maps (FCMs) for local knowledge.

Methods: This is an exploratory study for firm understanding of the target respondent's knowledge and opinions and test the readiness of the areas of interest by deploying wireless sensors around the community (Fig. 1).

References

1. Gold mining in South Africa, http://www.chamberofmines.org.za/mining-industry/gold
2. Oelofse, S., Hobbs, P., Rascher, J., Cobbing, J.: The pollution and destruction threat of gold mining waste on the Witwatersrand - A West Rand case study (2010)
3. Olsson, P.; Folke, C.: Local ecological knowledge and institutional dynamics for ecosystem management: a study of Lake Racken watershed, Sweden. Ecosystems 85–104 (2001)

An Application of the Triangular Hough Transform and the Rectangular Hough Transform in Noisy Analytical Straight Line Recognition

Abdoulaye Sere[✉], Lassina Coulibali, Mamadou Diarra, Oumarou Sie, and Frédéric T. Ouédraogo

Laboratoire de Mathématiques et d'Informatique,
BP 7021 av. C.D.Gaulle, Ouagadougou, Burkina Faso
{abdoulaye.sere,oumarou.sie}@univ-ouaga.bf,
lass.coul.k@gmail.com,diarra_md@yahoo.fr,
ouedraogo.tounwendyam@yahoo.fr

Abstract. This paper proposes an application of Triangular Hough Transform and Rectangular Hough Transform for the recognition of thick analytical straight line. The proposed methods compute the dual of virtual rectangles or virtual triangles that contain real pixels, to create accumulator data. The methods accept more noises in pictures.

1 Some Results

See Figs. 1 and 2

R. Glitho et al. (Eds.): AFRICOMM 2015, LNICST 171, pp. 227–229, 2016.
DOI: 10.1007/978-3-319-43696-8

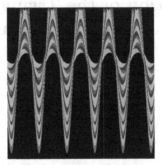

(a) The dual of virtual rectangles.

(b) A found straight line with $(\theta,p)=(100°,5)$, constituted of real pixels.

Fig. 1. Recognition for the virtual rectangles

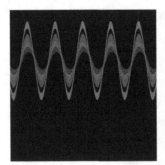

(a) The dual of virtual triangles. (b) A found straight line with $(\theta,p)=(39°,14)$, constituted of real pixels crossing the virtual triangles.

Fig. 2. Recognition for the virtual triangles

References

1. Sere, A., Sie, O., Andrès, E.: Extended standard hough Transform for analytical line recognition. Int. J. Adv. Comput. Sci. Appl. (IJACSA) **4**(3), 256–266 (2013)
2. Dexet, M.: Architecture D'un Modeleur Géométrique à Base Topologique D'objets Discrets et Méthodes de Reconstruction en Dimensions 2 et 3. Thèse en informatique, Université de Poitiers, France (2006)
3. Andres, E.: Discrete linear objects in dimension n: the standard model. Graph. Models **65**(1–3), 92–111 (2003)
4. Sere, A.: Transformations analytiques appliquées aux images multi-échelles et bruitées. Thèse en informatique, Université de Ouagadougou (2013)
5. Sere, A., Sie, O., Traore, S.: Extensions of standard hough transform based on object dual and applications. Int. J. Emerg. Trends in Comput. Inf. Sci. **6**(1), 20–24 (2015)

Author Index

Printed in the United States
By Bookmasters